ADDITIONS AND CORRECTIONS

TO THE

W.P.A.

INVENTORY

OF

ADAMS COUNTY, OHIO:

WEST UNION

Jana Sloan Broglin

HERITAGE BOOKS
2023

HERITAGE BOOKS

AN IMPRINT OF HERITAGE BOOKS, INC.

Books, CDs, and more—Worldwide

For our listing of thousands of titles see our website
at
www.HeritageBooks.com

Published 2023 by
HERITAGE BOOKS, INC.
Publishing Division
5810 Ruatan Street
Berwyn Heights, MD 20740

(Originally Titled)
INVENTORY OF THE COUNTY ARCHIVES OF OHIO
Prepared by
The Historical Records Survey
Division of Women's and Professional Projects
Works Progress Administration

No. 1 Adams County (West Union)

Columbus, Ohio
The Historical Records Survey
December 1938

International Standard Book Number
Paperbound: 978-0-7884-2877-7

County Offices and their Records

Journals and reports. Bridge and road records. County institutions and relief. Business administration of office. Miscellaneous.
Real property transfers: deeds; leases; mortgages; liens; registered lands; plat books and surveys. Personal property transfers. Corporations and partnerships. Business administration of office. Licenses and grants of authority. Miscellaneous.
Motor vehicles. Licenses and commissions. Elections, Business Administration of office. Miscellaneous.
Dockets. Records of trials. Miscellaneous.
Calendars and dockets. Court proceedings. Wills. Estates: appointments, bonds, and letters; inventories and sale bills; cost bills and settlements; original papers. Inheritance taxes. Assignments. Records of dependents. Vital statistics. Licenses, Fiscal accounts. Miscellaneous.

The Historical Records Survey

> Luther H. Evans, National Director
> John O. Marsh, State Director

Division of Women's and Professional Projects

> Ellen S. Woodward, Assistant Administrator
> Mildred M. Thrasher, State Director

WORKS PROGRESS ADMINISTRATION

> Harry L. Hopkins, Administrator
> Carl Watson, State Administrator

The *Inventory of County Archives of Ohio* is one of a number of bibliographies of historical materials prepared throughout the United States by workers on the Historical Records Survey of the Works Progress Administration. The publication herewith presented, an inventory of the archives of Adams County, is number 1 of the Ohio series.

The Historical Records Survey was undertaken in the winter of 1935-1936 for the purpose of providing useful employment to needy unemployed historians, lawyers, teachers, and research and clerical workers. In carrying out this objective, the project was organized to compile inventories of historical materials, particularly the unpublished government documents and records which are basic in the administration of local government, and which provide invaluable data for students of political, economic, and social history. The archival guide herewith presented is intended to meet the requirements of day-to-day administration by the officials of the county, and also the needs of lawyers, business men, and other citizens who require facts from the public records for the proper conduct of their affairs. The volume is designed so that it can be used by the historian in his research in unprinted sources in the same way he uses the library card catalog for printed sources.

The inventories produced by the Historical Records Survey attempt to do more than give merely a list of records – they attempt further to sketch in the historical background of the county or other unit of government, and to describe precisely and in detail the organization and functions of the government agencies whose records they list. The county, town, and other local inventories for the entire country will, when completed, constitute an encyclopedia of local government as well as a bibliography of local archives.

The successful conclusion of the work of the Historical Records Survey, even in a single county, would not be possible without the support of public officials, historical and legal specialists, and many other groups in the community. Their cooperation is gratefully acknowledged.

The Survey was organized and has been directed by Luther H. Evans, and operates as a nation-wide project in the Division of Women's and Professional Projects, of which Mrs. Ellen S. Woodward, Assistant Administrator, is in charge.

HARRY L. HOPKINS, Administrator

2nd Edition

In 1929 after the stock market crash along with the Great Depression which followed, President Herbert Hoover and his successor Franklin D. Roosevelt formulated relief projects, the most successful was the establishment of the Works Progress Administration (WPA).

Established in 1935, the WPA was the largest of the many programs developed during Roosevelt's "New Deal." In 1939, the agency's name was changed to Works Progress Administration, and continued as such until its demise in 1943.

The Federal Writers' Project, a division of the WPA (known as Federal Project Number One), created jobs for many unemployed librarians, clerks, researchers, editors, and historians. The workers went to courthouses, town halls, offices in large cities, vital statistics offices and inventoried records. Besides indexing works, many records were transcribed. One of these many projects was the *Inventory of the County Archives* which has benefitted genealogists and historians. The inventories listed the records, either by volumes or file boxes and years per record type, within the office. Although the WPA oversaw this project, the information for each volume of records may differ significantly by the information submitted, i.e.: sections on the Sinking Fund, Soldier's Relief Commission, etc.

This project was to encompass all of Ohio's eighty-eight counties although approximately thirty of these inventories have been located while others may not have been done.

The original WPA volume for Adams County contained maps showing the evolution of Ohio judicial districts, flow charts, and Index to County History and Office Essays which have been omitted.

PREFACE
2nd Edition

The information herein is verbatim except for obvious spelling errors. Records listed may have met the requirement for retention and have been destroyed as per the records retention act, while other records are considered permanent records. (*See:* **https://codes.ohio.gov/ohio-revised-code** Ohio Revised Code, sections 149.31 and 149.34). Records considered "open" to the public, such as lunacy, idiotic, and juvenile cases, may be "closed" due to a revision of state laws. However, the records may be opened to family members with adequate proof of lineage.

The addresses and website section of this edition list an up-to-date location guide to each office mentioned.

DISCLAIMER: The terminology in the section "Historical Sketch of Adams County" as well as other areas, is contemporary to the time and does not reflect the wording used today.

Jana Sloan Broglin
Fellow, Ohio Genealogical Society
Swanton, Ohio
2023

1st Edition

The Historical Records Survey began operations in Ohio in February 1936. General regulations and procedures applicable to all project units in the forty-eight states have been followed in Ohio. In the sixteen districts of the Works Progress Administration in Ohio, the project was organized and operated by district supervisors of the Writers' Project. In November 1936, the Survey became an independent part of Federal Project No. 1. Russell S. Drum, Assistant State Director, has been in charge of the administrative details of the project.

The objective of the Survey in Ohio has been the preparation of complete inventories of the records of the state and of each county, city, and other local governmental unit. Although a condensed form of entry is used, information is given as to the limiting dates of all extant records, the contents of individual series, and the location of records in statehouse, county courthouse, or other depository.

The *Inventory of the County Archives of Ohio* will, when completed, consist of a set of eighty-eight volumes with a separate number for each county in the state. The units of the series are numbered according to the respective position of the county in an alphabetical list of the counties. Thus, the inventory herewith presented for Adams County is number 1. The inventory of the State Archives and of municipal and other local records will constitute separate publications.

The principle followed in the inventory of county records has been to place a record in the office of origin rather than in the office of deposit. The records are arranged with those of the executive branch of the county government first, followed by judicial, law enforcing, fiscal, and miscellaneous agencies. Minor agencies are placed in the general arrangement according to function rather than according to constitutional or statutory responsibility to a major subdivision. The legal development of each office or agency has been treated in a prefatory section preceding the inventory of the records of the office.

The Historical Records Survey was inaugurated in Adams County in May 1936, under the immediate supervision of George Reichert, and the final careful rechecking of the county records was completed by Reichert in July 1938. The wholehearted cooperation of the county officials with the project workers has meant much in the thoroughness and completeness of the result. Members of the state editorial staff of the Historical Records Survey, under the supervision of Miss Winifred Smith, State Editor, compiled, arranged, indexed, edited, and reproduced the volume for distribution among public and semipublic institutions and organizations. The research for the historical data was conducted by Dr. Edward L.

PREFACE
1ˢᵗ Edition

Pross of the project. Dr. James H. Rodabaugh, also of the project staff, prepared the maps showing the evolution of Ohio judicial districts.

The various units of the *Inventory of County Archives of Ohio* will be issued in mimeographed or printed form for free distribution to state and local public officials and public libraries in Ohio, and to a limited number of libraries and government agencies outside the state. Requests for information concerning particular units of the *Inventory* should be addressed to The Historical Records Survey, Old Post Office Building, State and Third Streets, Columbus, Ohio.

John O. Marsh
State Director
The Historical Records Survey

Columbus, Ohio
December 20, 1938

AAA .... Agricultural Adjustment Administration
am. .... amended
Amer. .... American
Arch. .... Archaeological
Art. .... Article
assizes .... an action, writ, or verdict
bd. .... board
c. .... copyright
certiorari .... to be more fully informed
CCC .... Civilian Conservation Corps
cf. .... (confer) compare
comp. .... compiler
dept. .... department
ed. .... editor
eng. .... engineer
et al. .... (et alii), and others
(et) passim .... (and) here and there
ex officio. .... as a result of one's status or position
fee simple. .... full and irrevocable ownership
G.C. .... General Code
H. .... House bill
habeas corpus .... protection against illegal imprisonment
Hist. .... Historical
ibid. .... the same reference
in. .... inch
Loc. Cit. (loco citato) .... in the place cited
mandamus ... when an officer or authority is required to perform a duty
Mun. .... Municipal
n. .... north
Nat. .... National
n.d. .... no date
ne exeat .... a writ issued to restrain a person
from leaving the jurisdiction of the court or state
N.P. .... The Ohio NISI PRIUS REPORTS
n.p. .... no place of publication

LIST OF ABBREVIATIONS, LEGAL TERMS, SYMBOLS,
AND EXPLANATORY NOTES

n.s. . . . . new series
nolle prosequi . . . . notice of abandonment by a
plaintiff or prosecutor of all or part of a suit or action
Ohio Const. . . . . Ohio Constitution
Ohio State Arch. and Hist. Quarterly. . . . .
Ohio State Archives and Historical Quarterly
O.L. . . . . Laws of Ohio
op. cit. (opere citato). . . . . in the work cited
posse comitatus . . . . a group of citizens called upon to assist the sheriff
praecipes . . . . a written request for action
prima facie. . . . . on the first impression
procedendo. . . . . sends case from appellate court to a lower court
Pt. . . . . part
quo warranto . . . . by what authority or warrant
R. . . . . River
replevins. . . . . return of personal property
wrongfully taken or held by a defendant
R.S.. . . . . Revised Statute
S.b.. . . . . senate bill
scire facias. . . . . why a judgment regarding
a record or patent should not be enforced
sec(s) . . . . section(s)
Ser.. . . . . Series
sic. . . . . thus, following copy
St.. . . . . Saint, Street
supersedeas . . . . . . a stay of enforcement of a judgment pending appeal
supt. . . . . superintendent
U.S. . . . . United States
v.. . . . . versus
venires . . . . a group of people summoned for jury duty
vol(s) . . . . volume(s)
writ. . . . . a formal, legal document, a decree
WPA. . . . . Works Progress Administration
X. . . . . by
– . . . . to date, current

If a record has no title or a nondescriptive or misleading title an appropriate title has been assigned. Supplied titles have been enclosed in brackets. Explanatory additions to titles are enclosed in brackets with initial capitals.

If the title of a record varies, the current or most recent title is used but significant variations are shown in the title line.

Numbers and letters within parentheses following the quantity of the record indicate the labeling on volumes, file boxes, or bundles.

Title line cross references are used to complete series where a record is kept separately for a period of time or in other records for different periods of time. They are also used in all artificial entries which are made to show, under their proper office or subject heading, records kept in the same volume or file with unrelated records. In both instances, the description of the master entry shows the title and entry number of the record from which the cross reference is made. Dates shown in the description of the master entry are only for the part or parts of the record contained therein, and are shown only when they vary from those of the master entry.

Separate third paragraph cross references from entry to entry, and "see also" references under subject headings, are used to show prior, subsequent, or related records which are not a part of the same series.

Unless an index is self-contained an entry for the index immediately follows its record entry. Cross references are given for exceptions to the rule.

If no statement is made concerning the condition of the records, it is to be assumed that they are in good condition.

Dimensions given in each entry show the size of the volumes, file boxes, or maps mentioned in the title line and are expressed in inches unless otherwise indicated. The dimensions of volumes are given in order of height, width, and thickness; of file boxes in order of height, width, and depth.

On maps and plat records, the names of author and publisher, and information on scale have been omitted only when these data are not available.

Unless otherwise indicated all records are located in the county courthouse.

Adams County is located on the southern edge of the state and is bounded by the Ohio River on the south, Brown County on the west, Highland County on the north, and Pike and Scioto Counties on the east. It is rectangular in shape, has a total area of 546 square miles, and is composed of fifteen townships which are irregular in size and shape. The surface is generally uneven or hilly and in the eastern sections is almost mountainous. Ninety-three percent of the county's area is very steep and broken, four percent is hilly to very hilly, two percent is gently to heavily rolling, and only one percent is level to gently undulating. In the southeastern townships of Green and Jefferson there are high ridges and hills reaching an elevation of 1,000 to 1,200 feet. The highest point is Peach Mountain in Meigs Township with an elevation of 1,280 feet. The decline from the near-mountain altitudes to the Ohio River Valley level of 500 feet is very swift and steep.

The drainage system of most of Adams County empties directly into the Ohio River through the Ohio Brush Creek and its tributaries. The creek flows south to the Ohio across the center of the county. Several townships in the eastern part of the county are drained by the Scioto River tributaries. The valleys of the streams in Adams County are narrow and deep but they are very fertile.

Across the northwestern corner of the county runs the glacial boundary, marking the line beyond which the glaciers in their advance left no appreciable trace. The greater part of the region, therefore, is in the unglaciated plateau and lies on the edge of the great limestone area of the western half of the state, being covered by limestone of the Upper and Lower Silurian. The eastern portion of the county is covered with Devonian shales and Carboniferous sandstones. The residual soils are fifty-five percent limestone, thirty percent sandstone, and fifteen percent shales. The average annual production of commercial limestone from 1920 to 1930 was 156,451 tons. No other mineral resources have been exploited although iron ore was mined during the early years of settlement. Adams is one of the few counties of Ohio into which the Blue Grass region extends.[1]

---

1. J. A. Caldwell, comp., *Illustrated Historical Atlas of Adams County, Ohio* (Newark, 1880), 13. Hereafter cited, Caldwell's *Atlas*. Ohio Study of Local School Units, "A Study of the Public Schools of Adams County..." (mimeographed, Columbus, 1937), 4-5. Hereafter cited, "*Adams Schools Survey.*"

The earliest known inhabitants of this region were the so-called Mound Builders. Fifty-eight mounds, thirteen enclosures, ten village sites, thirty-one burials, two stone graves, one effigy, and two petroglyphs have been discovered in the county and remain as mute testimony as to the habitat of these aborigines. Several pictographs, mostly in the form of human footprints cut in the exposed rock surfaces, are to be seen along the Ohio River in Green Township. More interesting, however, is the great "Serpent Mound" which is one of Ohio's most remarkable prehistoric monuments. This is located in northern Bratton Township and occupies an eminence which terminates in a sheer precipice towering nearly one hundred feet above the bed of Brush Creek. The Serpent proper is 1,254 feet in length with a maximum height of five feet. There are three principal convolutions of the body, while the tail is curled twice around. The head is triangular in shape and before the mouth is an oval figure, 120 feet long and sixty feet wide, which the serpent apparently is about to swallow.[2] Many interesting conjectures have been made regarding the history of this work which at present is enclosed by a state park under the supervision of the Ohio State Archaeological and Historical Society.[3]

The Shawnees were the principal tribe of historic Indians to frequent the region of Adams County. There were noted summer camps on Ohio Brush Creek near its mouth, on the West Fork above the modern village of Newport, and above the Marble Furnace on the East Fork. There was also a well-known hunting camp on Scioto Brush Creek. As late as 1800, Indian families cultivated the bottom lands on West Fork but these camps were only temporary in nature, the Indians preferring the level lands of the Scioto Valley for their permanent villages.[4] By treaties made at Fort Stanwix in 1784, at Fort McIntosh in 1785, and at Fort Harmar in 1789, Indian claims to southern Ohio were extinguished but a few tribes, notably the Shawnee, remained hostile until the treaty made at Greenville in 1795.[5] As a result of the failure to placate the Shawnees, the surveys and early settlements in Adams County were made under extremely dangerous conditions.

---

2. William C. Mills, *Archaeological Atlas of Ohio* (Columbus, 1914), 1.

3. E. O. Randall, *The Serpent Mound, Adams County. Ohio* . . . (Columbus, 1905) 1-125, *passim*.

4. Nelson W. Evans and Emmons B. Stivers, *A History of Adams County, Ohio* (West Union, 1900), 29; David Meade Massie, *Life of Nathaniel Massie* (Cincinnati, 1896), 26.

5. Eugene Holloway Roseboom and Francis Phelps Weisenburger, *A History of Ohio* (New York, 1934), 69-99; [Jacob Burnet], *Notes on the Early Settlement of the North-Western Territory* (Cincinnati, 1847), 83-96.

Christopher Gist of the Ohio Land Company was one of the first white men to visit the region of the Adams County of today, passing through this territory in February 1751.[6] Several expeditions against the Indians marched through this county, the most important being those led by Colonel Robert Todd and Simon Kenton, in 1787, by Colonel Charles Scott in 1790, and by Simon Kenton in 1793.[7] However, before all Indian claims had been extinguished, land surveys were made in this region. All the lands within Adams County were included in the Virginia Military Reserve. Virginia claimed the Northwest Territory under a grant from the king of England, and when she yielded her claims in favor of the United States in 1783, reserved certain lands as bounties for Revolutionary War veterans from Virginia.

During the winter of 1787 John O'Bannon and Arthur Fox of Kentucky examined lands along the Ohio and Scioto Rivers. On November 19, 1787, O'Bannon certified to have surveyed 3,600 acres in Adams County in three surveys. In the following year Nathaniel Massie, an enterprising Virginian, and his parties of surveyors began operations. Extreme precautions had to be taken against Indian attack, and most of the work was done during the winter months when the savages were in their villages. The system of the government rectangular survey was not followed, the land in this region being first located and then surveyed. Bounty holders on their assigns were allowed to settle where they pleased, with the result that property holders for years were frequently involved in land title litigations.[8]

_____

6. William M. Darlington, ed., *Christopher Gist's Journals, with Historical, Geographical and Ethnological Notes and Biographies of his Contemporaries* (Pittsburgh, 1893), 46, 123.

7. Evans and Stivers, *op. cit.*, 31-32.

8. Henry T, Bannon, *Scioto Sketches; An Account of Discovery and Settlement of Scioto County. Ohio.* (Chicago, 1920), 57-59; W.P. Strickland, ed., *Autobiography of Rev. James B. Finley; or, Pioneer Life in the West* (Cincinnati, 1859), 128-29; John McDonald, *Biographical Sketches of General Nathaniel Massie. General Duncan McArthur. Captain William Wells and General Simon Kenton; Who were Early Settlers in the Western Country* (Cincinnati, 1858), 26; Nelson W. Evans, "Colonel John O'Bannon," *Ohio State Arch. and Hist. Quarterly.* XIV (1905), 321.

Nathaniel Massie realized that large scale surveying operations would be expedited by the establishment of a strong base within the Military Reserve. As an inducement to colonists he offered to the first twenty-five persons who would join him in making a settlement one inlot and one outlot in the village that he proposed to lay out, as well as one hundred acres near this settlement. Thirty persons accepted this offer, subscribing to the terms of a contract by which in return for land they promised to live for two years within this settlement. After various consultations with his friends Massie selected a location about twelve miles above the present Maysville, Kentucky, opposite the lower of three islands in the Ohio River. This village he named Manchester in honor of the English city of that name. By the middle of March 1791, the whole village was enclosed within strong pickets, firmly fixed in the ground, and with blockhouses located at each corner for defense. The lower of the three islands was cleared and planted in corn. This was one of the earliest settlements in Ohio, being antedated only by Marietta, Cincinnati, and possibly Gallipolis. [9]

The strength of Manchester's stockade and the vigilance of its defenders prevented an open attack by the Indians but danger was ever present. In the winter of 1791-1792 Massie and a party of surveyors narrowly escaped from a war party lurking in ambush along Brush Creek. In 1792 Israel Donalson was captured by the savages, and in 1793 Andrew Ellison was taken prisoner almost in the shadow of Manchester. In 1795 a band of Indians on Paint Creek was surprised by a party led by Massie, but the ensuing conflict proved to be the last Indian battle in this region.[10] From 1794 until 1798 mail boats plied the Ohio from Wheeling to Cincinnati but were often fired upon by lurking Indians. Sometimes they were lured to the shore by white men who were forced to act as decoys for the Indians who would hide until the boats were within easy range.[11]

---

9. McDonald, *op. cit.*, 31; Caldwell's *Atlas*, 12.
10. McDonald, *op. cit.*, 34-59.
11. S. P. Hildreth, *Pioneer History: Being an Account of the First Examinations of the Ohio Valley, and the Early Settlements of the Northwest Territory* (Cincinnati, 1848), 342-43; Bannon, *Scioto Sketches*, 25-28.

In the northwestern corner of the county there are many caverns which are said to have been the dwelling places of desperadoes when preyed upon emigrant boats and traders. Tradition records that James Girty, the renegade, at one time had his headquarters here.[12]

Despite these early dangers, by 1797 Manchester had become a thriving village of forty cabins,[13] and on July 10, 1797, Adams County, the fourth to be organized in Ohio, was created by Winthrop Sargent, secretary of the Northwest Territory, and then acting governor.[14] The county was named in honor of President John Adams, and was very large, embracing within its limits the whole of what later became eight counties and parts of twelve others,[15] Since 1797 Adams has lost much of its original area by the creation of Ross County in 1798, Scioto in 1803, Highland in 1805, Pike in 1815, and Brown in 1818.[16] The only addition ever made to the county was in 1798 when part of Hamilton County was attached to Adams.[17]

The first court was held at Manchester in September 1797, but the commissioners selected for the county seat an out of the way place, a few miles above the mouth of Brush Creek, called Adamsville. The place was situated where the village of Rome now stands, but at that time the region was almost a wilderness and in derision the county seat was termed "Scant." At the next session of the court its members became divided, a part sitting at Adamsville, and part at Manchester which had the backing of Massie and his friends for the location of the county seat. Governor St. Clair then moved the seat of justice to Washington, a tiny village platted by Noble Grimes, at the mouth of Brush Creek.

---

12. Evans and Stivers, *op. cit.*, 424.
13. Caldwell's *Atlas*, 32.
14. Salmon P. Chase, comp., *The Statutes of Ohio and of the Northwestern Territory, 1788-1833* (Cincinnati, 1833-35), III, 2096.
15. Caldwell's *Atlas*, 13.
16. Chase, *op. cit.*, III, 2097; *Laws of Ohio*. I, 8-9; III, 256-58; XIII, 52; XVI, 28-31.
17. Randolph Chandler Downes, "Evolution of Ohio County Boundaries," *Ohio State Arch. and Hist. Quarterly*, XXXVI (1927), 451.

In 1799 the territorial legislature passed an act making Manchester the county seat, but the governor refused to sign the bill, and the controversy waged until 1804 when the Ohio legislature selected West Union, a village platted by Thomas Kirker and others in 1804.[18]

In 1805 the first courthouse was built at West Union at a cost of $709,[19] but the settlement of this village was very slow. In 1807 there were only twenty cabins, and church services were held in the courthouse.[20] The basic importance of the county seat controversy was the fact that it was one of the causes for the cleavage between Massie and the Virginians as opposed St. Clair and the New Englanders at Marietta and Cincinnati. This dispute eventually led to the formation of political intrigue, the establishment of political parties in Ohio, the subsequent downfall of St. Clair, and the organization of the state of Ohio.[21]

The settlers of early Adams County were mostly from Virginia and the Scotch-Irish element predominated. About 1850 there was a small German immigration into the county,[22] but so firmly were the teachings of Jefferson ingrained in the inhabitants of this county that until the 1880s Adams was almost always strongly Democratic in its politics. Since that time the struggle between the two parties has been generally very closely contested.[23]

After the removal of the Indian menace by the treaty of Greenville in 1795, the early settlers left the protection of Manchester and many new villages were platted and settled: West Union in 1804, Jacksonville and Winchester in 1815, Newport in 1819, Rockville in 1830, Commercialtown in 1832, Rome and Locust Grove in 1835, Palestine in 1837, Louisville in 1838, Loudon, Bentonville, and Bradysville in 1839, Dunkinsville in 1841, Fairview in 1844, Unity in 1846,

---

18. Caldwell's *Atlas*. 13; Henry Howe, comp., *Historical Collections of Ohio...*, (Norwalk, 1896), I, 228; A. A. Graham, "Legislation in the Northwest Territory," *Ohio State Arch. and Hist. Quarterly*, I (1838), 309-10.

19. Caldwell's *Atlas*. 39.

20. F. Cuming, Sketches of a Tour to the Western Country . . . (Reuben Gold Thwaites, ed., *Early Western Travels. 1748-1846...*, Cleveland, 1904, IV), 202-8.

21. Massie, *op. cit.*, 67, 68, 71 ,74, *et passim*.

22. Evans and Stivers, *op. cit.*, 7.

23. Evans and Stivers, *op. cit.*, 234-41.

North Liberty in 1848, Harshaville in 1849, Eckmansville in 1850, Wamsley[ville] in 1874, Peebles in 1881, and Seaman in 1888.[24] In 1880 [sic] the population of the county was 3,432; in 1820, 10,406; in 1840, 13,183; in 1860, 20,309; in 1880, 24,005; and 1900, 26,328.[25] In 1930 this figure had fallen to 20,381 of whom 99.5 percent were native-born whites.[26] There was no city in the county in 1930, Manchester having population of 2,009, Peebles, 1,235, West Union, 1,094, Winchester, 821, and the other villages being somewhat smaller.[27] [In 2020 the population of the county was 27,542].

      Agriculture was the most important industry in early Adams County, a distinction that it has maintained up to the present time. All the hillsides and valleys in the eastern portion of the county were originally densely forested, but for many years squatters there eked out a precarious livelihood by cutting down fine oak and chestnut trees, peeling the bark which was used for tanning purposes, and leaving the valuable bodies of the trees to decay. In 1871 Congress gave all vacant lands in the Virginia Military Reserve to Ohio which in turn gave them to the Ohio State University. Her trustees had these lands investigated, surveyed, and sold out, and as a result of this policy, substantial settlers appeared in the eastern part of Adams County. In 1896 one half of the tobacco for which this region became noted was raised east of Brush Creek.[28] As early as 1868 Adams County was one of the most important tobacco sections in the state.[29] However, the hilly surface and relatively poor soil proved discouraging to many early farmers, and a traveler through this region in 1819 observed that while there were some good farms, many others had been abandoned for richer lands of Indiana and Illinois.[30] By 1880 wheat and corn had become the staple crops, and hogs and cattle were the most important livestock.[31]

---

24. Caldwell's *Atlas*. 16-58, *passim*.
25. *Twelfth Census of the United States*, 1900, *Population*. I, pt. I, 34.
26. *Fifteenth Census of the United States*, 1930, *Population*, III, pt. ii, 466. 479.
27. Simeon D. Fess, ed., *Ohio Reference Library* (Chicago and New York, 1937), III. 276.
28. Howe, op. cit., I, 231-33.
29. Ohio Secretary of State, *Annual Report*, 1869, 156.
30. Thomas Hulme, *A Journal* . . . (Reuben Gold Thwaites, ed., *Early Western Travels, 1748-1846*, Cleveland, 1904, X), 69,
31. Caldwell's *Atlas*. 13.

In 1930 there were 2,829 farms in Adams County,[32] valued at $9,873,693,[33] or about eighty-six percent of the 1934 grand tax duplicate of the county,[34] and raising products valued at $3,202,369.[35] Over eighty-four percent of the county was in farms, and of this are a 31.7 percent was in crop lands, 23.4 percent in woodlands, and 47.6 percent in pastures.[36] There were eight products of the county's farms which were equal to or exceeded the state average for production, the most important being tobacco, forest products, mules, chickens, eggs, and bees. The outstanding single product was tobacco, and 11.5 percent of all the weed raised in Ohio in 1929 was grown in Adams County.[37] However, this region is not one of Ohio's richest agricultural centers for only six counties in Ohio have lower farm valuations than Adams;[38] 22.6 percent of the farms were mortgaged in 1930,[39] and 33.5 percent were operated by tenants.[40] Of those gainfully employed in the county, nearly 60.5 percent were engaged in agriculture.[41] Despite the lack of abundant economic wealth this county's per capita relief cost in 1934 was only $4.61 in comparison with the state average of $9.22.[42]

The earliest industries in the county were based upon the primary products of timber and grain; saw and grist mills being erected during the earliest years of settlement.[43] Many distilleries were also opened, there being four in Green Township in 1804.[44] The iron industry was important during the early decades of the past century.

---

32. *Fifteenth Census of the United States. 1930, Agriculture.* III , pt. I, 279.

33. *Ibid.* 286.

34. Ohio Auditor of State, *Annual Report.* 1935, 555.

35. *Fifteenth Census of the United States. 1930, Agriculture.* III, pt. I, 294.

36. *Ibid.,* II , pt. I, 402.

37. *Ibid.,* 421-67, *passim.*

38. *Adams Schools Survey,* 6.

39. *Fifteenth Census of the United States. 1930, Agriculture.* II, pt. I, 468.

40. Ibid., 473.

41. *Fifteenth Census of the United States. 1930, Population.* III, pt. II 508.

42. *Adams Schools Survey.* 10.

43. Caldwell's *Atlas.* 16-59, *passim.*

44. Evans and Stivers, *op. cit.,* 422.

The Brush Creek Furnace, built by John Fisher in 1811, was the fourth established in Ohio, and the Steam Furnace, opened in 1814, was the first in the state to employ steam. The Marble Furnace was built in 1817, and a few others were constructed later but the dearth of coal and scarcity of iron ore soon caused their abandonment.[45] However, in 1836 there were three furnaces in operation in the county, as well as twenty-three water mills, one steam mill, six carding machines, two fulling mills, and several smaller enterprises.[46] At Manchester there was a carding mill established in 1808, flour mills in 1840 and 1869, and a pottery in 1846.[47] At West Union there was a tannery opened in 1805, flour mills in 1857, and woolen mills in 1866.[48] Prior to 1836 there had been no banks established in the county,[49] and one of the earliest was the G.B. Grimes and Company Bank, organized in West Union in 1865.[50]

At present the principal manufactured products of the county are furniture, pearl buttons, concrete blocks, tombstones, flour, and dairy products.[51] In 1929 there were nineteen establishments in the county, employing an average of 168 workers, and producing goods valued at $575,251.[52] Adams is not an important manufacturing county.

The Ohio River furnished the pioneers of Adams County with a ready means of transportation and by 1811 steamboats were running to Manchester.[53] Zane's Trace, the first important traveled thoroughfare across southern Ohio, reached the Ohio River at Manchester, continuing on to its terminal at Aberdeen opposite Maysville. West Union was laid out along this trail.[54]

---

45. Wilbur Stout, "Early Forges in Ohio," *Ohio State Arch, and Hist. Quarterly*. XLVI (1937), 27-31; Caldwell's *Atlas*. 16-59, *passim*; John Kilbourne, *The Ohio Gazetteer* . . . (Columbus, 1831), 75.

46. Warren Jenkins, *The Ohio Gazetteer and Travellers' Guide*;... (Columbus, 1841), 52.

47. Caldwell's *Atlas*. 32.

48. *Ibid*.., 40-44.

49. Caleb Atwater, *A History of the State of Ohio. Natural and Civil* (Cincinnati, c. 1838), 315.

50. Caldwell's *Atlas*. 44.

51. N.W. Ayer and Sons *Directory of Newspapers and Periodicals* (Philadelphia, 1937), 721, 734.

52. *Fifteenth Census of the United States, 1930, Manufactures*. III, 398.

53. Evans and Stivers, *op. cit.*, 442.

54. Clement L. Martzolff, "Zane's Trace," *Ohio State Arch, and Hist. Quarterly*. XIII (1904), 318

For some years Manchester was the meeting point between land travel by the Zane Road and the river traffic on the Ohio, as well as the point of transhipment on the great stage route east from Lexington to Maysville, Manchester, Chillicothe, Zanesville, Wheeling, and the East.[55] The first public road in Adams was the old post road over that portion of Zane's Trace which ran through the county. Afterwards the "New State Road," as it was called, was laid out over the same general line . In 1838 the Maysville and Zanesville turnpike was constructed along the general route of the old post road, and this was taken over by the county twenty-five years later. All the early roads in the county began at some one of the many ferries across the Ohio River and extended into the interior. In the days of the early iron furnaces their products were transported during a part of the year in barges down Brush Creek to the Ohio. At one time this traffic was so important that slackwater navigation on the stream was contemplated by the state.[56]

For the greater part of a century the turnpikes and the Ohio were the only outlets for the commerce of the county, but in 1877 the Cincinnati and Eastern Railroad was built across the northern part of the county running through Winchester.[57] This railroad, which eventually became a part of the Norfolk and Western system, is the only one in operation in the county,[58] but there are 1,107 miles of highway including one United States and seven state routes. However, over half of this mileage consists of dirt roads,[59] and the transportation problems of this county have not yet been completely solved.

---

55. Howe *op. cit.*, I, 230.
56. Evans and Stivers, *op. cit.*, 3, 114-23; Fess, *op. cit.*, III, 276,
57. Fess, *op. cit.*, III, 276; Evans and Stivers, *op. cit.*, 498.
58. Ohio Tax Commission, *Annual Report*, 1934. 34.
59. *Adams Schools Survey*, 10, 55,

The devout Covenanters among the early Scotch-Irish settlers established churches at an early date as did the pioneer Methodists. In 1797 in Jefferson Township on Scioto Brush Creek a Methodist meeting-house was built under the direction of Reverend Joseph Moore which is said to have been the first in Ohio of this denomination. Philip Gatch, Lewis Hunt, and Henry Smith were other early preachers in this church. Methodist meetings were also held in Tiffin Township under Reverend Simon Fields in 1797, in 1800 at West Union under Reverend John Collins, in 1804 in Liberty Township under Reverend O'Dell and Robert Dobbins, and in 1805 in Monroe Township under Reverend James Quinn. Presbyterian pioneer meetings were held in 1797 in Liberty Township, in 1799 in Wayne Township, in 1800 near West Union, in 1801 in Franklin Township, in 1805 at North Liberty, and at Manchester in 1806. William Baldridge, David Risk, William Williamson, John Dunlevy, Adam Rankin, and Robert H. Bishop were, among the early Presbyterian clergymen. A Baptist church was established in Tiffin Township in 1802 under Reverend Thomas Ellrod, and a Christian Union church was organized at West Union in 1808. [60]

In 1926 there were 6,040 church members in Adams County. Of this number 2,258 were Methodist Episcopal, 908 were Presbyterians, 552 were Disciples of Christ, and smaller numbers belonged to several other denominations.[61]

The first schools of the county were of the subscription type, the parents of the pupils paying a small fee for the tuition. Many of these schools were not of very high quality, the teachers frequently being intemperate or poorly educated.[62]

60. Caldwell's *Atlas*. 16-58, *passim*; Evans and Stivers, *op. cit.*, 413-500, *passim*.
61. Bureau of the Census, *Religious Bodies; 1926*. I, 656-59,
62. D.C. Shilling, "Pioneer Schools and School Masters," *Ohio State Arch. and Hist. Quarterly*. XXV (1916), 49.

Schools of the tuition type were established in 1794 at Manchester under William Dobbins and Israel Donalson, in 1802 in Meigs Township under James Lane, in 1803 in Liberty Township under Mrs. Dodson, in 1804 in Sprigg Township under Allen Gates, in 1805 at Winchester under Richard Cross, in 1807 in Scott Township under James McGill, and in other townships soon thereafter. No academies were chartered in the county prior to 1840,[63] but in 1848 or 1851 the North Liberty Academy in Wayne Township was opened. In 1882 this school offered normal school training, but in 1893 it was sold to the public schools of the district.[64] In 1856 the schools of Manchester and West Union were reorganized and graded, an example that was soon followed by the other districts in the county.[65] In 1935 there were 4,731 pupils enrolled in the county's schools,[66] and the percentage of illiteracy which had been 4.2 percent in 1920 had been reduced to 3.0 percent in 1930.[67] In 1934 the Alfred Holbrook College was transferred to Manchester.[68]

The first newspaper in the county was the *Political Censor*, printed in West Union in 1815 by James Finley. Other early papers of this village were the *Village Register* in 1823, the *Juvenile Journal* in 1825 (said to have been the first children's magazine west of the Alleghenies), the *Courier of Liberty* in 1831, and the *Register* in 1833. In 1835 appeared the first Whig paper, the *Free Press*. The first newspaper issued at Manchester was the *People's Intelligencer*, a Whig paper which appeared in 1852, and in 1867 the *Gazette* was published,[69] At present there are three newspapers issued in the county: the Manchester *Signal*, a Republican daily, founded in 1881; the West Union *People's Defender*, a Democratic weekly, established in 1866 and the *Adams County Messenger*, a Republican weekly, printed since 1928.[70]

---

63. W.W. Boyd, "Secondary Education in Ohio Previous to the Year 1840," *ibid.*, XXV (1916), 120; Edward A. Miller, "The History of Educational Legislation in Ohio from 1803 to 1850." *ibid.*, XXVII (1918), 100.

64. Evans and Stivers, *op. cit.*, 468-87,

65. Caldwell's *Atlas*. 33, 34, 41

66. *Adams Schools Survey*, 22.

67. *Fifteenth Census of the United States. 1930, Population*. Ill, pt. ii , 479

68. *Adams Schools Survey*, 3.

69. Caldwell's *Atlas*. 46-48

70. Ayer. *op. cit.*, 721, 724.

In the decades immediately preceding the War between the States the slavery question was a source of much acrimony in Adams County. Most of the early settlers had been Virginians, and in many cases had brought a few slaves with them who acted as servants but remained in virtual bondage.[71] A strong anti-slavery feeling developed in some sections, and in 1836 in Green Township the Sandy Springs Anti-Slavery Society was organized. The Covenanters who settled about Cherry Creek and Brush Creek under Reverend Dyer Burgess and others became ardent abolitionists, and there were many stations of the "Underground Railroad" in the county. There was an early anti-slavery organization at West Union, but later this part of the county became strongly pro-slavery in its sentiments. In 1836 the Reverend John Rankin, a noted abolitionist, was attacked at Winchester.[72] Despite these early differences the county proved very loyal to the Union cause during the War between the States.[73] In 1863 Morgan's Raiders passed through Adams County and caused considerable loss of property and life,[74] but such untoward incidents have been few in the history of this peaceful agricultural county.

---

71. Evans and Stivers, *op. cit.*, 404-5,

72. Paul R. Grim, "The Rev. John Rankin, Early Abolitionist," *Ohio State Arch, and Hist. Quarterly.* XLVI (1937), 232-33; Caldwell's *Atlas.* 27; Evans and Stivers, *op. cit.*, 406-8.

73. *Ibid.*, 330-64.

74. Emilius O. Randall and Daniel J. Ryan, *History of Ohio: The Rise and Progress of an American State* (New York, 1912), IV, 246.

The county as a political institution and as a subdivision of the state for purposes of political and judicial administration is of ancient origin.[1] In a form substantially similar in all general features and functions it has existed in England since early times, and in America since its settlement. As the tide of migration moved westward, following the American Revolution, the institutions of the seaboard states were transferred to the newer west, undergoing such alteration as best suited frontier conditions.[2]

The earliest provision for the settlement of counties in what is now the state of Ohio was contained in the Ordinance of 1787, by which the governor of the Northwest Territory was directed to "lay out the parts of the district in which the indian [sic] titles shall have been extinguished into counties and townships subject however to such alterations as may thereafter be made by the legislature."[3] The organization of county government, therefore, began before the organization of the state and before the adoption of a state constitution. Prior to statehood four counties, including Adams, were organized. The first county lines were drawn in 1788.[4] The last county lines were altered in 1888, exactly one hundred years later.[5]

The establishment of local government in the Northwest Territory was one of the first concerns of Governor St. Clair. The Ordinance of 1787 furnished the framework, but details of institutions had to be constructed. All county officials, under the provisions of the ordinance, were made appointive by the governor.

---

1. Edward Channing, *A History of the United States* (New York, 1905), I, 425-26.
2. Beverley W. Bond, Jr., *The Civilization of the Old Northwest: A Study of Political, Social, and Economic Development. 1788-1812* (New York, 1934), 58-59.
3. Clarence Edwin Carter, ed. and comp., *The Territorial Papers of the United States* (Washington, 1934), II, 44.
4. *Ibid.*, III, 279.
5. *Laws of Ohio*. LXXXV, 418; Randolph Chandler Downes, "Evolution of Ohio County Boundaries," *Ohio State Arch, and Hist. Quarterly*. XXXVI (1927), 449.

St. Clair, a former resident of Pennsylvania, in providing for local administration depended in a large part upon the Pennsylvania Code, which, in some instances, was altered to meet the needs of pioneer communities.[6] The provisions for local administration were, for the most part, simple and effective. In each county the court of general quarter sessions, composed of three or more justices of the peace, served as the fiscal and administrative board of the county, estimating county expenditure appointing tax commissioners, and providing for highway and bridge construction.[7] By the end of the decade the court was authorized to make and enter contracts for building or repairing the county jail and the courthouse.[8] Other county officials included a sheriff, a coroner, a recorder, a treasurer, a license commission, and justices and clerks of the various courts.[9]

Officers having been appointed, the next step in the organization of government was the establishment of a system of local courts. Evidence seems to indicate that the judicial system for the county had been carefully planned. The court of common pleas, composed of not less than three nor more than five appointive judges, was an inferior court having general common law jurisdiction, though concurrent in the various counties with the supreme court.[10]

---

6. The governor and judges were given power to "adopt and publish in the district such laws of the original states" as they thought necessary and these laws were to remain in force unless disapproved by Congress. In many cases the governor and judges had not adopted laws of the original states, as the Ordinance stipulated, but had passed measures that conformed in spirit. Since there was some question of the legality of these laws St. Clair, in 1795, after the lower house of Congress disapproved of the laws passed at the legislative session of 1792, called a legislative session to revise the territorial code. The commission, after sitting for three months, completed Maxwell's Code, named in honor of the printer, W. Maxwell. Few changes were made in the Maxwell Code by the territorial assembly which was elected in 1798. Carter, II, 43. The minutes of the legislative assembly were reproduced in *The Ohio State Arch, and Hist. Quarterly.* XXX (1921), 13-53.
7. Theodore Calvin Pease, *The Laws of the Northwest Territory 1788-1800* (Illinois State Bar Association Law Series. Springfield, 1925, I), 4, 36, 337; 69-70; 467-68; 74, 77, 453, 456, 485.
8. *Ibid.*, 485.
9. *Ibid.*, 8, 24-25, 61, 68-69, 197.
10. *Ibid.*, 7.

The court of general quarter sessions, besides serving as the fiscal and administrative board of the county, had jurisdiction in lesser criminal cases.[11] A probate court, composed of a single judge, was given jurisdiction in probate and testamentary matters.[12] In 1795, following St. Clair's revision of the territorial code, circuit courts were established; and orphans' courts were instituted .[13]

In the meantime the local government was further developed by the organization of civil townships. The governor and judges adopted a law from the Pennsylvania Code requiring the justices of the court of quarter sessions to divide each county into townships and appoint in each a constable to act in townships and the county, a clerk, and one or more overseers of the poor.[14]

The territory entered the second stage of administration when, in 1798, the population, having reached the requisite five thousand, the governor ordered the election of a representative assembly.[15] The system of local government continued, as established by the governor and judges and the transition was achieved without a disturbance of local administration.

The admission of Ohio as a state did not, in the main, materially affect county organization and administration. The system of local government having been organized by the governor and judges and the legislature of the Northwest Territory, the basic offices were continued and the transfer from the territorial status to statehood was achieved without incident to disturb the effectiveness of the system. Except for the provision for the election of a county sheriff and a county coroner in each county, two officials of utmost importance in pioneer communities, the constitution was silent on such matters as titles, number of officials, and duties.[16]

---

11. *Ibid.*, 4-7.
12. *Ibid.*, 9.
13. *Ibid.*, 157, 181-88.
14. *Ibid.*, 37-41, 338. The system of local governmental administration was the result of sectional compromise, since it combined the county system of the southern and middle states with the elements of the New England town. Dwight G. McCarty, *The Territorial Governors of the Old Northwest: A Study in Territorial Administration* (Iowa City, 1910). 53-54.
15. Carter, *op. cit.*, III, 514-15.
16. *Ohio Const. 1802*, Art. VI, sec. 1.

It resolved, therefore, upon the legislature to confer powers upon the county. In 1804 the legislature made provision for a board of county commissioners, composed of three members elected for a three-year term.[17] The board of county commissioners, supplanting the court of quarter sessions, became the administrative and fiscal board of the county. The legislature, in 1803, recognizing the need for a more adequate system of land records, provided for a recorder to be appointed by the court of common pleas for a seven-year term and for a surveyor also to be appointed by the court of common pleas.[18] Another act authorized the appointment of a county treasurer by the associate judges–later by the county commissioners.[19]

The legislature provided also, during its first session, for a prosecuting attorney to be appointed by the supreme court to prosecute cases in behalf of the state.[20] In 1805 the appointing power was transferred to the court of common pleas.[21]

A new office was created in 1820. The county auditor, first appointed by the legislature, had as his duty the preparation of the tax duplicate.[22] The county board of revision, the purpose of which was to correct some of the inequalities of assessments, was established in 1825. The first board of revision or equalization, as it was sometimes called, was composed of the commissioners, the auditor, and the assessors.[23]

The judicial power of the state in matters of law and equity was vested in the supreme court, the court of common pleas, and the justices' courts. The articles of the constitution, in regard to the judiciary, provided for a court of common pleas to be composed of a president and associate justices. The members of the court, appointed by a joint ballot of both houses of the general assembly, were to hold court in three judicial circuits into which the state was to be divided by the legislature.[24]

---

17. *Laws of Ohio.* II, 150.
18. *Ibid.*, I, 136, 90-93.
19. *Ibid.*, I. 97-98; XX. 154.
20. *Ibid.*, I, 50.
21. *Ibid.*, III, 47.
22. *Ibid.*, XVIII, 70.
23. *Ibid.*, XXIII, 68-69.
24. *Ohio Const. 1802.* Art. III, secs., 3, 8.

The court was assigned common law and chancery jurisdiction in all cases to be provided by law.[25] To the court was assigned jurisdiction in probate and testamentary matters granting administration and in the appointment of guardians, functions performed during the territorial period by the probate court.[26] Finally, the court was authorized to appoint a clerk.[27]

The county offices created by the legislature were designed to transact the business of a state as yet unaffected by transformations wrought by industrialism and the problems presented by large urban areas, aside from the maintenance of county poorhouses, the county had no functions in the administration of public welfare.

As the wave of democratic philosophy swept across the country in the 1820s and 1830s there arose a demand not only for an extension of the franchise but also for the election of public officials. Accordingly the auditor became an elective official in 1821, the treasurer in 1827, the recorder in 1829, and the prosecuting attorney in 1833.[28]

While the legislature responded to the general demand for the election of county officials, there arose a further demand for a revision of the constitution which failed to meet the needs of an expanding state. This movement came as a result of dissatisfaction with the judicial system which placed the burden of judicial administration upon four judges who had the task of holding court each year in all the counties. Then, too, there arose a demand for the election of all public officials, for the prohibition of charters that granted special privilege, and for a limitation on the legislature to create a state debt. In February 1850 the legislature, following a favorable popular vote on the proposition, called for the election of delegates to meet in convention in May. The constitution drafted by the delegates, was approved by a special election on June 17, 1851.

---

25. *Ibid.*, Art. III, sec . 3.
26. *Ibid.*, Art. III, sec . 5; Pease, op. cit. 9.
27. *Ibid.*, Art. III, sec . 9.
28. *Laws of Ohio*, XIX, 116; XXV, 25-32; XXVII, 65; XXXI, 13-14.

The constitution of 1851, like the constitution of 1802, failed to provide a definite form of county government and administration. Aside from the constitutional provision for the election of a county treasurer, sheriff, and clerk of courts and re-creating the probate court which had existed during the territorial period, the organic instrument was silent on the administrative duties of the county.[29] Again all matters pertaining to county government were entrusted to the legislature. While the legislature conferred powers upon the county, it was limited by constitutional provision which required all laws of a general nature to be uniform throughout the state.[30]

The present administrative organization of Ohio county government presents a picture of extraordinary complexity. Each county quadrennially elects, besides the board of county commissioners, nine administrative officials: the recorder, the clerk of courts, the probate judge, the prosecuting attorney, the coroner, the sheriff, the treasurer, the auditor, and the county engineer. While the above mentioned officials conduct a major portion of the county's business, there is a variety of appointive officers and boards, as well as *ex-officio* commissioners. For convenience the work of county government may be classified under the following general heads: administration, courts, law enforcing agencies, financial administration, health, welfare, and public works.

Administration

The board of county commissioners is the central feature of the present structure of county government. The functions of this board touch either directly or indirectly every other branch and department. The board is the agency in whose name actions for and against the county are brought. This board is empowered to determine certain policies for the conduct of county affairs such as adoption of the budget, establishment of services left optional by law, and the authorization of improvement.[31]

---

29. *Ohio Const. 1851.* Art. X, sec. 3; Art. IV, sec. 16; Art. IV, sec. 7.
30. *Ibid.,* Art. II, sec. 26.
31. G.C., sec. 2421.

Thus in a limited sense it constitutes the legislative branch. The commissioners, however, have no ordinance-making powers. The board also functions as the central administrative body although much of the administration, centered in other elective offices, is beyond its control. The county auditor was originally made secretary of the board and still functions as such in a majority of the counties.[32] Later provisions of the law permitted the board to appoint its own clerk, thus removing this duty from the auditor.

Judicial System

The constitution of 1851 made significant changes in the composition of the court of common pleas. The judges, heretofore appointed by the legislature, were made elective for a seven-year term. For the purpose of electing judges the state was divided into nine districts. Each district was divided into three parts, in each of which one common pleas judge was to be elected. Court was to be held in every district or county with such jurisdiction as should be provided by law.[33] The legislature made a provision for the districts but left the jurisdiction of the court much as it had been in the earlier years of its existence.[34] The constitutional amendment of 1912 abolished the divisions and subdivisions provided by the constitution of 1851, and authorized the election of one or more common pleas judges in each county.[35]

The judicial system was extended in 1851 by the creation of district courts composed of one supreme court justice and several common pleas judges in each district.[36] For administrative purposes the nine common pleas districts were apportioned into five judicial circuits.[37] The courts were assigned original jurisdiction in the same matters as the supreme court and such appellate jurisdiction as might be provided by law.[38]

---

32. *Ibid.*, 2566.
33. *Ohio Const. 1851.* Art. IV, sees. 3, 4.
34. *Laws of Ohio.* LI, 145.
35. *Ohio Const. 1851.* (Amendment), Art. 17, sec. 3.
36. *Ohio Const. 1851.* Art. IV, sec. 5,
37. *Laws of Ohio.* L, 69.
38. *Ohio Const. 1851.* Art. IV, sec. 6.

The district courts, abolished by the constitutional amendment of 1883, were superseded by the circuit courts which were given the same jurisdiction as their predecessors. The state was divided into seven circuits. In each circuit three judges were to be elected.[39] The judicial system was again altered in 1912 when, by constitutional amendment, the circuits were renamed courts of appeals.[40] The state is divided into nine appellate districts. There are three judges in each district elected by the people of the district for a six-year term.[41]

The constitution of 1851 re-created the probate court, which, existing during the territorial period, was abolished by the first constitution and its authority and jurisdiction vested in the courts of common pleas. Each county has one probate judge elected by the people for a four-year term.[42] The probate judge, by constitutional provision, has original jurisdiction in probate and testamentary matters, the appointment of guardians, the settlement of the accounts of executors, administrators, and guardians,[43] and the issuance of marriage licenses. An amendment to the constitution of 1912 authorized the common pleas judge, when petitioned by ten percent of the voters in counties having a population of less than 60,000, to submit to the voters at any general election the question of combining the probate and common pleas courts.[44] This combination exists in Adams, Henry, and Wyandot counties.

Due to an increased amount of juvenile delinquency, the legislature in 1904, authorized the judges of the court of common pleas, the probate court, and the insolvency courts where established to appoint one or more of their members as "juvenile judge" to hear cases involving neglected, dependent, and delinquent children.[45] In most Ohio counties including Adams, the probate judge, serves as judge of the juvenile court.

---

39. *Ibid.*, Art. IV, sec. 6.
40. *Ibid.*, Art, IV, sec. 6.
41. G.C. sec. 1514.
42. *Laws of Ohio*, CXIV, 320.
43. *Ohio Const. 1851.* Art. IV, sec. 8.
44. *Ibid.* Art, IV, sec. 7.
45. *Laws of Ohio*. XCVII, 561-62.

Law Enforcement

Closely related to the courts are the agencies of law enforcement in the county. Law enforcement is conducted by three officials: the sheriff, the prosecuting attorney, and the coroner. These officials are concerned primarily with the enforcement of state laws, leaving the enforcement of municipal ordinances, and, in some instances, state statutes in urban centers to municipal law-enforcing agencies.

The county sheriff, whose duties have been seriously curbed by municipal law-enforcing agencies and the state highway patrol, has as his duty the enforcement of state law:[46] he serves as custodian of the county jail,[47] and serves as an executive agent of the courts.[48] It has been estimated that approximately one half of the sheriff's time is devoted to duties connected with the courts. It has been charged that "little attempt is made by sheriffs to exert a preventive or repressive influence on the activities of criminals." This is due, in part, to the lack of scientific equipment which has become essential to law enforcement.[49]

The county prosecuting attorney, the most important personage in the enforcement of criminal law, is directed by law to "inquire into the commission" of crime within his county, and to prosecute on behalf of the state all complaints, suits, and controversies to which the state is a party.[50] In conjunction with the state attorney general, he prosecutes cases in the supreme court arising in his county.[51]

---

46. G.C. sec. 2833. The sheriff's authority extends to all parts of the county, although for obvious practical purposes he rarely makes an arrest in incorporated areas.

47. *Ibid.*, sec. 3157.

48. *Ibid.*, sec. 2834.

49. *The Reorganization of County Government in Ohio: Report of the Governor's Commission on County Government* (n.p., December 1934), 105. The sheriff system worked admirably in rural communities. From the standpoint of police administration, it is unsatisfactory in areas of dense population. In such areas there is need for a force of officers whose duty it is not merely to apprehend law violators but to prevent the infraction of the law by patrolling the territory. For an interesting discussion of some of the newer problems confronting law enforcing agencies see Donald C. Stone, "The Police Attack Crime," *Nat. Mun. Review.* XXIY (1935), 39-41.

50. G.C., sec. 2916.

51. *Ibid.*, sec. 2916.

He acts, also, in a civil capacity as the legal counsel for the commissioners and other county officials.[52] The prosecuting attorney may institute proceedings against an individual, but as a rule charges must be filed against the offender before action is taken. The prosecuting attorney has certain administrative duties such as serving as a member of the county budget commission and the board of sinking fund trustees.[53] In view of the importance of this office and the powers possessed by the incumbent, the political aspects of the prosecutor's office have attracted the unfavorable attention of those interested in improving judicial administration.[54] Despite the criticism leveled at this office, the prosecuting attorney remains one of the great bulwarks against modern gangland.

The county coroner has the ancient duty of determining the cause of death where death results from suspicious or unlawful means,[55] the making of the proper distribution of property found on or about the deceased,[56] and the management of the county morgue.[57] Since a large majority of the county coroners have had no medical training, it is impossible for them to execute their duties properly.[58] Indeed, the work of the prosecuting attorney is sometimes impeded by the acts of the coroner. It has been suggested, by authorities on county administration, that the office be abolished and the duties transferred to a medical examiner appointed by the prosecuting attorney.[59]

---

52. *Ibid.*, sec. 2917.

53. *Laws of Ohio*. CXI I, 399-400; CXV, pt. ii, 412; CX71, 565; CVIII, pt. I , 700-702.

54. Report of the Governor's Commission. 113-14, See also, W.F. Willoughby, *Principles of Judicial Administration* (Washington, 1929), 130.

55. G.C. sec. 2856,

56. *Ibid.*, secs. 2863, 2864.

57. *Ibid.*, sec. 2856-1,

58. The office of county coroner is one that requires two distinct qualifications on the part of the incumbent, those of a medical specialist and those of one familiar with legal principles and procedure. This combination of qualities is, indeed, rare. An investigation covering the state, made by the Governor's Commission in 1934, revealed that at least thirty-three of the eighty-eight county coroners were not members of the medical profession. It is not strange that undertakers, interested in the commercial aspect of the office, are always available candidates. *Report of the Governor's Commission*, 117. According to a recent act, effective June 8, 1937, only a licensed physician or a person who shall have previously served as coroner is eligible to fill the office. G.C. sec. 2856-3.

59. Willoughby, *op. cit.*, 165-73.

Law enforcement in the county is defective in two respects: first, there is little or no coordination between the three agencies of law enforcement, and second, there is little or no responsibility for neglect of duty. Evidence seems to indicate that the present inefficient aid antiquated system could be corrected by consolidating all law-enforcing agencies into a county department of law enforcement under the immediate supervision of the county prosecuting attorney.[60]

The administration of criminal justice in the county has grown up in more or less hit-or-miss fashion and is for the most part unsatisfactory and extremely cumbersome. Arrests are made by the sheriff, or other police officers, who are theoretically officers of the state, but who are under little or no supervision. The accused person is brought before a local magistrate for a preliminary hearing. In the event the accused is committed, it is necessary, in most cases, to receive an indictment before a grand jury. The prosecuting attorney is really the person who determines whether the person will be prosecuted after the indictments have been returned. A locally selected jury determines the question of guilt.[61]

Finance

There are three types of financial functions performed by county officers and employees: tax administration, handling of the fiscal affairs of the county, and the trusteeship of funds held for individuals in court procedure. The principal financial authorities are the board of commissioners, the auditor, and the treasurer. The commissioners levy taxes, appropriate funds, and authorize payments.[62] The auditor's primary duties are the keeping of accounts, the issuance of warrants, the valuation of real estate , and the preparation of the tax list.[63] The treasurer collects taxes, receives and has custody of county money, and disburses it upon warrant from the auditor.[64] Other functions relating to county finances are performed by the board of revision, budget commission, and board of sinking fund trustees.

---

60. *Report of Governor's Commission*, 117-22.
61. For a criticism of the administration of criminal justice, see Edwin H. Sutherland, *Principles of Criminology* (Chicago, 1934), chap. xiv; Willoughby, *op. cit.*, chaps., xi, xiv, xxxvi.
62. G.C. secs. 5630, 5637, 7419.
63. *Ibid.*, secs. 2570, 2573, 2583-2589.
64. *Ibid.*, secs. 2649, 2649-1, 2656, 2674.

The board of revision, or equalization, originally established in 1825, and continued by statutory enactments following the adoption of the constitution of 1851, is composed of the county treasurer, the county auditor, and the president of the county commissioners. It is the function and duty of this board to hear all complaints relating to the valuation or assessment of real property as appearing on the tax duplicate.[65]

Since the Ohio legislature, in 1911, established a tax rate limitation, it was necessary to establish a commission vested with the authority to reduce the amounts set up in the annual tax budgets when the overlapping districts required more than the aggregate maximum tax rate permits. This power was vested, in 1927, in the budget commissioners, consisting of the county auditor, the county treasurer and the prosecuting attorney.[66] The county auditor is prohibited from making up his tax list and duplicate, until the board has completed its work and has returned to him all the returns laid before it with revision.[67]

The board of trustees of the sinking fund, consisting of the prosecuting attorney, the auditor, and the treasurer, was created in 1919 to provide ways and means for the payment of all bonds issued by the county and the interest maturing thereon.[68]

---

65. *Ibid.*, sec. 5596
66. *Laws of Ohio.* CXII, 399-400.
67. G.C. sec. 5605.
68. *Ibid.*, secs. 2976-18, 2976-19.

Elections

Any discussion of county governmental organization would be incomplete without considering public elections. Public elections belong to the political branch of county government. Such a system, unknown in the common law, depends entirely upon regulation by constitutional and statutory provisions. The duty of providing machinery of elections devolves upon the legislature and the manner in which the privilege of the suffrage is exercised is subject to legislative control.

During the first nine decades of Ohio history the county sheriff was charged with the duty of announcing the time and place of holding elections, providing ballot boxes, ballots, and other supplies, and the township trustees were directed by law to serve as judges of the elections.[69] This system continued, with slight alterations designed to facilitate the conduct of elections in municipal centers until 1892. At that time there were created the offices of state supervisors of elections and deputy state supervisors of all elections with duties prescribed for the conduct and supervision of all elections in the state .[70] The secretary of state, designated as the state supervisor of elections, was authorized and instructed to appoint four deputy supervisors, who, in turn, appointed in all precincts four judges and two clerks of elections.[71]

Under the present election laws, provision is made for a chief election officer, a board of elections in each county, and judges and clerks in each precinct. The board of elections in each county consists of four qualified electors in the county, the members of which are appointed by the secretary of state, two of such members being appointed on the first day of March in the even-numbered years, to serve a four-year term.[72]

---

69. *Laws of Ohio*. I, 76-77; III, 331-32; VII, 113; XXIX, 44; L, 312; LXVIII,

70. *Ibid.*, LXXXIX, 455. This act, however, did not apply to the election of school director.

71. In 1892 each township, exclusive of the territory embraced within the limits of a municipal corporation which was divided into wards, composed an election precinct. See *Laws of Ohio*. LXVII, 47.

72. G.C. secs. 4785-6, 4785-8.

In making appointments to the membership of the board, equal representation is given to the political party casting the highest and the next highest number of votes for the office of governor in the last preceding state election. In this connection provision is made for party recommendations of persons for such appointments.[73]

Under the early election laws the canvassing board was composed of the clerk of the court of common pleas and two justices of the peace called by him to his assistance.[74] This practice continued until 1892 when the board of state supervisors of elections succeeded to the duties formerly performed by both the clerk of the court of common pleas and the county sheriff. The sheriff, however, continued to announce the time and place of holding elections in the county until January 1, 1930 when the board of elections assumed this historic duty.[75] The duty of canvassing the returns, under the present statutes, is performed by the board of elections. The board in each county is required, within five days after each general or special election, to canvass the returns, and to prepare abstracts of the votes cast.[76] A certified copy of the abstract is to be transmitted to the secretary of state, and another copy filed in the office of the board.[77] The board is required also to prepare and transmit to the president of the senate a separate abstract of the returns of election for governor, lieutenant governor, secretary of state, auditor of state, and attorney general.[78]

---

73. *Ibid.*, sec. 4785-9. Under the Ohio election law, it is the duty of the secretary of state to appoint persons so recommended, unless he should have reason to believe that such a person would not be a competent member of the board.

74. *Laws of Ohio*, I, 83; III, 336-37; VII, 119-20; XXIX, 49; L, 316; LXI, 68; LXXXII, 30.

75. G.C. sec. 4785-5; *Laws of Ohio*. CXIII. 307; LXXXIX, 455. The election laws of Ohio were revised and recodified by an act of the general assembly, passed April 5, 1929. *Laws of Ohio*, CXIII, 307-413.

76. G.C. secs. 4785-152, 4785-153.

77. *Ibid.*, sec. 4785-153.

78. *Ohio Const. 1851*. Art. III, sec. 3; G.C. sec. 4785-154.

Health

Prior to 1919 the county had few responsibilities in regard to health administration. With the development of urban centers with congested areas the problem of health administration was brought to the attention of the legislature. Prior to the enactment of the present health code in 1919, jurisdiction in matters of health was vested in the cities, villages, and townships. Under the act of 1919 all villages, and townships in the county were combined into a general health district under the supervision of a board appointed by the advisory council composed of the mayors of villages and chairmen of township trustees. Each city in the district is organized as a separate health district. Two general health districts or a general health district and a city health district located within such a district may combine.[79] All physicians are required to report communicable diseases to the district health commissioners who impose quarantines.[80]

The legislature has placed on the county the burden of responsibility in the treatment of tuberculosis. Any county, regardless of its size, may employ nurses, operate clinics, and care for patients in private, municipal, or county sanatoriums. Any county having a population of 50,000 or more inhabitants may with the consent of the state department of health, erect and operate sanatoriums, and two or more counties may form districts for the same purpose. The sanatoriums are operated by special boards appointed by the county commissioners.[81]

Besides establishing sanatoriums for the treatment of tubercular patients, counties are authorized to operate general hospitals. The county hospital is operated by a board appointed by the county commissioners.[82] Evidence seems to indicate that the county is the proper unit for hospital administration.

---

79. *Laws of Ohio*. CVIII, pt. I, 238; CVIII, pt. ii, 1885-86,,
80. *Ibid.*, CVIII, pt. ii , 1088-89.
81. G.C. secs. 3148-1, 3148-3.
82. *Ibid.*, secs. 3127-3138-4.

Public Welfare

The administration of public welfare presents one of the most complex and one of the most expensive functions of county government. The administration of institutional and outdoor relief is delegated to eight boards and commissions operating independently and with little regard for efficiency.

The county home, originally established by the legislative acts of 1816, is one of the most unprogressive institutions in the county. The administration of the county home is vested in the county commissioners and a superintendent, appointed from a list of names of persons eligible under civil service regulations.[83] Employees are appointed by the superintendent.

Although provision was made for the institutional care of the county's indigent as early as 1816, it was not until after the conclusion of the War between the States when hundreds of Ohio youngsters were left homeless, that the legislature enacted measures for the care of dependent children.[84] Previous to the act of 1865, the trustees of the poorhouses were authorized to apprentice dependent children. The administration of the children's home is vested in a board of trustees, appointed by the commissioners, and a superintendent appointed by the board of trustees.[85]

The board of county visitors, an agency for the examination of county institutions, was created by the general assembly in 1882. Until 1913 the board was appointed by the court of common pleas and after that date by the probate judge.[86] The board consists of six persons appointed for terms of three years.

In 1886 counties were required by law to provide relief for indigent soldiers and sailors and their indigent wives, children, and parents.[87] Soldiers relief is administered by a commission consisting of three persons appointed by the court of common pleas for terms of three years. This commission, in turn, selects township and ward committees.[88]

---

83. *Ibid.*, sec. 2523.
84. *Laws of Ohio* III, 276; VIII. 223-24. •
85. G.C. secs. 3081,3084
86. *Laws of Ohio* LXXXIII, 174; G.C. secs. 3082-1, 3085
87. *Ibid.*, LXXXIII, 232-34
88. G.C. secs. 2930, 2933

In 1884 the legislature made provision for a soldiers' burial commission in each county.[89] The administration of soldiers' burials is vested in a commission consisting of two persons in each township and ward appointed by the county commissioners.[90]

Counties maintain a system of pensions for the needy blind. Prior to 1936 blind relief was administered in the county by the probate judge (1904-1908), by a blind relief commission appointed by the probate judge (1908-1913), and by the county commissioners (1913-1936).[91] The present system originated in 1936 when the legislature accepted the provisions of the federal social security act. Blind relief is financed by federal, state, and local funds and is administered in the state by the Ohio commission for the blind and in the county by the county commissioners, who were designated as a blind relief commission.[92]

Prior to 1932 the county confined its relief activities to the institutional care of the indigent. Outdoor relief, except for those persons lacking a legal settlement, was provided and administered by the townships and cities. With the coming of the economic depression the resources of the municipalities and townships proved inadequate for financing relief activities. Accordingly, in 1932, the legislature conferred on all counties the authority to care for the poor in their own homes. Funds for such purposes were provided by the issuance of bonds and by a diversion of gasoline taxes for financing such services. While the state relief commission, created for administering state relief, is required to pass upon local relief budgets, the county relief offices, administered by the county commissioners, provide relief services in the county.

---

89. *Laws of Ohio*, LXXXI, 146-7
90. G.C. sec. 2950.
91. *Laws of Ohio*, XCVII, 392-94; XCIX, 56-58; CIII, 60.
92. *Ibid.*, CXVI, pt. ii, 195-200

Old age pensions are relieving the counties of the increased burdens of institutional relief. This system, originating in 1933, provides for persons sixty-five years of age or over. The person applying for the pension must have no property of net value over $3,000 nor an annual income of over $300.[93] The old age pension system is financed by state and federal funds and is administered by a division of the department of public welfare through county boards of aid to the aged.[94] Under the provision of the initial act the county commissioners served as *ex-officio* members of the board of aid for the aged in the county. Since May 1, 1937 the chief of the division has been required by law to appoint an advisory board in each county consisting of five members. This board, appointed for a two-year term, succeeded to the duties formerly performed by the county commissioners.[95]

Aid to dependent children, although provided for by the legislature in 1913 in the form of mothers' pensions, assumed a new significance, when, in 1936, the legislature accepted the provisions of the federal social security act. Aid to dependent children is financed by federal, state, and local funds. The administration of the act is delegated to the department of public welfare and in Adams County to the juvenile judge.[96]

The welfare facilities of the county outlined above have been adopted one after another as the result of the demands occasioned by a changing society. When a new function of county government has been needed to be performed, a new bureau or commission has been created with little regard for efficiency or economical administration. There is some difference of opinion, but the trend of thought seems to favor a consolidation of all relief responsibilities under a single head. This would eliminate the duplication of work, and centralize responsibility, which, at present, rests with eight separate boards with overlapping jurisdiction.

---

93. *Ibid.*, CXV, pt. ii, 431-39.
94. *Ibid.*, CXV, pt. ii . 431-39.
95. G.C. sec. 1359-12.
96. *Laws of Ohio*, CXVI, pt. ii. 188-96.

Public Works

The responsibility for the administration of public works in the county rests with the board of county commissioners, the county engineer, and the sanitary engineer. The county commissioners, since the inauguration of county government, have had the responsibility for the authorization and financing of public works. With the immense development of highway improvement, occasioned by the introduction of automobiles and trucks as means of transportation, public works became one of the most important functions of the county commissioners and consequently the county engineer, who, during the first 120 years of his office, had as his principal duty the surveying of lands, received new duties and responsibilities with respect to the construction of roads, culverts, ditches, and in most cases bridges.[97] Within the last two decades the township roads, under the joint authority of the county and the township trustees, have been gradually absorbed by the county state system of highways.[98]

Authorities on county administration are agreed that the organization of county public works is defective. The overlapping jurisdiction of the county commissioners and the county engineer makes it impossible to place responsibility for neglect of duty.

The Ohio counties were formed to meet the needs of rural pioneer communities with a population spread relatively uniformly over the entire state. Recent decades have, of course, brought remarkable changes. Many sections of the state have become thoroughly industrialized, and, as a result of the change, have been forced to treat of such problems as housing, health, sanitation, police administration, scientific transportation, and sewage disposal. These problems with which the county organization has been unable to cope are rapidly taking the forms of city problems.

---

97. *Laws of Ohio*. XCVIII, 245-47; CVIII, pt. I, 497.
98. The centralization of highway construction was guaranteed under the road law of 1915. The township trustees, at one time one of the most important agencies in local highway construction, have become a local improvement board with powers to authorize but not to supervise road construction. *Laws of Ohio* CV, 589-94.

When it is considered that in 1930, of the 1,201,455 persons in Cuyahoga County 900,429 were in Cleveland, that of the 361,055 people in Franklin County 290,564 were in Columbus, that of the 589,356 people in Hamilton County 541,160 were in Cincinnati, and that of the 347,709 people in Lucas County 290,718 were in Toledo, it is not strange that demands were made for a reorganization of county government to eliminate the waste and confusion occasioned by overlapping jurisdiction of county and municipal functions.[99]

In view of the growth of large cities and the confusion occasioned by the conflict of county and municipal powers, there has been an attempt to work out a more satisfactory relationship between the two organs of local government. This took the form of a constitutional amendment, which, defeated in 1919, was placed on the ballot in 1933 by initiative petition and adopted by the electorate. The amendment provides:

> "The General Assembly shall provide by general law for the organization and government of counties, and may provide by general law— alternative forms of county government. No alternative form shall become operative in any county until submitted to the electors thereof and approved by a majority of those voting thereon under regulations provided by law. Municipalities and townships shall have authority, with the consent of the county, to transfer to the county any of their powers or to revoke the transfer of any such power, under regulations provided by general law, but the rights of initiative and referendum shall be secured every measure... giving or withdrawing such consent."[100]

The constitutional amendment of 1933 altered the status of the county. Where the status of the county was formerly fixed by statute, it is now subject to local determination in the same manner as municipalities.

---

99. *Fifteenth Census of the United States. 1930, Population.* III, pt. ii, 518, 520, 521, 525. C.A. Dykstra "Cleveland's Effort for City-County Consolidation," *Nat. Mun. Review.* VIII, (1919), 551-56.
100. *Ohio Const. 1851* (Amendment, adopted November 7, 1933) Art. X, sec. 1.

The arguments advanced in favor of the system fall under three heads:

1. It makes possible a different form of government for urban centers
   where political, social, and economic conditions differ from those
   of rural counties.
2. It promotes efficiency and economy by the elimination of duplicate
   officers and employees.
3. It promotes efficiency by the centralization of power and
   responsibility.[101]

A commission on county government was appointed by Governor White in 1933 to formulate optional plans of county government for submission to the legislature.[102] Accordingly, in 1935, the commission submitted to the legislature ten bills embodying its recommendations as to matters of county reorganization. The major bills authorized three optional forms of county government, subject to adoption by the local electorate: (1) a county manager plan, (2) the elective plan, (3) the appointive executive plan.[103] Of the ten bills presented, two became laws, one of these authorized the transfer to the county of any local governmental activity by voluntary agreement between the county and a local subdivision within the county. This measure, of course, opened the way for the consolidation of such activities as welfare, police, and sewer construction which need unification in counties having a large urban population.[104] The other act authorizes the charter county to take over health administration, noninstitutional relief, and park construction.[105]

---

101. *Ohio State Journal*, October 9, 1933; C.A. Dykstra, lc. Cit.,551-56
102. R.C. Atkinson, "County Home Rule Developments in Ohio" *Nat. Mun. Review*, XXIII (1934), 235.
103. R.C. Atkinson, "Ohio - Optional County Legislation," *Nat. Mun. Review*, XXIV (1935), 228.
104. *Laws of Ohio*, CXVI, 102-4.
105. *Ibid.*, CXVI, 132-35.

While the amendment offers an opportunity for the improvement of local government in counties in which large municipalities have developed, no use has been made of the provision.[106] At present Franklin County with a population of 361,055 has essentially the same type of county government as Vinton County with a population of 10,287.[107]

While unsuccessful attempts have been made to correct some of the defects of county administration in areas containing large urban populations, little consideration has been given to rural counties where, due to a constant decline in population, the old governmental organization has become unduly expensive and ill-suited to the needs of the population. This is particularly true in the counties located in the southeastern and northwestern portions of the state where the population has steadily declined since 1880. There is a question as to whether the services of modern government in such counties can continue to be maintained without the consolidation of contiguous territory for purposes of administration. The Ohio Constitution, from its beginning in 1802 has contained a restriction upon the legislature in regard to the minimum area of counties. None could be formed with less than 400 square miles–or reduced below that size.[108] With the development of modern means of transportation and communication this area is ridiculously small. The combination for administrative purposes of sparsely populated counties, having common social and economic interests would eliminate waste, overhead, and duplication of personnel.

Governmental service is constantly requiring the employment of better trained officials. Evidence seems to indicate that only by enlarging the size of the administrative area to make possible the specialization in work can the requisite degree of training and skill be secured in the performance of public service.[109]

---

106. Home rule charters were submitted to the voters in Hamilton, Cuyahoga, Lucas, and Franklin counties. Advocates of home rule attributed the defeat of these measures to politicians who saw in the scheme the destruction of the spoils system. See R.C. Atkinson, "Ohio - County Charter Elections," *Nat. Mun. Review.* XXIV (1935), 702-3.
107. *Fifteenth Census of the United States, 1930. Population*, III, pt. ii, 520, 531
108. *Ohio Const, 1851.* Art. II, sec. 30; *Ohio Const. 1802.* Art. VI, sec. 3.
109. H. Eliot Kaplan, "A Personnel Program for County Service," *Nat. Mun. Review*, XXV (1936), 596-600.

The relation of the county to the state is also a matter of importance. As a result of radical changes in economic life, matters which were at one time a purely local interest and concern have become of statewide importance. During recent years the old type of county organization has proved inadequate to meet the needs of modern civilization. Recognition of this fact is found in the steady growth of state control of such matters as public accounting, health and welfare administration, and law enforcement.

At the same time the county has definitely supplanted the township as the administrative unit. This is particularly noticeable in the substitution of the general health district for the township district, and the transfer of tax assessment from the township assessors to the county auditor. The county-state administration of highway maintenance and public welfare have been affected. Although many deplore the passing of the little red schoolhouse, the substitution of the county school district for the township area has resulted in better educational advantages for children residing in rural areas.

It is significant that modern invention has removed the necessity for the rural administrative units of such small proportions. The transfer of power from the smaller to the larger unit has arisen out of the desire for better service and economy. Little remains to justify the retention of the township.

Records System

Indispensable to the operation of county government is a scientific system of records and accounts. Such records and accounts offer statistical records for county officers, enabling them to view past actions and to plan future work in terms of actual cost. It is unnecessary to point out that for students of history, political science, and sociology, etc., they are invaluable sources of information.[110]

---

110. Dr. Robert C. Binkley, professor of history, Western Reserve University, in an annual address before the eighty-eighth annual meeting of the Minnesota Historical Society, called attention to the importance of local documentary materials in the writing of a history for a democracy. Robert C. Binkley, "History for a Democracy," *Minnesota History; A Quarterly Magazine."* XVIII (1937), 1-27. See also, Carl Becker, "Everyman His Own Historian," *The Amer. Hist. Review.* XXXVII (1932), 221-36.

It has been the duty of most officials since the beginning of county government to keep a record of the business of their offices. These early records bear mute testimony to the efficiency and inefficiency of portions of the early governmental machinery and display in a remarkable degree the training and intelligence of the public officials. The difference in population, however, forced a wide variance in the recording as evidenced by the fact that several types of records were kept in the same book in some counties, and in others were kept in separate books. As indicated in detail in the office essays, preceding the records of each office, the legislature eventually prescribed not only what records were to be kept but also the content. In this field there was a remarkable advance following the adoption of the constitution of 1851. Such legislation assured some uniformity in the county records system.

There are three strictly clerical officers whose work consists mainly in the preparation and custody of records: the recorder, the clerk of courts, and the judge of the probate court. All three have some part in the recording of documents and instruments affecting the title of property and of other documents presented for record. The last two have as their principal duty the keeping of court records; the clerk of courts serving as clerk of both the court of common pleas and the court of appeals, and the probate court looking after its own records.

It is the duty of the county recorder to copy, index, and file documents authorized to be recorded in his office. The system of recording is prescribed in detail by law. In most counties recording is done by typewriter with considerable use of printed forms. The photographic method of copying is in use in Clark, Hamilton, Lucas, Montgomery, and Summit counties. Deeds, mortgages, plats, and leases must be copied into separate books, and indexed direct and reverse.[111] The recorder is required, also, to prepare daily an alphabetical index to such instruments.[112]

---

111. G.C. secs. 2757, 2764.
112. *Ibid.*, secs. 2764, 2766.

The principal records of the clerk of courts are prescribed by statute. They include an appearance docket, a trial docket, an execution docket, a journal, and a complete record of proceedings, a system of indexes, end a file of original papers.[113] The clerk is responsible for a variety of non-judicial records work of which the filing and indexing of automobile bills of sale was the major item. The bill of sale law was repealed by an act effective January 1, 1938, requiring the clerk to issue certificates of title to motor vehicles in triplicate and to file a duplicate of the certificate.[114] At present the clerk of courts acts as the agent of the state for the sale of hunting, trapping, and fishing licenses,[115] and also issues auctioneers and ferry licenses.[116]

The clerical portion of the probate court performs the following services; the recording of miscellaneous instruments, including marriage licenses,[117] and certificates of physicians, surgeons, and nurses to practice their professions in the county.[118] The court record system of the office, originating in 1853 and continued by the probate code of 1931, is prescribed by statute and involves the proper keeping of papers in each case and copying materials in appropriate record books.[119] Few records are prescribed for the law-enforcing agencies. The county sheriff is required by law to keep at least three books; a foreign execution docket,[120] a cash book,[121] and a jail register.[122] Indexes, direct and reverse, to the foreign execution docket were prescribed in 1925.[123]

---

113. *Ibid.*, secs. 2878, 2885, 2884.
114. *Ibid.*, sec 6290-6.
115. *Ibid.*, sec 1432.
116. *Ibid.*, secs. 5868-5869, 5947-5950.
117. *Ohio Const. 1851.* Art. IV, sec. 8.
118. *Laws of Ohio*, XCII, 45-47; XCIX, 499; CVI, 193.
119. *Ibid.*, CXIV, 321-22.
120. *Ibid.*, sec. 2837.
121. *Ibid.*, sec. 2839.
122. *Laws of Ohio*, XLI, 74; G.C. sec. 3158.
123. *Laws of Ohio*, CXI, 31.

The system of recording is prescribed by statute. The county coroner's records consist of two: a report of findings in cases of unlawful death,[124] and an inventory of articles found on the person or about the deceased.[125] Such records are prescribed by law and the contents of the records minutely prescribed.

It has generally been found that the records of the county prosecuting attorney are unbusiness-like and inadequate for the efficient administration of the office. Indeed, in many counties no records or files are kept and individual memoranda are disposed of by the incumbent. In some of the counties including Adams the records of the prosecuting attorney, kept on standard forms, include such records as a grand jury docket, a grand jury testimony record, and a criminal court docket. Since the county prosecuting attorney is vested with large discretionary powers, there is need of special records and files. Such records according to authorities on judicial administration should include, among others, a permanent record of the names and addresses of witnesses, the deputy or division handling the case, and the reason for failure to prosecute, and the reason for which a *nolle prosequi* was asked and granted.

The records of the financial agencies of county government are prescribed by statute. Although records were kept in the earlier years, it was not until 1902 that the manner of keeping and the content of such records attracted the attention of the legislature. It was evident that accounts had not only been poorly kept but there had been little uniformity among the counties of the state. Accordingly, in 1902, the legislature enacted the most important and far-reaching laws on the subject. This act provided for a uniform system of accounting, auditing, and reporting, under the supervision of a newly created bureau of inspection located in the office of the auditor of state. The act further provided for the annual examinations of the finances of all public offices.[126]

---

124. G.C. sec. 2857
125. *Ibid.*, sec. 2859
126. *Laws of Ohio* XXUV. 511-15

The governor's commission on the reorganization of county government, after studying the county records system and noting the illogical combination of administrative. Judicial, and financial functions, made the following recommendations:[127]

1. County charters and optional forms of government should provide for a department of records and court service to take over the functions of the recorder and clerk of courts, the nonjudicial record work of the probate court, and the functions of the sheriff as a court officer.
2. The issuance of licenses should be transferred from the clerk of courts to the department of finance.
3. Wider use should be made of the photographic process of recording in large counties.
4. Legislation should be adopted permitting the destruction of chattel mortgages and after they have ceased to have effect.
5. The requirement of three systems of indexes of cases in the clerk's office should be the code and of pending suits and living judgments should be required.
6. Provisions should be made in the rules of the common pleas court for service of process by mail and that method should be brought into general use.

Concurrently with the development of a records system, steps were taken to assure the proper restoration of damaged or dilapidated records treating of lands and surveys. The county engineer, when directed by the county commissioners, is required by law to transcribe any and all dilapidated maps and the records of plats and field notes of surveys from the records of the courts of common pleas, auditor, recorder, or other officer in the state where they may be procured.[128]

---

127. Reports of Governor's Commission. 186-87. See also, R. E. Heiges, *The Office of Sheriff in the Rural Counties of Ohio* (Findlay, 1933), 55-56, 60-61.
128. G.C. sec. 2804.

Similarly, the county recorder, when authorized by the county commissioners, is required to transcribe from the records of the counties all deeds, mortgages, powers of attorney, and other instruments of writing, for the sale, conveyance, or encumbrance of lands, tenements, or hereditaments situated within his county.[129]

The large accumulation of county records, occasioned by increasing governmental service, presents a serious problem. It is important, on the one hand, that valuable space in county courthouses and other county depositories be not cluttered up with vast quantities of useless materials. On the other hand, it is more important that every precaution be taken to prevent public officials from destroying valuable public records in order to make space for current business.

Within recent years photography has become an increasingly important aid in archival administration. The Ohio legislature, following the modern trends in recording, has enacted measures looking forward to the conservation of space in the county courthouses by permitting county officials to destroy records which have been reproduced photographically. Under this act, passed in 1937, any county official charged with keeping public records may, when the space requires it, have such records copied or reproduced by any photographic process and destroy the original papers. The original records, however, must be preserved until the time for filing legal proceedings based upon the documents shall have elapsed.[130]

---

129. *Ibid.*, sec. 2763.
130. *Ibid.*, sec. 32-1.

While the legislature has attempted to enact legislation looking forward to the conservation of much needed space in county courthouses a significant trend is to be observed in the increasing interest which is being displayed for a department of county archives where all noncurrent records may be properly housed, classified, listed, and made more readily accessible to those interested in consulting them. The arguments advanced in favor of such a system are:

1. that the preservation of county records should be viewed as a distinct function of county government,
2. that the administration of county archives should be under the direction of those qualified to serve efficiently and effectively both the needs of the administration and historians,

3. that the construction of county archives buildings for noncurrent records would make available more space for current business, which, at present, is seriously curtailed.

In the field of archival administration the state, rather than the county, has been the experimental laboratory and the results have been eminently successful.[131]

---

131. For an interesting and informative article on the administration of state archives, see Charles M. Gates, "The Administration of State Archives," *The Pacific Northwest Quarterly*. XXIX (January 1938), no. 1; also in *The American Archivist*, I (July 1938), 130-41.

Although the county seat of Adams County was located successively at Manchester, 1797, Adamsville, 1798, and Washington, 1798, it was not until 1802 that the commissioners made provision for the construction of a county courthouse. Previous to that time, privately owned log cabins had been rented for transacting business and taking care of records. When, in 1804, the county seat was established at West Union, a log cabin continued to serve the needs of the county until the completion of a courthouse in 1805. This two-story building, measuring approximately 24 by 30 feet, served the needs of the county until 1811 when Thomas Metcalf, a stone mason who later became governor of Kentucky, was awarded the contract for erecting a two-story stone courthouse. This building was succeeded by a brick structure in 1876.[1]

The courthouse built in 1876 was completely destroyed by fire in the early months of 1910. All records, except a few volumes and original papers of the probate court, the clerk of courts, and the recorder, kept in the only steel safe in the building, were consumed. After a dispute between the citizens of West Union and Peebles over the question of removing the county seat to the latter village, the legislature authorized a $50,000 bond issue for the construction of a new courthouse at West Union.[2] The legislature also passed an act on April 10, 1910, providing for similar emergencies. This law authorizes county commissioners to issue bonds up to $50,000 without submitting the question to the voters, for rebuilding an infirmary or courthouse destroyed by fire. It also requires the commissioners to install and use fireproof vaults for preserving valuable records in all newly constructed courthouses.[3] The present courthouse, erected in 1911, complied with the conditions prescribed by this law.

---

1. Evans and Stivers, *op. cit.*, 133-36
2. Portsmouth "Blade." February 26, 1910
3. *Laws of Ohio*. CI, 135-36.

It is a two-story structure of buff brick, with a basement in which are located the board of elections, county agricultural agent, the soil conservancy bureau, the basement vault, storage bin, the furnace and coal rooms. The building is surmounted by a tower and town clock. The lot covers the full city block bounded by Mulberry on the north, Market on the east, Main on the south, and Cross on the west, and is 594 feet north and south by 396 feet east and west. The building itself is 60 feet by 90 feet and fronts on Main Street with wide, tile-floored corridors running north and south. It was designed by T.S. Murray and Son, architects, and erected by James Shene and Company, building contractors. The space not occupied by the building is landscaped and equipped for a small public park.

The various county departments described below, except as otherwise noted, are in the courthouse at the points designated.

County Commissioners. The commissioners' office is on the east side of the first floor, between the auditor's on the south, and probate court's on the north. A door connects with the former; another leads to the lobby and adjoins the entrance to the probate judge's office. The room is commodious, with space for expansion. A north door opens into the auditor's fireproof vault. While this vault is crowded, facilities are ample to meet the needs of officials and the convenience of the public. Congestion has been minimized by removal of seldom-consulted records to the basement vault.

Recorder. The recorder's office is in the northwest corner of the first floor, with both northern and western exposure, and five windows admitting ample natural light. All records are carefully housed in the fireproof vault which has double steel doors. It contains records dating from 1797 which were saved during the courthouse fire of 1910. It is reached from the recorder's office through a small research room equipped with table and chairs to facilitate the work of consultants. A stenographer also occupies this room. The entrance to the recorder's office from the corridor also has double steel doors.

Clerk of Courts. The clerk of the court of common pleas occupies a single room located on the northeast corner of the second floor. The clerk's records are neatly filed in a fireproof vault equipped with steel shutter windows and double steel doors. There is ample room for expansion in the clerk's office, although many unbound records, including vouchers, are stored in the basement in vaults or storeroom where additional shelving is badly needed.

Probate Court. The office of the probate division of the common pleas court is in the northeast corner of the first floor. The records of this division include those of aid to dependent children. With both northern and eastern exposure and six windows, the natural light and ventilation are ample. Most of the records are housed in a small fireproof vault. A few records, antedating the fire of 1910, are included. Additional filing equipment is needed. Facilities for consultants of the records are satisfactory.

Prosecuting Attorney. No office is designated by the county for this official. He uses the office in which his private law practice is conducted, but his permanent records are kept in the vault of the clerk of courts and the basement vault.

Coroner. Current coroner's records are located in the office of the present incumbent, Dr. E.T. Gibboney, on West Main Street in West Union, There is no permanent coroner's office.

Sheriff. The sheriff's office is in the northwest corner of the second floor. His records, few in number, are stored, partly in the sheriff's office filing cabinet, partly in the basement, and partly in the county jail office. Practically all records prior to 1910 were destroyed in the fire of that date. Many records of transactions since that date are missing; particularly those of fingerprints, arrests for parole violation, monthly reports to the commissioners, and records relating to dogs.

Treasurer. The treasurer occupies two rooms in the southwest corner of the first floor and west of the main entrance. The smaller room is the treasurer's private office and adjoins the treasurer's vault. The main office is cramped for space. The capacity of the treasurer's vault could be increased to good advantage by the construction of additional shelves for which there is adequate space. However, the records are neatly and systematically filed, and facilities for consultation are satisfactory.

Auditor. The auditor's office is in the southeast corner of the first floor, across the hall from the treasurer's office. A doorway connects it with the commissioners' room and another leads to the lobby. The records are systematically arranged and carefully filed, some in the auditor's fireproof vault and others in the basement vault.

Board of Elections. The records of this department are in the board's office in the southwest corner of the basement of the courthouse. Ample filing space is afforded by a steel safe.

Board of Education. The board of education records are kept in the office of the county superintendent of schools in the north end of the second floor east of the main stairway. They are kept in ample steel filing cabinets.

Board of Health. The office is on the first floor of the frame building at the southeast corner of Mulberry and Market Streets, West Union. The records are in metal filing cabinets. There are no records prior to 1921.

County Home. The county home is one and one-half miles southwest of West Union on State Route 41. The office of the superintendent, on the first floor, contains a small wooden cabinet in which the records are filed. The county's relief records are also filed in this office.

Children's Home. The Wilson Children's Home, a two-story brick building constructed in 1884, is located on State Route 125 near the eastern limits of West Union. The office of the superintendent, on the first floor, has a wooden cabinet for records of the institution.

Board of Aid for the Aged. The office of the board of aid for the aged is conveniently located on West Main Street, West Union. Two well-lighted rooms furnish adequate space for housing of records and for the needs of the office. The unbound records are filed in steel cabinets.

County Engineer. The office of the engineer is on the west side of the first floor, between the offices of the recorder and the treasurer. The current records, few in number, are kept in a steel safe, while older records are stored in the basement vault. The engineer's office furnished space for WPA certification and CCC records. No additional space or equipment is needed.

Agricultural Extension Agent. The office of the agricultural extension agent is in the northwest corner of the basement. The records are kept in steel filing cabinets. There is ample space for expansion.

Dog Warden. The records of this official are found in the auditor's vault.

Basement Vault. The basement vault of the courthouse measures approximately 8 by 14 feet. The ninety-seven feet of wooden shelving available carries fifty-five feet of bound volumes and forty-two feet of unbound records. Wooden file boxes, measuring 15 by 15 by 22 inches also contain unbound records. The vault contains records for the commissioners, recorder, clerk of courts, court of appeals, probate court, prosecuting attorney, sheriff, treasurer, auditor, and engineer. There is a pressing need for additional storage space and some facilities for consultation of the records.

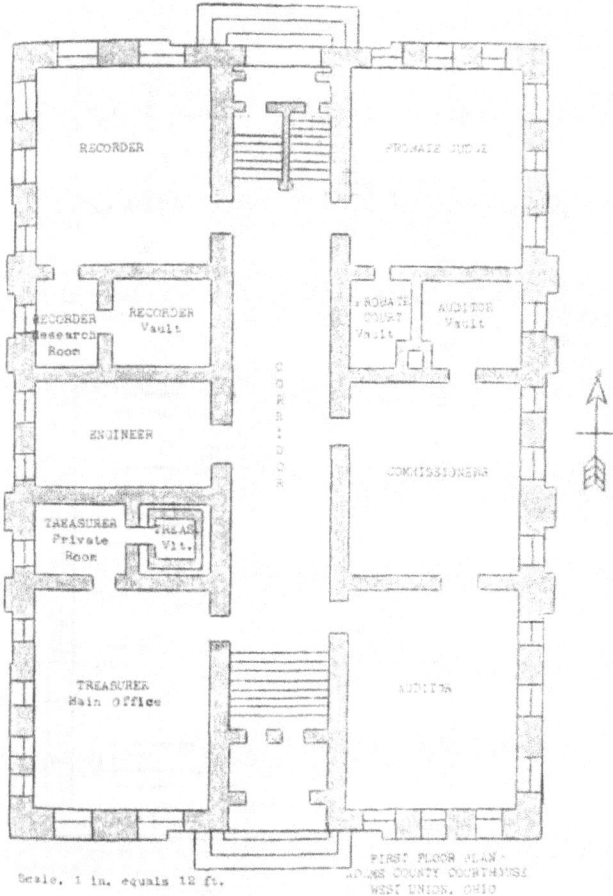

Adams County Courthouse, First Floor, 1938

64

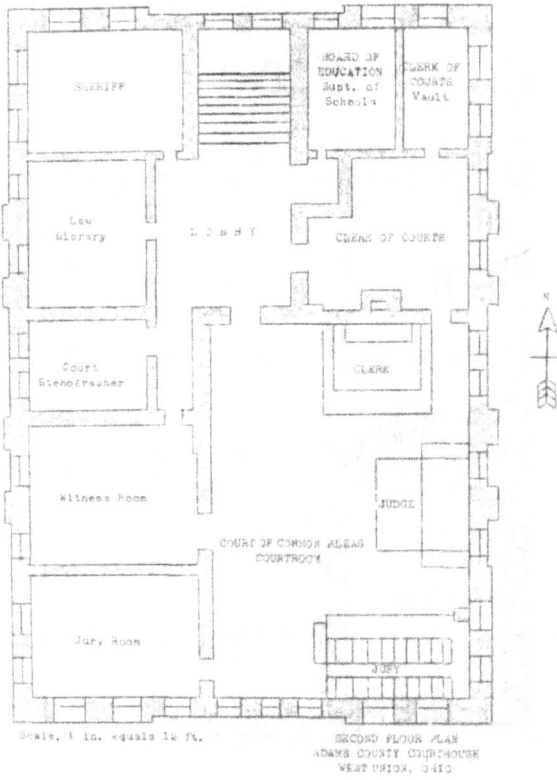

Adams County Courthouse, Second Floor, 1938

55

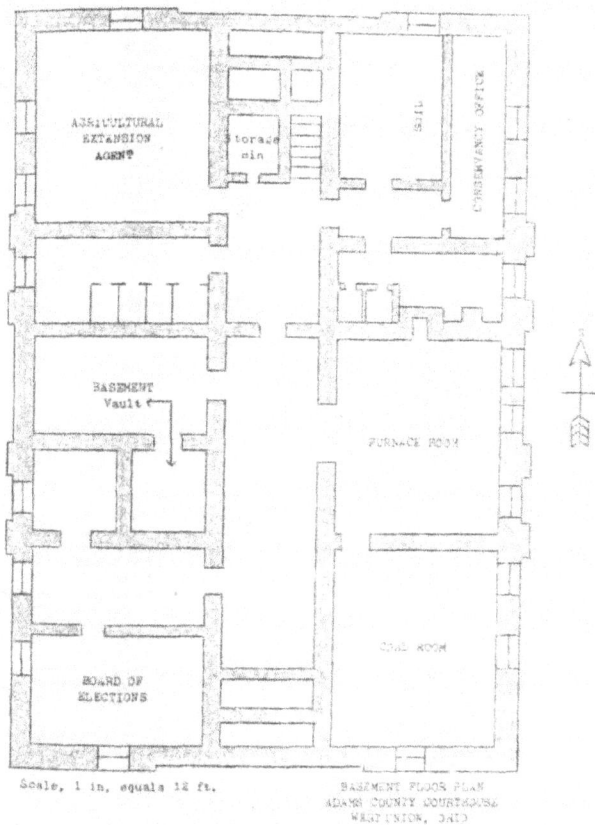

Adams County Courthouse, Basement, 1938

The local governmental system for the Northwest Territory comprising the present state of Ohio established the office of county commissioners. This office, created by the territorial act of 1792, consisted of two appointive commissioners who were directed to compile a tax list, levy taxes for the county, and draft plans for and supervise the construction of a "court-house jail pillory whipping-post and several stocks."[1]

The governmental system established in 1802, under the first constitution of Ohio, made no provision for the office and its existence is due entirely to statutory enactment. By an act of the legislature passed in 1804, the territorial office was re-created and was to be composed of three members elected for a three-year term.[2] Three years later the commissioners were made a corporate body invested with the power to sue and be sued.[3] They were required to keep a record of their proceedings; to assess taxes for the support of the county; appoint a county treasurer; and to supervise the construction of bridges.[4] They were paid on a per diem basis. Moreover, during the same period they were given the task of constructing courthouses, jails, and offices for the clerk of courts, court of common pleas, the sheriff, the auditor, and the treasurer.[5] Of these earlier duties the commissioners retain all but one: that of appointing a county treasurer. However, since 1831 they have been authorized to examine and compare the accounts of the county treasurer and county auditor and to examine the condition of county finances.

Besides the duties regarding construction and finance, the commissioners were given the task of constructing local highways when so authorized by the legislature. During the first thirty years of Ohio history the duties of the commissioners in this respect were local in nature. But as the system of road construction expanded they were given the additional duty of converting free turnpikes into state roads.[6]

---

1. Theodore Calvin Pease , comp., *The Laws of the Northwest Territory 1788-1800* (Illinois State Bar Association Law Series, Springfield, 1925, I), 76.
2. *Laws of Ohio,* II , 150.
3. *Ibid.*, V. 97.
4. *Ibid.*, V. VIII, 45-46
5. *Ibid.*, II, 154-57; XXIX, 315.
6. *Ibid.*, XLIV, 74.

During the 1840s and 1850s private companies were authorized by the legislature to construct plank roads.[7] When these companies were caught in the stringency of a financial depression in 1857, the commissioners were authorized to purchase their holdings. If such transaction was made, the transfer signed by the president of the company was to be deposited with the county auditor.[8] In the 1870s the commissioners, although earlier subjected to regulatory measures by the legislature, were prohibited from levying taxes for roads to exceed three and a half mills on the dollar on the taxable property in the county.[9] Later, in 1885, they were authorized to levy taxes not to exceed five mills on the dollar on all taxable property in the county for the maintenance of roads which had been damaged by excessive wear or were damaged from other causes.[10]

With the development of modem means of transportation, scientific principles were applied to road construction and maintenance. Although the county surveyor, now the county engineer, had in earlier years furnished the commissioners with estimates for bridge construction, it was not until the latter part of the nineteenth century that they were authorized to utilize his scientific knowledge in road construction.[11] At the opening of the present century the surveyor was directed to appoint a maintenance engineer, with the consent of the commissioners, to supervise the repairing of improved roads in the county.[12]

Although the county commissioners have never been closely associated with the administration of criminal justice, their earlier duties in regard to the construction of county jails qualified them, in the earlier period, for additional duties in this respect. During the middle of the nineteenth century the commissioners of Cuyahoga County were authorized to employ persons on construction work who were confined in the county jails.[13]

7. *Ibid.*, LIV, 198.
8. *Ibid.*, LIV, 198
9. *Laws of Ohio*, LXVIII, 117.
10. General Code, sec. 7419; *Laws of Ohio*, LXXXII, 171.
11. *Laws of Ohio*, LXXVIII, 285; XCVIII, 245-47. See also p. 181.
12. *Laws of Ohio*, CVIII, pt. I , 497.
13. *Ibid.*, November 2, 2023 XXXVII, 54.

While this provision was repealed by the criminal code, adopted in 1853, either earlier functions applicable to all counties were continued. Since 1843 the Commissioners have provided equipment and fixtures for places of incarceration, food and clothing for prisoners, and appointed a jail physician.[14] Since 1869 they have been authorized to offer a reward for the detection or apprehension of any person charged with a felony in the county.[15] Since 1892 the commissioners in any county where there is no workhouse may, under certain conditions, release or parole an indigent person confined in the jail.[16] With the extension modern crime into the rural areas in the form of small-town bank robbing, the commissioners were given the duty of furnishing motorcycles to the sheriff and his deputies in an attempt to compete with the high powered equipment used by modern gangs. One of the latest functions in this respect is the contracting with radio stations for the broadcasting of descriptions of fleeing criminals.[17]

Besides providing for those who have violated the laws, the commissioners were given the duty of caring for persons who, because of poverty or physical or mental defects, became public charges. Since 1816 they have established and maintained "poor houses."[18] Since 1908 the commissioners have been authorized to issue warrants for the relief of the blind in sums varying from $100 to $400 per year.[19] Since 1913 they have been authorized, in any county containing a city which has an infirmary, to contract with the director of public safety for the care of the county's indigent.[20] In 1933 the commissioners were designated as a board to administer the state law providing aid for the aged.[21] Two years later, in 1935, the commissioners were authorized to provide noninstitutional support, care, assistance, or relief for the indigent in the county and were authorized to establish a suitable agency or office for such purposes.[22]

---

14. *Ibid.*, XLI, 74; LXXXVII, 186.
15. *Ibid.*, LXVI, 321.
16. *Ibid.*, LXXXIX, 408; CXIII, 203.
17. G.C. sec. 13431-1
18. *Laws of Ohio.* XIV, 447.
19. See p. 171.
20. G.C. sec. 2419-1.
21. *Laws of Ohio*, CXV, pt. ii , 431-39. See also p. 175.
22. *Ibid.*, CXVI, 134.

In addition to furnishing financial aid to the civilian population the commissioners were authorized, in 1886, to levy a tax for the relief of indigent Union soldiers, sailors, or marines of the Civil War, or if such veterans were deceased, for their dependents.[23] In 1919 the provisions of the original act were amended to include all indigent veterans of the World War.[24] The commissioners were authorized also, in 1884, to defray the funeral expenses of any honorably discharged soldier, sailor, or marine who died indigent.[25] Ten years later, in 1894, the provisions of the act were extended to include the mother, wife, or widow of any soldier, sailor, or marine; and war nurses.[26]

The humanitarian duty of caring for the county's dependent and neglected children was delegated to the county commissioners. Since 1866 they have been authorized to establish and maintain children's homes. At the beginning of the present century, when the treatment of children was undergoing a remarkable change, they were authorized to place dependent and neglected children in private homes or institutions where they would receive food, clothing, and medical and dental treatment.[27] The development of the juvenile court system added new responsibilities. In order to segregate completely juvenile offenders from adults being tried in the regular criminal courts, the commissioners were authorized to provide a separate building to be known as the "juvenile court."

The commissioners, by the authority conferred upon them to construct public buildings, were given duties regarding educational advancement. Since 1871 they have been authorized to accept bequests for the construction of county libraries, and since 1923 to issue bonds, after submitting such questions to the voters, for the construction of libraries, or to contract with existing libraries for the use of people in the county.[28] Moreover, in 1913 they were authorized to provide and maintain civic centers in the county and to employ an expert director to supervise and administer them.[29]

---

23. *Ibid.,* LXXXIII, 232. See also p. 167.
24. *Ibid.,* CVIII, pt. I , 633.
25. *Ibid.,* LXXXI, 146.
26. *Ibid.,* XC. 177.
27. *Ibid.,* CIX. 533.
28. G.C. secs. 2434-1, 2454, 2455; *Laws of Ohio.* CX, 242.
29. G.C. sec. 2457-4.

Other duties not closely related to the original duties of the commissioners have been added from decade to decade. For example, in 1850 they were authorized to subscribe for one leading newspaper of each political party in the county and cause them to be bound and deposited with the county auditor as public archives.[30] The newspapers on file in the auditor's office have not been listed in this inventory as they are to be the subject of a separate survey. An amendment to the original act, passed in 1923, provided for the preservation of such newspapers for a period of ten years, after which they may be removed to the Ohio State Archaeological and Historical Society library.[31] They have been authorized also to promote historical research by appropriating annually a sum not to exceed $100 to defray the expenses of compiling and publishing historical data for historical societies not incorporated for profit.[32]

During the early years of the twentieth century the commissioners were given the duty of providing facilities for county sanitation, which, in previous years had been sadly neglected. In 1911 they were authorized to lay out, establish, and maintain one or more sewer districts within the county. Since 1917 no sewer or sewerage treatment works may be constructed outside of any incorporated municipality by any person, persons, firms, or corporations until the plans have been approved by the commissioners.[33]

The commissioners were authorized in 1908 to establish a county tuberculosis hospital and in1909 to cooperate with the commissioners of other counties for the establishment of a district tuberculosis hospital. In 1913 they were empowered to appoint, with the approval of the state department of health, one or more instructing and visiting nurses to visit the homes or places housing tubercular patients, and since 1917 have been authorized to establish tuberculosis dispensaries and provide by tax levies the necessary funds for their establishment and maintenance.[34]

---

30. *Laws of Ohio*. XLVIII, 65.
31. *Ibid.*, CX, 4.
32. G.C. sec. 2457-1.
33. *Ibid.*, sec. 6602-1; *Laws of Ohio*. CVII, 440.
34. G.C. secs, 3153-4, 3153-5, 3148-1.

Finally, the county commissioners have acted in a supervisory capacity over other county officials. Since the middle of the nineteenth century they have been authorized to compare the annual reports and statements made to them by the prosecuting attorney, the clerk of courts, the sheriff, and the treasurer; take measures to rectify errors, correct discrepancies, and record in their journal the results of such examinations. Such reports were to be filed with the county auditor who has custody of their official, acts and proceedings.[35] Moreover in the latter part of the same century (1896) the commissioners were given their present duty of visiting hospitals, detention homes, private asylums, and any other institution exercising a reformatory or correctional influence over individuals, and reporting on the sanitary conditions and the treatment of inmates. These reports, required to be filed with the county prosecuting attorney, and kept open to the inspection and examination of the public, were not located.[36]

The board of county commissioners offers a typical example of an office. which, designed primarily for an agricultural society, has expanded to meet the needs and requirement of modern society. At the present the commissioners are elected for a four-year term.[37]

---

35. G.C. sec . 2504; Revised Statutes. 886; *Laws of Ohio*. XLVIII, 66.
36. G.C. secs. 2498, 2499; *Laws of Ohio*. XCII, 212.
37. *Laws of Ohio*. CVIII, pt. ii , 1300.

Journals and Report

1. COMMISSIONERS' JOURNAL
1893—. 8 vols. (1-8). Missing: 1895-1904.

Record copies of minutes of meetings of board of county commissioners showing date, names of members present, yea and nay votes on each proposal or resolution introduced; copies of all petitions filed by freeholders in connection with establishing, changing, or vacating of roads and ditches; copies of specifications of proposed construction or repair of county projects; record of all appropriations of county funds; itemized account of all expenditures authorized by board; approval of bills and claims; copies of all contracts entered into by board; and copies of annual reports by county officials. Also contains: record of receipts and expenditures of county home and children's home funds, 1893-1912; Soldiers' Relief Record, 1924, entry 301. Chronologically arranged. For index to bills and contracts, 1910—, see entry 2; otherwise, no index. Handwritten. Average 630 pages. 16 x 12 x 4. 1 volume, 1893-1895, Basement vault; 7 volumes, 1905—, Auditor's vault.

2. INDEX TO COMMISSIONERS' JOURNAL
1910—. 3 vols.

Index to bills and contracts as entered in Commissioners' Journal, entry 1, showing volume and page numbers of record, name of creditor, amount of bill, name of contractor, what contract, and amount of contract. Alphabetically arranged by names of creditors or contractors. Handwritten. Average 480 pages. 18 x 12 x 3.5. Auditor's vault.

3. ANNUAL REPORTS
1910—. 2 file boxes.

Copies of commissioners annual financial reports showing date, receipts, expenditures, and balances of various funds. Chronologically arranged. No index. Handwritten on printed forms. 5 x 10 x 14. Auditor's vault.

4. REPORTS
1910—. 11 file boxes.

Copies of annual reports by county officials to commissioners showing what office or department, name of official, date filed, and date approved. Chronologically arranged. No index. Handwritten on printed forms. 5 x 10 x 14. Auditor's vault.

5. AUDITOR'S MONTHLY STATEMENTS
1910—. 7 file boxes. Prior records missing.
Auditor's monthly financial statements to county commissioners showing date, receipts and expenditures of each county fund for each thirty-day period. Chronologically arranged. No index. Handwritten on printed forms. 5 x 10 x 14. Auditor's vault.

6. SOLDIERS' BURIAL RECORD
1884—. 5 vols.
Record of burial, by the county, of indigent soldiers, sailors, marines, and of their widows, mothers, or minor children, showing date , name, company, rank, service, and itemized account of cost. Chronologically arranged. Alphabetical index by names of decedents. Handwritten on printed forms. Average 400 pages. 14 x 11 x 13. 4 volumes, 1884-1923, Basement vault; 1 volume, 1924—, Auditor's vault.

Bridge and Road Records
(See also entries 241-243)

7. TURNPIKE DIRECTORS' JOURNAL
1912-1915. 1 vol. Discontinued.
Record of minutes of meetings of turnpike directors (board of county commissioners organized as board of turnpike directors) showing names of members present, and yea and nay votes on resolutions and motions; also record of appropriations and expenditures for construction and repair of free turnpikes in Adams County. Chronologically arranged. No index. Handwritten. 480 pages. 16 x 12 x 3.5. Auditor's vault.

8 . ROAD JOURNAL AND RECORD
1875—. 5 vols.
Record of proceedings incident to establishing, changing, and vacating roads by county commissioners, showing copies of petitions by freeholders to commissioners; reports of road viewers on each project; and county engineer's reports with plat and cross section drawings for construction of improved roads, culverts, and bridges; also engineer's estimates on cost of proposed construction.

Chronologically arranged. Alphabetical index by names of roads and bridges. Handwritten. Average 400 pages. 18 x 12 x 3.5. Auditor's office

9. SPECIFICATIONS AND ESTIMATES
1910—. 9 file boxes (labeled by subjects).
Original specifications and estimates submitted by county engineer on road and bridge projects showing what project and date. Chronologically arranged. No index, Handwritten on printed form. 5 x 10 x 14. Auditor's office.

10. CONTRACTS
1910—. 2 file boxes (labeled by subjects).
Original contracts entered into by county commissioners with contractors for furnishing materials and labor for county projects showing date and terms of contract. Chronologically arranged. No index. Handwritten on printed forms. 5 x 10 x 14. Auditor's vault.

County Institutions and Relief

11. COMMISSIONERS' INFIRMARY AND CHILDREN'S HOME JOURNAL
1913—. 2 vols.
Commissioners record in connection with the two institutions showing appropriations made for institutions and itemized expenditures as certified by institution superintendents showing dates and amounts. Chronologically arranged. No index. Handwritten. Average 470 pages. 16 x 12 x 3.5. Auditor's vault.

12. RECORDS OF WORTHY POOR
1893 -1895. 1 vol. Discontinued.
Commissioners' records of aid to worthy indigent of county showing name and address of recipient, date, and amount and kind of aid given. Chronologically arranged. No index. Handwritten. 585 pages. 18 x 12 x 4. Basement vault.

13. RECORD OF BLIND
1905-1936. 1 vol.
Record of blind relief showing name and address of client, degree of blindness, physician's certificate, amount of award, record of payments made, date, and

warrant number. Chronologically arranged. No index. Handwritten. 160 pages. 14 x 9 x 1. Auditor's vault.

For related records, see entries 249, 302.

Business Administration of Office

14. BUDGETS
1911—. 3 file boxes.
Certified copies of yearly budgets for various subdivisions of county. Chronologically arranged. No index. Handwritten on printed forms. 5 x 10 x 14. Auditor's vault.

15. APPROPRIATIONS
1911—. 6 file boxes (labeled by subjects)
Original copies of appropriations to various county funds by commissioners showing date, what fund, amount appropriated the preceding year, amount expended, and amount appropriated for ensuing year. Chronologically arranged. No index. Handwritten on printed forms. 5 x 10 x 14. Auditor's vault.

16. CLAIMS
1911—. 2 file boxes.
Claims presented for animals injured or killed by dogs showing name of claimant, date of claim, number and kind of animals killed or injured, and amount of claim; also automobile accident claims against county showing name of claimant, place and cause of accident, amount of claim, and date filed. Chronologically arranged. No index. Handwritten on printed forms. 5 x 10 x 14. Auditor's vault.

17. BILLS
1911—. 3 file boxes.
Original cost bills presented by sheriff for food furnished county jail inmates; also cost bills certified by clerk of courts for prosecution of criminal cases showing date and itemized costs. Chronologically arranged. No index. Handwritten on printed forms. 5 x 10 x 14. Auditor's vault.

18. INVOICES

1911—. 6 file boxes (labeled by subjects).
Original invoices submitted by state institutions for maintenance of persons committed from Adams County showing date of invoice, what institution, names of inmates, and itemized statement of account due. 2 file boxes contain invoice for equipment and furnishings for county institutions. Chronologically arranged. No index. Typed on printed forms. 5 x 10 x 14. Auditor's vault.

19. VOUCHERS

1911—. 22 file boxes (labeled by subjects)
Original vouchers for payment of bills incurred by commissioners including those for county institutions, showing date, voucher number, to whom, for what and amount of voucher. Chronologically arranged. No index. Handwritten on printed forms. 5 x 10 x 14. Auditor's vault.

20. REJECTED ACCOUNTS

1911—. 3 file boxes (labeled by subjects)
Original bills and accounts filed against the county on which county commissioners refused payment showing date of bill or account, name of claimant, for what, and amount of claim. Chronologically arranged. No index. Typed on printed forms 5 x 10 x 14. Auditor's vault.

Miscellaneous

21. APPLICATION FOR PAROLE

1915—. 1 file box. Prior records missing.
Original applications for paroles by persons confined in county jail showing date, name of prisoner, term of sentence, time served, and signatures of applicant and those recommending parole. Chronologically arranged. No index. Handwritten on printed forms. 5 x 10 x 14. Auditor's vault.

22. TRANSFERS

1920—. 1 file box.
Original orders by commissioners authorizing transfer of funds from one fund to another showing date, name of fund from which transferred, name of fund to which

transferred, and signatures of county commissioners. Chronologically arranged. No index. Handwritten on printed forms. 5 x 10 x 14. Auditor's vault.

23. LEGAL NOTICES
1911—. 2 file boxes.

Copies of legal notices posted for hearings on various proposals showing date and nature of each proposal. Chronologically arranged No index. Handwritten on printed forms. 5 x 10 x 14. Auditor's vault.

24. MISCELLANEOUS RECORDS
1803-1910. 2 wooden boxes. Discontinued.

Original petitions by freeholders for establishing, extending, or changing public roads; contracts between commissioners and individuals or firms covering construction of roads and bridges; reports by county surveyor to commissioners on condition of bridges and culverts in county; and orders for payment of bills and claims allowed by commissioners. No systematic arrangement. No index. 1803-1870, handwritten; 1871-1910, handwritten on printed forms. Condition poor. 15 x 15 x 22. Basement vault.

The office of county recorder, although not unknown as an early English institution for the registration of land titles, developed in colonial America, where, because of the mobility of the restless pioneers, changes in land titles were frequent and some system was needed to protect purchasers against previous encumbrances. Public land registers, established in most of the colonies during the colonial period and continued by the states following independence, served as a model of land registration for the territory of which the present state of Ohio was then a part. Thus the office of county recorder was established by an act of the Northwest Territory, effective August 1, 1795. This act, adopted from the Pennsylvania code, provided for the appointment by the governor of a recorder in each county whose principal duty was the recording of the deeds.[1]

When Ohio entered the Union in 1803 no constitutional provision was made for the continuance of the office, but the legislature during its first session passed an act providing for a recorder in each county to be appointed by the judges of the court of common pleas for a seven-year term.[2] The recorder continued to be an appointive officer until 1829, when, by an act of the legislature , he became elective for a three-year term.[3] The tenure of office remained at three years until the constitutional amendment of November 7, 1905, which provided for the election of all county officers in the even-numbered years.[4] The term of office was fixed at two years, and so continued until the amendment of 1933, which extended the tenure of the incumbent until January 1937, at which time the recorder, elected at the regular election in November1936, began to serve a four-year term.[5]

The first county recorder was directed by statute to record "all deeds, mortgages and conveyances of lands and tenements," lying within his county, and also all instruments and writings required by law to be recorded.[6] In 1805 he was directed to record all plats and maps of newly laid-out villages.[7]

---

1. Pease, *op. cit.* I, 197- 99.
2. *Laws of Ohio.* I, 136.
3. *Ibid.*, XXVII, 65.
4. *Ohio Const. 1851*, (Amendment, 1905). Art. XVII. sec. 2.
5. *Laws of Ohio*, XCVIII, 271, CXV, 191.
6. Ibid., I, 137.
7. *Ibid.*, III, 213-15.

In 1835 he was permitted, when authorized by the county commissioners, to transcribe from the records of other counties all deeds, mortgages, and other instruments of writing for the sale or conveyance of lands, tenements, or hereditaments affecting land titles in his county.[8]

Since the establishment of the office many duties besides those of recording land titles have been added. The present practice of recording powers of attorney began in 1818.[9] Although the mechanics of Cincinnati were authorized to file mechanics' liens with the recorder as early as 1823, it was not until 1843 that the privilege was extended to the laborers of Adams County.[10] Successive acts in 1865, 1872, 1881, 1884, 1904, and,1923 added new duties to the office in the recording of soldiers' discharges,[11] copies of certificates of compliance authorizing insurance companies not incorporated under the laws of Ohio to transact business in the state, and certified copies of renewal as granted by such companies to their agents,[12] limited partnership agreements,[13] stallion keepers liens,[14] oil and gas leases,[15] partition fence records,[16] and federal tax liens.[17] The recording of chattel mortgages and conditional sales began in 1846. Such instruments were to be deposited with the township clerk where the mortgagor was a resident. In all townships, however, in which the recorder maintained his office such instruments were to be deposited with him.[18] Since 1906 chattel mortgages have been filed with the county recorder exclusively. It is provided that in order to be valid against subsequent mortgages, the chattel mortgage must be deposited with the county recorder of the county where the mortgagor resides at the time of its execution, and to retain its validity the mortgage must be renewed every three years.[19]

---

8. *Ibid.*, XXXIII. 8, XXXV, 11.
9. *Laws of Ohio*, XVI, 155-56.
10. *Ibid.*, XXI, 8-10; XLI, 66 .
11. *Ibid.*, LXII, 59.
12. *Ibid.*, LXIX, 32, 148; XCVII, 405.
13. *Ibid.*, LXXVIII, 248.
14. *Ibid.*, LXXXI, 43.
15. *Ibid.*, LXXXV, 179.
16. *Ibid.*, XCVII, 140.
17. *Ibid.*, CX, 252.
18. *Ibid.*, XLIV, 61.
19. G.C. sec. 8565.

In 1936 the legislature passed an act authorizing the recorder to destroy such instruments six years after the time of refiling has expired.[20]

In the latter part of the nineteenth century an important extension of the method of recording land titles was provided by an act of the general assembly. The "Torrens System," as provided by the act of 1896,[21] was declared unconstitutional by the supreme court of Ohio as being contrary to section 16 of the bill of rights of the state constitution.[22] The act of 1913, amended in 1913 and 1915, provides for the examination of land titles by the recorder and the issuance, if the title prove to be held in fee simple, of a certificate of title by the courts. The official certificate becomes the title of ownership and is indefeasible. However, in the event an interest is found in the land, after the issuance of the certificate, a claim is allowed to the legal claimant from a fund created for that purpose at the time of registration.[23] The recorder of Adams County has kept a register of land titles since 1854. This system, although adopted by a few counties, is not used as widely as it might be because of the difficulty of replacing the traditional complicated system.

The recorder, like other county officials, had been required in earlier years to keep records of the business of his office, but it was not until the middle of the nineteenth century that the legislature, looking forward to some uniformity in land registration, enacted measures prescribing the form and contents of such records. Since 1850 the recorder has been required to keep a record of deeds in which is recorded all deeds, powers of attorney, and other instruments of writing for the unconditional sale of land, tenements, or hereditaments.[24] The same year saw the beginning of a record of mortgages in which was recorded all mortgages, powers of attorney, and other instruments of writing by which, land, tenements, or hereditaments "shall or may be mortgaged" or otherwise conditionally sold; and a record of plats in which was to be record all plats and maps of town lots and of the subdivisions thereof, and of other divisions or surveyed lands, in like regular succession according to the priority of their presentation.[25]

---

20. *Laws of Ohio*, CXVI, 324.
21. *Ibid.*, XCII, 220.
22. *Ohio State Reports* (Cincinnati, 1852—), LVI, 575.
23. G.C. secs. 8572-34 - 8572-56; *Laws of Ohio*. CVI, 24; CXV, 443.
24. *Laws of Ohio*. XLVIII, 64.
25. *Ibid.*, XLVIII. 64.

Since 1851 the recorder has been required to keep separate record of deeds and mortgages denominated respectively as "Record of Deeds" and "Record of Mortgages."[26] Fourteen years later in 1865, began the separate recording of leases in which the recorder was and is required to record all leases.[27] The present practice of keeping a daily register of deeds and a daily register of mortgages had its beginning in Adams County in 1879 although not required by statute until 1896. In this record are entered in alphabetical order the names of grantors of all deeds and mortgages affecting real estate.[28]

Although indexes had been prepared in earlier years, the present system of indexing had its beginning in 1851 and took practically its present form in 1896.[29] At present the recorder, at the beginning of each day's business, is required to make and maintain a general alphabetical index, direct and reverse, of all names of both parties of all instruments recorded by him. The indexes show the kind of instruments, the date, the range, the township and section, the survey number and the number of acres or the lot and sublot numbers and the part thereof, of each tract or lot of land described in any such instrument of writing; the name of each grantor is entered in the direct index under the appropriate letter and followed on the same line by the name of the grantee; the name of each grantee is entered in the reverse index under the appropriate letter and followed on the same line by the name of the grantor.[30]

Since 1859 the county commissioners have been authorized to provide sectional indexes to the records of all real estate in the county, beginning with some designated year and continuing through a period of years as may be specified.[31]

The present duties of the recorder do not differ, in the main, from those prescribed in the middle of the nineteenth century. His records, bound in large bulky volumes, are open to the inspection of the public and are transferred to his successor.

---

26. *Ibid.*, XLIX, 103.
27. *Ibid.*,170
28. *Ibid.*, XCII, 268
29. *Ibid.*, XLIX, 103, XCII, 268, CII. 288
30. G.C. sec. 2764.
31. G.C. sec. 2766; *Laws of Ohio*, LXIV, 256; LXXVI, 49; CII, 289.

All records are located in the recorder's vault, unless otherwise specified.

Real Property Transfers
(See also entries 209, 210)

Deeds

25. DEEDS AND MORTGAGES
1803—. 1 box, 9 file boxes.
Original copies of deeds and mortgages which have been transcribed into the volume records. Box, no systematic arrangement; file boxes, chronologically arranged. No index. 1803-1823, handwritten; 1824—, handwritten and typed on printed forms. Box. 15 x 15 x 22; file boxes, 5 x 10 x 14. 1 box, 1803-1910, Basement vault; 9 file boxes, 1911—. Recorder's vault.

26. DEED RECORD
1797–. 143 vols. (1-143).
Record copies of instruments conveying title to real estate showing names of grantor and grantee, kind of instrument, date, description of real estate, consideration, names of witnesses, and notarization. Also contains: record copies of town plats, 1799-1849; Sheriff's Deed Record, 1797-1907, entry 28; Sheriff's Deeds in Partitions and Affidavits for Transfers, 1797-1907, entry 30; Church and Cemetery Deeds, 1797-1847, entry 31; Administrators and Executors Deed record, 1797-1909, entry 32; Lease Record, 1797-1864, entry 34; Mortgage Record, 1797-1849, entry 35, chronologically arranged. For index, see entry 27; for index to sheriff's deeds, 1797-1907, and to town plats, 1799-1849, see entry 29. 1797-1924, Hand written; 1925—, typed. Average 600 pages. 18 x 12 x 3.5.

27. INDEX TO DEEDS
1797–. 16 vols, (1-16).
Direct and reverse index to Deed Record showing date, names of grantor and grantee, volume and page numbers of record, and kind of instrument or document. Alphabetically arranged, direct, by names of grantors, and reverse, by names of grantees. Handwritten. Average 590 pages. 18 x 12 x 3.5.

28. SHERIFF'S DEED RECORD

1908—. 1 vol. 1797-1907 in Deed Record, entry 26.

Record of deeds executed by sheriff in foreclosure proceedings showing case number, names of litigants, description of real estate consideration; notarization, and date recorded. Chronologically arranged. Alphabetical index by names of grantees. Handwritten on printed forms. 640 pages. 18 x 12 x 4.

29. INDEX TO SHERIFF'S DEEDS

1797-1907. 1 vol.

Index to sheriff's deeds as recorded in Deed Record, entry 26, showing volume and page numbers of record, survey number, watercourse, and number of acres. This is also an index, 1799-1849, to town plats recorded in Deed Record, entry 26, showing volume and page numbers of record, by whom platted, number of acres, and date recorded. Alphabetically arranged by names of grantees. Handwritten. 400 pages. 18 x 14 x 3.25.

30. SHERIFF'S DEEDS IN PARTITIONS AND AFFIDAVITS FOR TRANSFERS

1908 2 vols. 1797-1907 in Deed Record, entry 26.

Sheriff's deeds in partition proceedings and affidavits of transfers of real estate to heirs of estates, each showing case number, names of litigants, name of decedent, description of real estate, consideration, notarization, and date recorded. Chronologically arranged. Alphabetical index by names of decedents. Handwritten on printed forms. Average 430 pages. 18 x 12 x 3.

31. CHURCH AND CEMETERY DEEDS

1848—. 2 vols. 1797-1847 in Deed Record, entry 26.

Record of deeds to church property, cemeteries, and cemetery lots, showing names of grantor and grantee, date, description of tract or lot, consideration, notarization, and date recorded. Chronologically arranged. Alphabetical index by names of grantees. 1848-1918, handwritten; 1919—, handwritten on printed forms. Average 380 pages. 16 x 11 x 2.5.

32. ADMINISTRATORS' AND EXECUTORS' DEED RECORD

1910—. 1 vol. 1797-1909 in Deed Record, entry 26.

Record of deeds executed by administrators and executors of estates, showing case number, name of decedent, date, description of real estate, consideration, name of administrator or executor, notarization, and date recorded. Chronologically arranged. Alphabetical index by names of grantees. Handwritten on printed forms. 600 pages. 18 x 13x 4.5.

33. REGISTER OF CONVEYANCES

1879—. 12 vols.

Daily register of deeds and mortgages presented for record showing date, kind, of instrument, names of grantor and grantee, consideration or amount of mortgage, and town or township. Chronologically arranged and alphabetical thereunder by names of grantors. No index, Handwritten. Average 226 pages. 18 x 12 x 2.

Leases

34. LEASE RECORD

1865—. 6 vols. (1-6). Missing: 1907-16. 1797-1864; in Deed Record, entry 26.

Record copies of leases and right-of-way grants showing names of grantor and grantee. description of property leased, terms of lease or grant, notarization and date recorded. Chronologically arranged. Alphabetical index by names of lessors. 1865-1928, handwritten; 1929—, typed. Average 500. 18 x 12 x 4.

Mortgages

35. MORTGAGE RECORD

1850—. 57 vols. (A-Z, A1-Z1, A2-E2). 1797-1849 in Deed Record, entry 26.

Record copies of mortgage deeds conveying title to real estate as security for value received showing names of grantor and grantee, description of real estate, amount of mortgage, notarization, and date filed. Also contains Mortgage Discharge Record, 1850-1891, entry 41 . Chronologically arranged. Handwritten. Average 500 pages. 18 x 12 x 3.5.

36. INDEX TO MORTGAGES

1850—. 7 vols. (1-7)

Direct and reverse index to Mortgage Record showing date recorded, amount of land, amount of mortgage, description of tract, and volume and page numbers of record. Direct index in front half of each volume, and reverse index in back half of each volume. Alphabetically arranged direct, by names of grantors, and reverse, by names of grantees. Handwritten. Average 640 pages. 18 x 12 x 4.

37. MORTGAGE RECORD, ADAMS COUNTY BUILDING AND LOAN COMPANY

1911—. 1 vol. Prior records missing.

Record copies of mortgage deeds to real estate given to Adams County Building and Loan Company showing name of grantor, date, description of real estate conditions of mortgage, amount of mortgage, notarization, and date recorded. Chronologically arranged. Alphabetical index by names of grantors. Handwritten and typed on printed forms. 650 pages. 18 x 12 x 4.5.

38. MORTGAGE RECORD, FEDERAL LOAN BANK

1917-1928. 1 vol. Discontinued.

Record copies of mortgage deeds to real estate given to Federal Farm Loan Bank, Louisville, Kentucky, showing date, name of grantor, description of real estate, conditions and amount of mortgage, notarization, and date recorded. Chronologically arranged. Alphabetical index by names of grantors. Handwritten on printed forms. 480 pages. 18 x 12 x 3.5.

39. MORTGAGE RECORD, CITIZENS' BUILDING AND LOAN COMPANY

1919—. 2 vols.

Record copies of mortgage deeds to real estate given to Citizens' Building and Loan Company showing date, name of grantor, description of real estate, conditions and amount of mortgage, notarization, and date recorded. Chronologically arranged. Alphabetical index by names of grantors. Handwritten on printed forms. Average 600 pages. 18 x 12 x 4.

40. MORTGAGE RECORD, MISCELLANEOUS

1911—. 1 vol. Prior records missing.

Record copies of mortgage deeds to real estate given to miscellaneous building and loan companies showing names of grantor and grantee, date, description of real estate, conditions and amount of mortgage, and date recorded. Chronologically arranged. Alphabetical index by names of grantors. Handwritten on printed forms. 510 pages. 18 x 12 x 4.5.

41. MORTGAGE DISCHARGE RECORD
1891—. 2 vols. 1850-1890 in Mortgage Record, entry 35.
Record of releases or partial releases of real estate mortgages and certificates of release by courts showing names of grantor and grantee, date of release, description of real estate, amount of mortgage, amount released, and date recorded. Chronologically arranged. Alphabetical index by names of mortgagors. 1891-1931, handwritten; 1932—, typed. Average 430 pages. 18 x 12 x 3.5.

Liens

42. MECHANICS' LIENS
1890—. 3 vols. (1-3). Prior records missing.
Record of liens on buildings, machinery, and other property for labor and material furnished showing names of lienor and lienee, itemized account of claim, description of property attached, notarization, and date recorded, Chronically arranged. Alphabetical index by names of lienors. 1890-1933, handwritten;, 1934—, typed. Average 450 pages. 16 x 11 x 3.5.

43. TAX LIENS
1914—. 1 vol.
List and description of real property on which tax liens are held showing name of owner amount of lien, and date of delinquency. Chronologically arranged. Alphabetical index by names of property owners. Handwritten. 500 pages. 18 x 12 x 3.5.

Registered Lands

44. REGISTERED LANDS, REGISTER OF TITLE
1854—. 1 vol.
Copy of original certificates of title and instruments relating to registered land titles showing date, name of owner, registry number, description of real estate , and plat of survey. Plats prepared by county engineer. Chronologically arranged. 1854-1923,

handwritten and hand drawn; 1924——, typed; plats hand drawn. Scales vary. Approximately 325 pages. 18 x 14 x 3.5.

45. RECORDER'S INDEX TO REGISTERED LANDS
1854——. 1 vol.

Index to Registered Lands, Register of Title, showing name of owner, registry number or folium number of record, and date. Numerically arranged by registry numbers. Handwritten. Approximately 325 pages. 22 x 16 x 3.5.

Plat Books and Surveys (See also entries 211, 212)

46. ADAMS COUNTY SURVEYS, VIRGINIA MILITARY WARRANTS
1788-1851. 1 vol. Discontinued.

Record copies of original surveys transferred by military warrants showing plat of survey with landmarks designated, dimensions and area, name of owner, survey number, date of survey, names of surveyor and chairmen, and date recorded. Chronologically arranged. Alphabetical index by names of surveys. Handwritten. 300 pages.17 x 12 x 3.

47. PLAT BOOKS
1830——. 3 vols. (2-4). Prior records missing.

Record copies of plats of townships, towns, and additions showing boundary lines and markers; also area of plats. Prepared by county engineer. Alphabetically arranged by names of towns, townships, or additions. Chronologically index by dates of surveys showing what survey, survey number, and page of record. Handwritten and hand drawn. 362 pages. 2 ½ x 17 x 3.

48. PARTITION FENCE RECORD
1908——. 1 vol. Prior records missing.

Record of proceedings and findings in partition or line fence controversies showing names of parties involved, description of lands divided, names of fence viewers in each case, date viewed, copy of viewers' decision in case, and date recorded. Chronologically arranged. Alphabetical index by names of petitioners. Handwritten. 328 pages. 18 x 12 x 2.5.

Personal Property Transfers

49. CHATTEL MORTGAGES
1906—. 1vol .
Record of mortgages on personal property and chattels showing names of grantor and grantee, date, description of property, amount of mortgage, and date recorded. Chronologically arranged. Alphabetical index by names of grantors. Handwritten. 550 pages. 18 x 12 x 4.

50. CHATTEL MORTGAGES
1906—. 104 file boxes (labeling varies).
Original copies of chattel mortgages filed showing date, names of grantor and grantee, itemized list of chattels, amount of mortgage, terms of mortgage, and date filed. Chronologically arranged by dates of filing. No index. 1906-1920, Handwritten on printed forms; 1921—, typed on printed forms. 5 x 10 x 14.

51. INDEX TO CHATTEL MORTGAGES
1906—. 9 vols. (1-9).
Direct and reverse index record of chattel mortgages showing names of mortgagor and mortgagee, amount secured, date of filing, date of refiling, and date cancelled. Alphabetically arranged, direct in front half of volume, by names of mortgagors, and reverse in back half of volume by names of mortgagees. Handwritten on printed forms. Average 640 pages. 19 x 13.5 x 3; 2 volumes 1906-1923, Recorder's vault 7 volumes 1923—, Recorder's office.

52. DAILY REGISTER OF CHATTEL MORTGAGES
1904—. 5 vols. Prior records missing.
Daily record of chattel mortgages presented for recording showing amount of mortgage, date, hour filed, and names of grantor and grantee. Chronologically arranged. No index. Handwritten. Average 250 pages. 18 x 12 x 1.75.

Corporations and Partnerships

53. CORPORATION RECORD
1866—. 3 vols.
Record of incorporation of business concerns, churches, and societies showing

name and address of incorporation, date, names of incorporators, and dates filed and recorded. Chronologically arranged. 1866-1875, no index; 1876—, alphabetical index by names of incorporations. Handwritten. Average 250 pages. 12 x 8 x 1.5. 1 volume, 1866-1875, basement vault; 2 volumes, 1876—, Recorder's vault .

54. PARTNERSHIP RECORD
1864—. 2 vols.

Record of partnerships formed showing names of partners, kind of business, location of business, and dates filed and recorded. Chronologically arranged. Alphabetical index by names of partnerships. Handwritten. Average 180 pages. 18 x 12 x 1.25.

Business Administration of Office

55. RECORD OF FEES
1891—. 9 vols. Missing:1894-1906.

Daily record of fees received for services showing date and amount of fees for recording, filing, searching, and sundries. Chronologically arranged. No index. Handwritten. Average 250 pages. 16 x 11 x 1.75.

Licenses and Grants of Authority

56. POWER OF ATTORNEY
1893—. 1 vol.

Record copies of power of attorney granted to an individual by another to act as his agent in specified cases showing date, terms, and names of grantee and grantor. Chronologically arranged. Alphabetical index by names of grantors. Handwritten. 540 pages. 18 x 12 x 4.

57. CERTIFICATES OF COMPLIANCE [and Insurance Agents' Licenses]
1927—. 1 filing cabinet of 30 pigeonholes. Prior records missing.

Record copies of certificates issued by state superintendent of insurance to insurance companies certifying that the insurance regulations have been complied with; also record copies of licenses granted by state superintendent of insurance to individuals to write insurance showing name of insurance agent, name of insurance company represented, and name of employer. Alphabetically arranged by names of insurance companies or agents. No index. Typed on printed forms. 30 x 36 x 12.

58. REGISTER OF LIFE AND FIRE INSURANCE AGENTS
1905-1906. 1 vol. Prior and subsequent records missing.
Record of filing certificates of compliance by insurance companies operating in Ohio showing date and names of Adams County agents. Chronologically arranged. No index. Handwritten. 200 pages. 12 x 8 x 1 1.25. Basement vault.

Miscellaneous

59. DISCHARGE RECORD
1865—. 2 vols.
Record of soldiers' discharges showing name of soldier, date of enlistment, service record, and date and place of discharge. 1 volume 1865-1933, is a record of discharges of Civil War, Spanish-American War, and National Guard; 1 volume 1918—, is a record of discharges of soldiers and sailors of the World War. Chronologically arranged by dates of discharges. For index, 1865-1933, see entry 60; 1918—, no index. Handwritten on printed forms. Average 603 pages. 17 x 11.25 x 4.

60. INDEX TO DISCHARGE RECORD
1865—. 1 vol. Last entry 1933.
Index to volume for 1865-1933 of Discharge Record, entry 59, showing date, name of soldier, and page number of record. Alphabetically arranged by names of soldiers Handwritten on printed forms. 75 pp, 15 x 8 x .75

61. MISCELLANEOUS RECORD
1930—. 1 vol.
Record copies of the following instruments not recorded under other titles: contracts for labor and material in construction of buildings; land agreements, agreements including those to dissolve partnerships, prenuptial agreements and separation agreements between husbands and wives; sale records covering transfer of chattels or stocks, each showing names of principals, date , copy of notarization , date filed, and date recorded. Chronologically arranged by dates of recording. Alphabetical index by names of grantees showing names of grantors, or names of principles. Typed. 500 pages. 18 x 12 x 3.

The office of clerk of courts, an ancient English institution originating before the time of Edward I[1] was transplanted to America during the colonial period. The American Revolution made no radical change in the political heritage derived from England, and the office was continued by the states. The duties of the office were modified, however, because of a separation, in the newer states, of administrative and judicial functions, which under the English system had been combined.

The sections of the Ohio constitution of 1802 creating the judicial system for the state provided for the appointment of a clerk of courts by the judges of the court of common pleas. He was to serve a seven-year term, but was subject to removal by the appointing power for a breach of good behavior.[2] The constitution of 1851 made the office of clerk elective with a three-year term,[3] A constitutional amendment in 1905 provided that the terms of all elective offices should be for an even number of years not exceeding four. In compliance with this amendment, the general assembly passed an act fixing the term of office of the clerk at two years.[4] The term remained at two years until 1936 when it was extended to four years.[5] The remuneration of the office was by fees until 1906 when the legislature prescribed a definite salary.[6]

The duties of the clerk of courts, like those of other county officers are prescribed by statute. In 1853 a code of civil procedure was adopted summarizing the earlier duties and forming the basis for the present ones in most respects similar to those prescribed during the earlier years of the office. The clerk of courts was directed to issue all writs and orders for provisional remedies; endorse the date upon all papers filed in his office; keep the journal, record books, and papers appertaining to the court and record its proceedings, and keep five books to be called the appearance docket, the trial docket and a printed duplicate of the trial docket, the journal, the record, and the execution docket.[7]

---

1. Sir Frederick Pollock and Frederic William Maitland, *The History of English Law Before the Tine of Edward I* (Cambridge, 1895), I, 184.
2. *Ohio Const. 1802*, Art. III , sec. 9.
3. *Ohio Const. 1851.* Art. IV. sec . 16.
4. *Laws of Ohio*. XCVIII. 273.
5. *Ibid.*, CXVI, pt. II, 184.
6. *Ibid.*, XCVIII, 94, 117.
7. *Ibid.*, LI, 107, 158-59; LXXVIII, 108; LXXIX, 115; LXXXVI, 174.

The present practice of keeping an index, direct and reverse, to judgments began in 1866.[8] In 1871, the clerk was made official custodian of the law reports and books furnished by the state for the use of the court and bar, and was made liable in the event of their destruction.[9]

Some of the duties of the clerk as defined by the civil code of 1853 are still effective, others have been added by subsequent legislation. Thus, for example, in 1858 the clerk was directed to receive notary commissions for record.[10] He was required, also, to receive for record special police commissions (1867), timber trade-marks (1883), partnership agreements (1894), copies of judgments of federal courts (1898), marks of ownerships [trade-marks] (1911), motor vehicle bills of sale (1921), and certificates of judgments to operate as a lien (1935).[11] On the other hand, many of the earlier duties of the clerk have been transferred to other departments of local government or have been abolished. The clerk issued marriage licenses and ministers' licenses until 1852, after that date they have been issued by the probate court, to which court the records have been transferred. Moreover the clerk issued peddlers licenses until the decade of the 1860s, since that time they have been issued by the auditor.[12] These records were not found in the inventory. The practice of recording in the office of the clerk, the names of black or mulatto persons to be used as certificates of freedom was, of course, discontinued after the close of the War between the States in 1865.

In 1856 the clerk was directed by the legislature to preserve a list of births, marriages, and deaths as returned to his office by the assessors, and to transmit on or before the first day of June annually a copy of such statistics to the secretary of state. From these county lists, the secretary of state prepared tabular statements showing the vital statistics in each county. The clerk received 10 copies of the report, one of which he was required to preserve in his office.[13]

---

8. *Ibid,*. LXIII, 10; LXXV, 103; LXXVIII, 88; LXXXII, 33; LXXXVI, 26.
9, *Ibid,*. LXVIII, 109.
10. *Ibid,*. LV, 13 ; XCIII, 406.
11. *Ibid,*. LXIV, 60; LXXX. 195; XCI, 357; XCII. 25; XCIII, 285; CI1, 513-14; CIX. 333; CXVI, 274. See p . lii.
12. *Ibid,*. LIX, 67.
13. *Ibid,*. LIII, 73-75

The clerk was relieved of the task of collecting and preserving vital statistics, when, in 1867, such powers and duties were vested in the probate judge.[14]

The clerk of courts was given other duties in addition to those of serving the court of common pleas and receiving documents for record. Since 1850 he has been required to report each year to the county commissioners all fines assessed by the county in criminal cases, together with the names of the parties to each case, and the amount of money he has paid to the treasurer.[15] Duplicate copies of these reports have not been preserved in the clerk's office but the commissioner's copies are listed in entry 4. Moreover, since 1867 he has been required to report annually to the secretary of state the number of crimes committed in his county, the number of pending cases, and the amount of fines collected.[16] An act of 1927, amending the act of 1867, directed the clerk to report on any matters which the secretary of state might require, and to forward a duplicate copy of his report on crime in his county to the state board of clemency, [board of pardons and parole].[17] The state board of clemency was abolished in 1921 and its duties were assigned to a board of pardons and parole within the department of public welfare.[18]

The county clerk of courts, like the county prosecuting attorney, is one of the important persons in the judicial system. His significance and influence, however, was not recognized until recent years.

---

14. *Ibid.*, LXIV, 63-64
15. *Laws of Ohio.* XLVIII, 66; LVIII, 69; LXXXVI, 239.
16. *Ibid.*, LXIV, 17.
17. *Ibid.*, CXII, 203.
18. *Ibid.*. CIX, 111, 124.

Motor Vehicles

62. BILLS OF SALE AND SWORN STATEMENTS OF OWNERSHIP
1921-December 1937. 36 bundles, 42 file boxes (labeled by inclusive document nos.).

Duplicate bills of sale or sworn statements of ownership of new and used motor vehicles filed with clerk of courts showing bill of sale number, date, names of grantor and grantee, name of manufacturer, manufacturer's number, engine number, type, horsepower, and date filed. Numerically arranged by bills of sale numbers. Handwritten and typed on printed forms. Bundles, sizes vary; file boxes, 5 x 10 x 14. 36 bundles, 1921-1930, Basement vault; 42 file boxes, 1931-December 1937, Clerk of courts' vault.

63. INDEX TO MOTOR VEHICLE BILLS OF SALE AND SWORN STATEMENTS OF OWNERSHIP
1921-December 1937. 9 vols.

Direct and reverse index to Bills of Sale and Sworn Statements of Ownership showing names of grantor and grantee, date filed, make of vehicle, model, and horsepower. Direct index in front half of each volume and reverse index in back half of each volume. Alphabetically arranged direct, by names of grantors, and reverse, by names of grantees. Handwritten. Average 425 pages. 12 x 16 x 3.5. Clerk of courts' vault.

64. CERTIFICATE OF TITLE TO MOTOR VEHICLES
1938—. 4 file drawers.

Record of certificates of title to motor vehicles showing previous number, county, state, certificate number filed numerically, name and address of owner, description of motor vehicle, year of make, body type, number of cylinders, motor number, manufacturer's serial number, model, horsepower, acquired from whom, previous owner's name and address; on which motor vehicles are the following liens mortgages, or encumbrances: first lien, nature of lien, amount, held by, holder's address, date of notation, clerk of courts' signature, lien discharge date, date of cancellation, signature of lien holder, and by whom; record of other liens; type of safety glass if vehicle manufactured after January 1, 1936; if dealer, vendor's license number, amount of delivered price , amount of Ohio sales tax or use tax; date issued, seal, notarization , date, and signature of clerk of courts by deputy. Also contains receipt book of fees paid for certificate of title, receipts for fees paid for notation of lien; receipts for fees paid for cancellation of lien, and applications for certificates of titles motor vehicles. Numerically arranged by certificate numbers. For index, see entry 66. Typed on printed forms. 8 x 16 x 24. Clerk of courts' office.

65. DAILY REPORT OF FEES COLLECTED FOR CERTIFICATE OF TITLE [Motor Vehicles]
1938—. 1 vol.

Record of fees collected for issuance of certificates of title, motor vehicles, showing name of office, clerk of courts, county, state, date, month, year, signature of clerk of courts, certificate of title number; record of fees for issuing certificate of title, notation of lien, memoranda certificate, cancellation of lien, application, certified copy, and total fees; also contains clerk's fee and state registrar's fee; daily report of clerk of courts to state bureau of motor vehicles of certificate of titles issued, notation of lien receipts, cancellation of lien receipts and total amount of fees for each. Chronologically arranged by dates of entry. No index. Handwritten on printed forms. 150 pages. 14 x 10 x 1. Clerk of courts' office.

66. CARD INDEX TO CERTIFICATES OF TITLES, MOTOR VEHICLES
1938—. 1 file drawer.

Card index record to Certificate of Title to Motor Vehicles, entry 64, showing previous number, county, state, serial number, name and address of owner, year, make, body type, number of cylinders, motor number, manufacturer's serial number, model, horsepower, name and address of previous owner, and date issued by clerk, Alphabetically arranged by names of owners. Typed on printed forms. 7 x 14 x 24. Clerk of courts' office.

Licenses and Commissions

67. REGISTER OF JUSTICES' COMMISSIONS
1910—. 1 vol. Prior records missing.

Record copies of commissions of justices of peace and of justices surety bonds showing name of official, date; names of sureties, and amount of bond. Chronologically arranged. Alphabetical index by names of justices. Handwritten on printed forms. 240 pages. 14 x 9 x 1.5. Clerk of courts' office.

68. RECORD OF NOTARY COMMISSIONS

1910—. 2 vols. Prior records missing.
Record copies of notary public commissions granted by governor of Ohio showing name of appointee, date of commission, and oath of notary. Chronologically arranged. Alphabetical index by names of notaries. Handwritten on printed forms. Average 292 pages. 14 x 9 x 1.75. Clerk of courts' office.

69. EMBALMERS' LICENSE RECORD

1911-1925. 1 vol Discontinued.
Record copies of embalmers licenses issued and recorded in Adams County showing date, name of licensee, and date filed. Chronologically arranged. Alphabetical index by names of licensees. Handwritten on printed forms. 193 pages. 14 x 9 x 1 1.25. Clerk of courts' vault.

70. HUNTERS' LICENSE RECORD

1913—. 2 vols.
Record of licenses issued to hunt and trap showing date issued, applicant's name and address, physical description of licensee, and fee. Chronologically arranged. No index. Handwritten on printed forms. Average 200 pages. 16 x 11 x 1.5. 1 volume 1913-1923, basement vault; 1 volume 1924—. Clerk of courts' vault.

71. FISHING LICENSE RECORD

1926—. 1 vol. Prior records missing.
Record of licenses issued to fish with rod and reel showing name, address, and physical description of licensee, date issued, and license number. Chronologically arranged. No index. Handwritten on printed forms, 100 pages. 12 x 9 x 1. Clerk of courts' vault.

72. OPTOMETRY RECORD

1925—. 1 vol. Prior records missing.
Record copies of licenses granted by state board of optometry to persons qualified to practice optometry in Adams County showing license number, name of licensee, and date issued. Chronologically arranged. Alphabetical index by names of licensees. Handwritten on printed forms. 208 pages. 14 x 9 x .5. Clerk of courts' vault.

73. REGISTER OF REAL ESTATE BROKER
1936—. 1 vol. Prior records missing.

Record of licenses issued to buy, sell, and trade real estate for clients showing date issued, name of licensee, name of salesman or broker, name of employer, and license number. Alphabetically arranged by names of brokers or agents. No index. Handwritten. 100 pages. 15 x 8 x 1. Clerk of courts' vault.

Elections

(See also entries 268, 269)

74. POLL BOOKS AND TALLY SHEETS
1925—. 648 vols. (labeled by years, names of subdivisions, and precinct nos.).

Precinct poll books and tally sheets for general and primary elections. 324 volumes, general elections: poll books showing names and addresses of electors voting at general elections; tally sheets showing tabulated vote received by each candidate and for each proposal, 324 volumes, primary elections: poll books showing names and addresses of Republican and Democratic electors casting ballots; tally sheets showing tabulated vote received by each candidate. Poll books, alphabetically arranged by names of electors; tally sheets, arranged by office. Handwritten on printed forms. Average 30 pages. 26 x 14 x .25. 288 volumes, 1925-1930, Basement vault; 360 volumes, 1931—. Clerk of courts' vault.

Business Administration of Office

75. CASH BOOK
1910—. 12 vols. Prior records missing.

Daily record of cash receipts and disbursements by clerk of courts; receipts showing from what source received, to whom due, date, and amount; disbursements showing to whom paid, date, and amount. Chronologically arranged. No index. Handwritten. Average 200 pages. 18 x 16 x 1.5. Clerk of courts' vault.

76. RECORD OF ACCRUED FEES
1910—. 4 vols. Prior records missing.

Record of fees due clerk of courts showing date accrued, case number, for what, to whom charged, amount, and date paid. Chronologically arranged. No index.

Handwritten. Average 250 pages. 18 x 12 x 1.75. Clerk of courts' vault.

77. CRIMINAL COST BOOK
1910—. 11 vols. Prior records missing.
Itemized record of costs in criminal cases showing case number, date, offense charged, name of defendant, and total costs. Chronologically arranged. Alphabetical index by names of defendants. Handwritten on printed forms. Average 480 pages. 18 x 12 x 3.25. Clerk of courts' vault.

78. CIVIL COST BOOK
1910—. 6 vols. Prior records missing.
Itemized record of costs in civil cases showing case number, date, names of litigants, kind of action, to whom charged, and total cost. Chronologically arranged. Alphabetical index by names of plaintiffs. Handwritten on printed forms. Average 470 pages. 16 x 12 x 3.5. Clerk of courts' vault.

79. CERTIFICATES
1910—. 17 bundles, 7 file boxes (labeled by subjects) Prior records missing.
Carbon copies of certificates issued by clerk of courts for payment of witness and jury fees, showing date, certificate number, case number, name of payee, for what, and amount. Bundles, no systematic arrangement; file boxes. Chronologically arranged. No index. Handwritten on printed forms. Bundles, sizes vary; file boxes, 5 x 10 x 14. 17 bundles, 1910-1925, Basement vault; 7 file boxes, 1926—, Clerk of courts' vault.

Miscellaneous

80. ESTRAYS AND DRIFTS

1910—. 1 vol. Prior records missing.
Record of stray animals reported found showing description of animal and by whom found and held; also of craft found drifting on the Ohio River showing date, description of craft, and name of holder. Chronologically arranged. No index. Handwritten. 300 pages. 16 x 11 x 2. Clerk of courts' vault.

81. CORONER'S REPORTS

1910—. 5 file boxes. Prior records missing.
Reports by county coroner on investigations and inquests held in cases of accidental, sudden, and homicidal deaths, showing name of decedent, age, color, sex, date of death, place of death, names of witnesses, date of inquest, findings as to cause of death by coroner or coroner's jury, and itemized cost bill of each case. Chronologically arranged. No index. Handwritten on printed forms. 5 x 10 x 14. Clerk of courts' of vault.

For related records, see entries 168, 180.

The court of common pleas, like many other county institutions, originated in England during the reign of Henry II.[1] Established in America during the colonial period, the office was continued by the states following the War of American Independence.

The Northwest Ordinance of 1787 established a government consisting of a governor, a secretary, and three judges all appointed by Congress. The judges were to form a court, known as the general court, which had common law jurisdiction and together with the governor were authorized, to draw up a code of civil and criminal law. The territorial act of 1788, establishing the American colonial policy in the newer west in respect to the judiciary, contained sections authorizing the establishment in each county of a common pleas court to be composed of not less than three nor more than five members. These members appointed and commissioned by the territorial governor were given jurisdiction in all civil matters.[2] The same act established in each county a primary court called the court of general quarter sessions of the peace to be composed of no more than five nor less than three justices of the peace, appointed and commissioned by the governor.[3] This court, which had limited jurisdiction in criminal matters, was not re-established by the constitution of 1802.

When a constitution was drafted for Ohio in 1802, preparatory to the entrance of the state into the Union, provision was made for a continuation of the territorial court of common pleas.[4] The articles of the Ohio constitution, regarding the judiciary, provided for a court of common pleas in each county to be composed of a president and associate judges. For each county[5] not more than three nor less than two associate judges were to be appointed, with one president for each of the three judicial districts into which the counties were grouped. The associate judges were not as a rule men who had a legal education.[6]

---

1. George Burton Adams, *Constitutional History of England* (New York, 1921), 109, 134.

2. Pease, *op. cit.,* 7.

3. Pease, *op. cit.,* 4

4. *Ohio Const. 1802,* Art. Ill, sec. 1.

5. At this time there were eight counties in the state.

6. Francis J. Amer, *The Development of the Judicial System in Ohio from 1787 to 1932* (Johns Hopkins University. Baltimore, 1932, "Institute of Law Bulletin" no. 8, 17.

The members of the court, appointed by joint ballot of both houses of the general assembly, were to hold court in three judicial districts into which the state was to be divided by legislative action. Their term of office was seven years "if so long they behave well."[7]

For many years there were no significant changes in the structure of the common pleas courts. However in 1838 the superior court of Cincinnati was established as a special, local court, and was given concurrent jurisdiction with the common pleas court of Hamilton County in all civil cases at common law and in chancery, in which the older court had original jurisdiction.[8]

It was almost half a century before any significant changes were made in the structure of the court. The constitution of 1851 provided that judges of the common pleas were to be elected for a seven-year term. For the purposes of their election the state was divided into nine districts composed of three or more counties. Each district, in turn, was to be subdivided into three parts, in each of which one common pleas judge was to be elected. The court of common pleas was to be held by one or more of these judges in each county in the district.[9] Power was given to the general assembly to increase or diminish the number of districts of the court of common pleas, the number of judges in any district and to change the districts or the subdivisions there of, whenever two thirds of the legislature concurred therein.[10] Provision was made for the removal of judges by a concurrent resolution of two-thirds of the members elected to each house of the legislature.[11] An appellate court known as the district court was created, and was to be composed of one supreme court judge and the several common pleas judges of the district. This court was to be held in each county of the district at least once in each year or at least three annual sessions in not less than three places.[12] The district courts were not a success, and after many attempts at revision the circuit courts, staffed by a separate group of elected judges, were adopted by vote of the people in 1883, thus relieving the common pleas judges of this appellate work.[13]

---

7. *Ohio Const. 1802,* Art. Ill, sec. 8.
8. *Laws of Ohio.* XXXVI, 95; XLVI, 17, 21 .
9. *Ohio Const. 1851,* Art. IV, secs. 3, 4.
10. *Ibid.,* Art. IV, sec. 15.
11. *Ibid.,* Art. IV, sec. 17.
12. *Ibid.,* Art. IV, secs. 5, 6.
13. Amer, *op. cit.,* 31-33; *Laws of Ohio,* LXXXI, 168

The juvenile court was created in 1904 with jurisdiction in special matters relating to minors and was to be held by a judge of the common pleas, court of insolvency, or probate court who should be designated by the judges to hold such court.[14]

At the opening of the twentieth century sweeping changes in the organization of the courts were made. Constitutional amendments adopted in 1912 abolished the divisions and subdivisions of the common pleas provided by the constitution of 1851, and authorized the election of one or more common pleas judges in each county.[15] The chief justice of the supreme court was given authority to determine the disability or disqualification of any judge of the court of common pleas and also to assign any judge to hold court in any county.[16] Ten years later the selection of a chief justice of the court of common pleas was authorized. Under an act of March 13, 1923, in counties where there were two or more common pleas judges, a chief justice was designated by vote of the judges. The justice so designated by his colleagues was to serve in such capacity until the expiration of his term, after which time the office was to be an elective one. The elective section of the act was nullified by the supreme court on the grounds that the creation of a new elective office was unconstitutional. Accordingly, in 1927 an amendment was passed eliminating the elective provision of the act.[17] In recent years attempts have been made to improve the efficiency of the court imposing stricter qualifications upon those who seek election to the bench. In 1917 an act was passed providing that a common pleas judge shall have been admitted to practice as an attorney-at-law for a period of six years preceding his election.[18]

The salary of the office was also increased to $3,000 per year plus an amount based on the population of the county.[19] This making the position financially attractive, especially as the term of office is six years.[20]

---

14. *Laws of Ohio*. XCVII, 562.
15. *Ohio Const. 1851*, Art. IV, sec. 3.
16. *Ibid.,* Art. IV, secs. 3,6.
17. State ex rel. v. Powell, *Ohio State Reports*, CIX, 383; G.C. sec. 1558.
18. *Laws of Ohio*, CVII, 164.
19. G.C. sec. 2251-52.
20. *Ibid.,* sec. 1532.

In addition to their regular salaries, common pleas judges may be paid a per diem and expenses when assigned to special duty by the chief justice of the supreme court in a district not their own. When dockets become crowded or judges are incapacitated or disqualified, such assignments may be made.[21] In a few large counties certain common pleas judges have specialized duties such as domestic relations and juvenile court which promotes judicial efficiency.

The jurisdiction of the court of common pleas has also been the product of a long period of historical development. The territorial law of 1788 which created the court provided that the judges so appointed and commissioned shall hold pleas of *assizes, scire facias, replevins*, and hear and determine all manner of pleas, actions, suits, and causes of a civil nature, real, personal, and mixed, according to the constitution and laws of the territory. Individually, each judge of the common pleas was given jurisdiction over contract actions not exceeding five dollars.[23] The probate court was established by an act adopted August 30, 1788, and two of the judges of the court of common pleas sat with this judge in ruling on contested points, definitive sentences, and final judgments.[24] Under the laws of 1788 the common pleas had no criminal jurisdiction, and the quarter sessions of the peace had no civil jurisdiction . There was no provision for an appeal from one court to another except from the probate court to the general court.

In 1795 the judicial system underwent the first general revision and this increased the duties of the common pleas, A single justice of the peace or judge of the common pleas was given jurisdiction to hear certain civil, actions up to $12.00. Actions under $5.00 were exclusive with the judges or justices and there was no appeal from their judgment. Actions between $5.00 and $12.00 could be appealed to the court of common pleas. In 1799 this jurisdiction was raised to $20.00, and appeals could be taken to the common pleas if the judgment was over $2.00. If the judgment was for plaintiff, he could appeal only if the original demand was $4.00 more than the sum recovered.[25]

---

21. *Ohio Const. 1851* (Amendment, 1912), Art. IV, .sec. 3.

22. G.C. sec. 1532.

23. Salmon P. Chase, *The Statutes of Ohio and of the Northwestern Territory, 1788-1833* (Cincinnati, 1833-1835), I, 94.

24. *Ibid.*, I,96.

25. Chase, *op. cit.*, I, 143, 233. 307.

Appeal from the common pleas to the general court was not provided for until 1800, and could not be taken unless the title to land was in question or when the amount in controversy exceeded $50.00.[26]

The constitution of 1802 gave the court of common pleas jurisdiction in such common law and chancery cases as should be directed by law. In addition it was given jurisdiction of all probate and testamentary matters, and the appointment and supervision of guardians.[27] Moreover the court of common pleas and supreme court were assigned original cognizance of criminal cases as might be provided by law.[28] Appeals in civil cases might be made from the county commissioners, justices of the peace and other inferior courts, to the court of common pleas.[29]

An act of the first general assembly in 1803 provided for the organization of the courts and defined their jurisdiction.[30] The court of common pleas was given original jurisdiction in all cases, both in law and in equity, when the matter in dispute exceeded the jurisdiction of the justices of peace; of all probate, testamentary, and guardianship matters; and of all criminal matters exceeding the jurisdiction, of the justice of peace, except when the punishment of the crime was capital. It was allowed to review certain cases from the justices of peace and also to review the decisions of the county commissioners in highway matters. In addition, the court had the same power to issue remedial and other process, writs of error and *mandamus* excepted, as had the supreme court. In 1804 the court's jurisdiction in chancery cases was limited to cases involving less than $500.00.[31] and in 1805 it was given appellate jurisdiction from the justices of peace in all cases regardless of the amount involved.[32] In 1806 crimes wherein the punishment was capital could be tried in the common pleas court if the accused so elected.[33] In 1807 it was given jurisdiction in all chancery cases and concurrent jurisdiction with the supreme court in such cases involving over $500.00.[34]

---

26. Chase, *op. cit.*, I, 306.
27. *Ohio Const. 1851*, Art. III, secs. 3, 5.
28. *Ibid.*, Art. III, sec. 4.
29. *Ibid.*, Art. III, sec. 3.
30. Chase, *op. cit.* I, 355.
31. *Laws of Ohio*. II, 261.
32. *Ibid.*, III, 14.
33. *Ibid.*, IV, 57.
34. *Laws of Ohio*, V, 117.

In 1810 all cases in which the common pleas had original jurisdiction were permitted to be appealed to the supreme court.[35] By this act the right to appeal was established in Ohio in all civil cases. However the business of the supreme court increased so rapidly that in 1845 the right to appeal from a judgment of the common pleas court to the supreme court in actions at law was abolished. Instead, new trials were allowed "when law and justice require it."[36] Even earlier, appeals to the common pleas from inferior courts had been limited.[37] The chancery act, adopted in 1824, conferred general chancery powers on the court,[38] and in 1843 it was given concurrent jurisdiction with the supreme court in cases of divorce and alimony.[39]

The constitution of 1851 left the jurisdiction of the common pleas court to be fixed by law.[40] The jurisdiction conferred on this court by subsequent legislation was essentially the same as that exercised since 1810, with the exception of the jurisdiction transferred to the probate court,[41] and the addition of jurisdiction in divorce and alimony cases.[42] The court of common pleas was denied jurisdiction in cases of probate, testamentary, and guardianship matters, but final orders, judgments, and decrees of the probate court could be reviewed in common pleas on appeal or by writ of *certiorari*.[43] In 1853, the court of common pleas was given original jurisdiction of all crimes and offenses except minor criminal cases, the exclusive jurisdiction of which was vested in the justice of peace or other minor courts.[44] In the same year the court was given exclusive jurisdiction in divorce cases.[45]

---

35. *Ibid.*, VIII, 259.
36. *Ibid.*, XLIII, 80.
37. *Ibid.*, XXXVIII, 27.
38. *Ibid.*, XXII, 75.
39. *Ibid.*, XLI, 94.
40. *Ohio Const. 1851.* Art. IV, secs. 3, 4.
41. *Laws of Ohio*, L, 67.
42. *Ibid.*, LI, 377.
43. *Ibid.*, L, 64; LI, 145.
44. G.C. sec. 13422-5; *Laws of Ohio.* LI, 474; LII, 73.
45. *Laws of Ohio.* LI, 377.

The creation of criminal, mayors' and police courts also made certain changes in the powers and duties of common pleas courts.[46] The right of appeal from common pleas to the district court was restored in all civil actions in which the common pleas had original jurisdiction,[47] but by an act of 1858 appeals were allowed to the intermediate court only in non-jury cases. However, the same act provided for a second jury trial in common pleas as a matter of right in jury cases. This was granted upon demand made by either party at the close of the first trial on condition of his giving bond.[48] The abuse of this privilege led to its abolition in 1875.[49]

This period witnessed the re-establishment of superior courts in the state which were given the same jurisdiction as the courts of common pleas with certain exceptions.[50] At the same time as the superior court was established at Cincinnati, the legislature abolished the criminal court and transferred its jurisdiction to the common pleas court.[51] The criminal jurisdiction of the probate court was transferred to the common pleas court in 1857,[52] and a limitation was placed on the right to appeal from probate court to common pleas,[53] this being repealed, however, in 1856.[54]

For many years there were few changes in the powers of the court of common pleas except in the forms of appeal to higher courts,[55] and such added powers as resulted from the decline in the number of superior courts.[56]

---

46. *Ibid.*, L, 90, 240, 246, 251, 253.
47. *Ibid.*, L, 93.
48. *Ibid.*, LX. 81.
49. *Ibid.*, LXXII, 34.
50. *Ibid.*, LII, 34; LIII, 38; LIV, 37.
51. *Ibid.*, LII, 107.
52. *Ibid.*, LIV, 97.
53. *Ibid.*, LII, 104.
54. *Ibid.*, LIII. 8.
55. *Ibid.*, LXXIV, 359; LXXXII. 230.
56. *Ibid.*, LXII, 58; LXXII, 89, 105; LXXXII, 85.

In 1894 the probate court in certain counties was given concurrent jurisdiction with the common pleas court in divorce, alimony, foreclosure, and partition cases,[57] and in 1906 it was given coordinate jurisdiction with common pleas in a ll counties in the trial of misdemeanors and all proceedings to prevent crimes.[58] Certain other special courts, as insolvency courts, shared certain powers with common pleas.[59]

Since 1906 the court of common pleas has had jurisdiction in naturalization proceedings. In that year the federal statute was amended to limit jurisdiction in the granting of naturalization to the United States district courts and state courts having a clerk, a seal, and jurisdiction in matters of law and equity in which the amount of controversy is unlimited.[60]

Constitutional amendments adopted in 1912 had little effect upon the jurisdiction of the court of common pleas; this power being determined by law.[61] However the establishment of municipal courts, beginning in 1910, relieved common pleas courts in many cities of certain civil jurisdiction,[62] but this was balanced in 1911 by the abolition of the jurisdiction of the probate court in certain counties in divorce, alimony, foreclosure, and partition.[63] In the same year the juvenile courts were given jurisdiction of all misdemeanors against minors and certain other offenses.[64] Provision was also made for error proceedings from juvenile court to the court of common pleas.[65] The jurisdiction of the common pleas court of today is essentially the same as that of 1913. The few changes that have been made in the judicial system are found in the local, special courts, particularly in the rapidly developing municipal courts.

The common pleas court has never possessed extensive appointive powers. The constitution of 1802 authorized each court to appoint a clerk,[66] and in 1805 it was directed to appoint a county prosecuting attorney.[67]

----

57. *Ibid.*, XCI, 799.
58. *Ibid.*, XCVIII, 49.
59. *Ibid.*, XCI, 844; XCII, 475; XCIV, 353.
60. *United States Statutes at Large*, XXXIV, pt. I, 596.
61. *Ohio Const. 1851.* Art. IV, sec. 6.
62. *Laws of Ohio*, CI. 364; CIII, 279.
63. *Laws of Ohio.* CII, 100.
64. *Ibid.*, CII, 425.
65. *Ibid.*, CIII, 875.
66. *Ohio Const, 1802.* Art. III, sec. 9.
67. *Laws of Ohio*, Ill, 47.

During the first three decades of Ohio history, the movement for the extension of the popular election of public officers deprived the court of common pleas of the privilege of appointing the county recorder (1829), the county surveyor (1831), and the county prosecutor (1833).[68] The court continued to appoint a clerk of courts until 1851. In recent years, however, as new functions have been added to the county government, the court has again been given a limited appointive power. Successive acts in 1886, 1891, 1913, 1914, and 1925 authorized the court to appoint a soldiers relief commission, a jury commission, an assignment commissioner, a conservancy district board, and a probation officer.[69] Other appointments authorized in 1911 are those of court interpreter and criminal bailiff.[70]

Since 1929 the court, in counties having a population in excess of 300,000, has been authorized to appoint one or more psychiatrists, psychologists, or other examiners or investigators who hold their offices at the will of the court, and receive such compensation as the judge may determine, not exceeding the amount appropriated by the county commissioners.[71] The court may also appoint a court reporter (or reporters),[72] and may cooperate with the county commissioners for the establishment of a county department of probation, in which case the court appoints certain probation officers and supervises their work.[73] In case the sheriff is absent, disabled, or disqualified from serving the court's warrant, the judge may appoint temporarily on official for this service.[74] By and large, however, the patronage power of the court of common pleas is a negligible factor in county government.

---

68. *Ibid.*, XXVII, 65; XXIX,399; Chase, *op. cit.*, III,1935
69. *Laws of Ohio*, LXXXIII, 232; LXXXVIII, 200; CIII, 512; CIC, 13-64; CXI, 423.
70. G.C. sec. 1541.
71. *Ibid.*, sec. 1541.
72. *Ibid.*, secs. 1546-1554.
73. *Ibid.*, secs. 1554-1 - 1554-6.
74. *Ibid.*, sec. 2828.

The keeping of the records of the common pleas court presented no particular difficulties for many decades. However, with the increased number of issues presented to the court in recent years the problem of judicial administration has become greater. This problem was solved in part by the creation of a chief justice of the court of common pleas who has been given the duties of superintending the business of the court, classifying it, and distributing it among the judges. Beside the duties enumerated, the chief justice annually makes a report to the clerk of courts showing the work performed by the court and by each judge in the preceding calendar year. Moreover, he reports such other data as the chief justice of the supreme court may require.[75]

Judges of the common pleas court are also required to issue an annual order as to the exact time of sessions. The clerk of courts is required to make this information public and also send a copy to the secretary of state. The law sets certain requirements as to the sessions of the court and the power of the Judge to call special sessions.[76] The records of the court are deposited for safekeeping with the clerk of courts. The clerk is custodian also of all law reports and books furnished by the state for use of the court and the bar and is made liable in the event of their destruction.[77]

All records are located in the clerk of courts' vault unless otherwise specified.

---

75. *Ibid.*, sec. 1558.
76. *Ibid.*, secs. 1533-1539.
77. *Laws of Ohio*, LXVIII, 109.

Dockets

82. INDEX TO PENDING SUITS AND LIVING JUDGMENTS
n.d. 3 vols.
Index to pending suits and living judgments showing names of litigants, case number, amount of judgment, and volume and page numbers of docket, journal, and record. Alphabetically arranged by names of plaintiffs. Code index showing pages and case numbers. Handwritten. Average 600 pages. 20 x 12 x 4.

83. JUDGMENT INDEX, DIRECT
1910—. 2 vols. Prior records missing.
Direct index to judgments showing names of plaintiff and defendant, amount of judgment allowed, case number, cause of action, volume and page numbers of Execution Docket, entry 89, Journal, entry 95, and Common Pleas Record, entry 98, date execution issued, and date judgment satisfied. Alphabetically arranged by names of plaintiffs. Handwritten. Average 425 pages. 18 x 14 x 3.25.

84. JUDGMENT INDEX, REVERSE
1910—. 2 vols. Prior records missing.
Reverse index to judgments showing names of defendant and plaintiff, amount of judgment allowed, case number, cause of action, volume and page numbers of Execution Docket, entry 89, Journal, entry 95, and Common Pleas Record, entry 98, date execution issued, and date judgment satisfied. Alphabetically arranged by names of defendants. Handwritten. Average 425 pages. 18 x 14 x 3.25.

85. CIVIL APPEARANCE DOCKET
1854—. 9 vols. (6-9, 23-27). Missing: 1883-1909.
Appearance docket showing names of litigants, trial date, kind of action, case number, and volume and page numbers of Execution Docket, entry 89, and Journal, entry 95. Chronologically arranged. Alphabetical index by names of plaintiffs. Handwritten. Average 600 pages. 18 x 12 x 4. 1 volume. 1854-1882, Basement vault; 8 volumes , 1910—, Clerk of courts' vault.

86. CRIMINAL APPEARANCE DOCKET
1879—. 5 vols, (one unnumbered, 4, 5, 8, 17). Missing:1892-1909.
Appearance docket showing name of defendant, trial date, offense charged, case

number, and volume and page numbers of Journal entry 95.Chronologically arranged. Alphabetical index by names of defendants. Handwritten. Average 600 pages. 18 x 12 x 4, 1 volume. 1879-1891, Basement vault, 4 volumes 1910—, Clerk of courts' vault.

87. CIVIL DOCKET

1910—. 12 vols. Prior records missing.
Court dockets showing case number, date, names of litigants and attorneys, title of case, judge's decision or jury's verdict, and volume and page numbers of Journal, entry 95, and Common Pleas Record, entry 98. Chronologically arranged. Alphabetical index by names of plaintiffs. Handwritten. Average 400 pages. 16 x 13 x 3.

88. CRIMINAL DOCKET

1910—. 16 vols. Prior records missing.
Court docket showing case number, date, name of defendant, names of attorneys, offense charged, verdict, and volume and page numbers of State [Criminal] Record, entry 101. Chronologically arranged. Alphabetical index by names of defendants. Handwritten. Average 400 pages. 16 x 12 x 3. 13 volumes 1910-1925, Basement vault. 3 volumes, 1926—, Clerk of courts' vault.

89. EXECUTION DOCKET

1910—. 4 volumes (12-15). Prior records missing.
Record of executions ordered by court to satisfy judgments showing case number, names of litigants, kind of action, amount of judgment, and sheriff's return; also record of sales of property by sheriff to satisfy judgments. Chronologically arranged. Alphabetical index by names of plaintiffs. Handwritten. Average 300 pages. 18 x 12 x 2.25.

90. WITNESS DOCKET

1910—. 6 vols. Prior records missing.
Record of witnesses subpoenaed to appear before grand jury or to testify in common pleas or appeals court showing date, kind of action. names of litigants, number of days in attendance, mileage, and total fee due. Chronologically arranged. Alphabetical index by names of plaintiffs or defendants. Handwritten. Average 300 pages. 18 x 12 x 2.25. 2 volumes, 1910-1918, Basement vault; 4 volumes, 1919—,

Clerk of courts' vault.

91. MOTION DOCKET
1910—. 4 vols.

Record of motions in common pleas court showing date, names of attorneys litigants, nature of motion, find remarks. Chronologically arranged. Alphabetical index by names of plaintiffs. Handwritten. Average 380 pages. 16 x 11 x 2.25.

92. PRAECIPE DOCKET
1911—. 2 vols.

Record of praecipes issued showing names of litigants, kind of writ and action, names of attorneys, and date issued. Chronologically arranged. No index. Handwritten on printed forms. Average 300 pages. 15 x 9 x 2.

93. CERTIFICATE JUDGMENT DOCKET
1935—. 1 vol.

Record of certificates, issued on judgment liens showing kind of action, case number, names of litigants, name of court, date judgment was rendered, amount, costs, volume and page numbers of Journal, entry 95, date filed, and to whom issued, Chronologically arranged. Alphabetical index by names of plaintiffs. Handwritten on printed forms. 410 pages. 20 x 12 x 3.

Record of Trials

94. COURT RECORDS
1801—. 5 boxes, approx, 750 bundles, 185 file boxes (1-185 and also labeled by inclusive case nos,).

Original papers in civil and criminal cases; 1910—, criminal records in red jackets, civil cases in white jackets, showing case number, names of litigants, title of case, date issued, and date filed. Records, 1801-1910, were salvaged from the courthouse fire. 1801-1910, no systematic Arrangement; 1910—, numerical arrangement by case numbers. No index. 1801-1852, handwritten; 1852-1924, handwritten on printed forms; 1925—, typed on printed forms, 1801-1910, condition fair. Boxes, 22 x 15 x 15; bundles, sizes vary; file boxes, 5 x 10 x 14. 5 boxes and 750 bundles, 1801-1910, Basement vault; 185 file boxes, 1910—, Clerk of courts' vault.

For original papers, divorce cases, see entry 100.

95. JOURNAL

1910—, 16 vols. (33-48). Prior records missing.

Journal entries of proceedings in civil and criminal cases including affidavits, pleas, motions, and all court orders and decrees, showing names of litigants, date, case number, and title of case. Chronologically arranged. Alphabetical index by names of plaintiffs. 1910-1926, handwritten; 1927, typed. Average 600 pages. 18 x 12 x 4.

96. JURY BOOK

1910—. 2 vols. Prior records missing.

Records names of persons drawn for grand and petit jury duty from regular and special venires. Chronologically arranged by dates of court terms and alphabetical thereunder by names of jurors. No index. Handwritten. Average 420 pages. 16 x 12 x 3.

97. RECORD OF JURORS

1932—. 1 vol. Prior records missing.

Records names of jurors who served, who were discharged, or who were excused, showing if for grand or petit duty, number of days, mileage, and total fees due, Chronologically arranged by date of court terms and alphabetical thereunder by names of jurors. No index, Handwritten. 250 pages. 17 x 14 x 1.50.

98. COMMON PLEAS RECORD

1910—. 23 vols. (46-68). Prior records missing.

Complete record of all civil cases heard in common pleas court showing names of litigants, title of case, case number, date case filed, and date of trial. Chronologically arranged. Alphabetical index by names of plaintiffs. 1910-1923, Handwritten; 1924—, typed. Average 490 pages. 18 x 12 x 3.5.

99. PARTITION RECORD

1910–. 7 vols. (11-17). Prior records missing.

Complete record of proceedings in partition cases showing names of litigants, case number, name of decedent, and date tiled, Chronologically arranged. Alphabetical index by names of plaintiffs. 1910-1924, handwritten; 1925—, typed. Average 630 pages. 16 x 12 x 4.25.

100. COURT RECORDS, DIVORCE
1910—. 18 file boxes (labeled by inclusive case nos.). Prior records
missing.
Original papers issued in divorce proceedings showing names of litigants, case
number, date case filed, and date each paper issued. Numerically arranged by case
numbers. No index. 1910-1926, handwritten on printed forms; 1927—, typed on
printed forms. 5 x 10 x 14.
For other original papers, see entry 94.

101. STATE [Criminal] RECORD
1910—. 16 vols. (9-24). Prior records missing.
Complete record of all criminal cases tried in common pleas court including copies
of affidavits for arrest, transcripts of preliminary hearings, magistrates orders,
sheriff's returns, indictments, trial proceedings, verdicts, sentences, and
commitment orders, showing name of defendant, offense charged, date case filed,
and trial date, 1910-1911, 10 volumes, are records of election bribery cases.
Chronologically arranged. Alphabetical index by names of defendants. 1910-1928,
handwritten; 1929—, typed. Average 480 pages. 18 x 12 x 3.5. 10 volumes, 1910-
1911, Basement vault; 6 volumes, 1910—, Clerk of courts' vault.

Miscellaneous

102. ALIMONY AND SUPPORT BOOKS
1930—. 2 vols. Record initiated 1930.
Weekly entries of alimony and support payments showing names of payer and
payee, date of payment, and amount. Chronologically arranged. Alphabetical index
by names of payees. Handwritten. Average 270 pages. 16 x 9 x 1.5.

103. RECOGNIZANCE RECORD
1910—. 3 vols. Prior records missing.
Record copies of bonds imposed by common pleas court for appearance in court of
accused persons for trial showing date, names of principals and sureties, amount of
bond, and offense. Chronologically arranged. Alphabetical index by names of
defendants. Handwritten on printed forms. Average 450 pages. 14 x 9 x 3.5.

The constitution under which the state of Ohio operated for the first half century of its existence provided for a supreme court consisting of three judges appointed by a joint ballot of the legislature for a seven-year term. This court was required to hold sessions at least once a year in each county.[1] The number of judges, according to constitutional provisions, might be increased to four after a period of five years, in which case the judges were permitted to divide the state into two circuits. Accordingly, in 1808, the membership of the court was increased to four and the state was divided into the requisite number of circuits.[2] Two years later, in 1810, the membership of the court was reduced to three;[3] in 1824 it was again increased to four.[4]

By constitutional provision, this court was given original and appellate jurisdiction in "both common law and chancery" cases, and in such cases as should be provided by law. Accordingly, by statutory provision, the court was assigned exclusive cognizance of all cases of divorce and alimony and concurrent jurisdiction of all civil cases both of law and equity where the title to land, or the matter in dispute exceeded $1,000; and appellate jurisdiction from the court of common pleas "in all cases respecting the title of lands, or where the matter in controversy exceeds the value of one thousand dollars, and all cases where the proof or validity of wills or the right of administration shall be in question." During the first half century of Ohio history the legislature granted decrees of divorce. Although the constitution of 1802 did not prohibit the legislature from exercising such jurisdiction, the supreme court prohibited the practice in 1848.[5] The constitution of 1851, Art. II, sec. 32, contained a prohibiting clause. Moreover the court was given original cognizance in the trial of capital offenses.[6] All cases in which the title to land or freehold was in question were to be tried in the county where the land was situated. Furthermore the court was given appellate jurisdiction from the court of common pleas in all cases in which the court of common pleas had original jurisdiction.[7]

---

1. *Ohio Const. 1802,* Art. Ill, secs. 2, 8.
2. *Laws of Ohio,* VI, 32.
3. *Ibid.,* VIII, 259.
4. *Ibid.,* XXII, 50.
5. "Bingham v. Miller," *Ohio Reports,* XVII, 445.
6. *Laws of Ohio,* I, 36-37.
7. *Ibid.,* XIV, 310-54.

In 1831 the supreme court was directed to meet annually in the town of Columbus for the final adjudication of all such questions of law as may have been reserved in any county for decision. This session of the court, known as the court in bank, was required to have its decisions in each case reduced to writing, and transmitted to the clerk of the supreme court in each county in which such question was reserved. The clerk was directed to enter such decisions "on the journal of the said court" and such proceedings were to be taken as if such decisions had been made in the county.[8] Six years later, in 1837, an act was passed providing that the final judgments in the supreme court, held within any county within the state, could be re-examined and reversed or affirmed in the court in bank upon a writ of error.[9]

This judicial arrangement continued until the adoption of the constitution of 1851, which provided a judicial system modeled upon the federal system existing at the time. The supreme court, as established in 1851, became for the first time in Ohio history, a reviewing court of last resort in the state. At the same time the jurisdiction of the supreme court was restricted. In 1853 the court of common pleas, rather than the supreme court, was given original cognizance of all crimes and offenses, except minor crime cases, the exclusive jurisdiction of which was vested in the justices of the peace and other minor courts.[10] The supreme court, which, between the years 1803 and 1843, had had exclusive original cognizance in divorce and alimony cases and from 1843 to 1853 had concurrent jurisdiction with the court of common pleas in such cases, was denied such jurisdiction in 1853 when the latter court was granted exclusive jurisdiction in these cases.[11]

The opinions of the supreme court on circuit and the decisions of the court in bank, as transmitted to the clerk of the supreme court in each county, are in the offices of the respective clerics of courts.

All records of the supreme court on circuit in Adams County were destroyed in the courthouse fire of 1910.

---

8. *Laws of Ohio*, XXIX, 93-94.
9. *Ibid.*, XXXV, 60-62
10. G.C. sec. 13422-5; *Laws of Ohio*, LI, 474; LII, 72.
11. *Laws of Ohio*, XLI, 94; LI, 377.

Until 1851 the judicial power of the state of Ohio in matters of both law and equity was vested in the supreme court, the court of common pleas, and the justices courts. During the first fifty years of Ohio history the supreme court served as a court of appeals, holding court in each county annually. When a new constitution was adopted in 1851 the judicial system was extended by the creation of district courts composed of one supreme court justice and several common pleas judges in the district. These courts were assigned original jurisdiction in the same matters as the supreme court, and such "appellate jurisdiction" as might be provided by law.[1] Thus by constitutional provision the courts were assigned original cognizance in *quo warranto, mandamus, habeas corpus*, and *procedendo*.[2] In addition to this, in 1852 the legislature authorized the courts to issue writs of error, *certiorari, supersedeas, ne exeat*, and all other writs not specially provided by statute, whenever such writs were necessary for the exercise of its jurisdiction. The same act gave the courts appellate jurisdiction from the court of common pleas in civil cases wherein the latter court had original jurisdiction.[3]

For the purposes of the district courts the nine common pleas districts were apportioned into five judicial districts. A judge of the supreme court was designated to preside at the sessions of the district courts; in case no judge of the supreme court was present, as was often the case, the judge of the court of common pleas in whose subdivision court was being held was directed to preside.[4]

The district courts failed to function properly. Evidence seems to indicate, that the increasing numbers of cases coming before the supreme court made it difficult for the justices to attend the meetings of the district courts. Indeed, six years before the creation of the district courts, the supreme court dockets were overcrowded. In 1845 the legislature found it necessary to afford temporary relief by prohibiting appeals from the courts of common pleas to the supreme court.[5]

---

1. *Ohio Const. 1851*, Art, IV, secs. 5, 6.
2. *Ibid.*, Art. IV, sec. 2.
3. *Laws of Ohio*, L, 69.
4. *Ibid.*, L, 69.
5. *Ibid.*, XLIII, 80.

A similar condition of overcrowding existed in the 1860s; so that, in 1865, the supreme court justices were relieved of the duty of attending the meetings of the district courts for that particular year.[6] The judicial system had become slow and cumbersome. The courts declined rapidly after 1865 and were finally abolished.

Following the complete collapse of the district courts an amendment to the constitution, adopted in 1883, made provision for circuit courts. "The circuit courts," stated the amendment, "shall be the successors of the district courts, and all cases, judgments, records, and proceedings pending in said district courts, in the several counties, of any district, shall be transferred to the circuit courts." The district courts, however, were to continue in existence until the election and qualification of the judges of the circuit court.[7] The circuit courts were assigned the same original jurisdiction with the supreme court, and such appellate jurisdiction as may be provided by law. The composition of the courts and the number of circuits was left to the discretion of the legislature. Accordingly, in 1884, an act was passed dividing the state into seven circuits, and providing for the election of three judges in each circuit.[8]

The circuit courts, in addition to the jurisdiction conferred upon them by the constitution,[9] were authorized by the legislature to issue writs of *supersedeas* in any case, and all other writs not specially provided by statute when they were necessary for the exercise of their jurisdiction.[10] Moreover, the courts were authorized to make and publish, as they deemed expedient, rules of procedure in their respective circuits, not in conflict with the law or rules of the supreme court. The legislature directed that all cases taken to the circuit courts were to be entered on the docket in the order in which they were commenced, received, or filed, and "be taken up and disposed of in the same order." However, cases in which persons seeking relief were imprisoned or were convicted of a felony; cases involving the validity of any tax levy or assessment; cases involving the constitutionality of a statute; and cases involving public right and proceedings in *quo warranto, mandamus, procedendo,* or *habeas corpus,* could be taken up in advance of their assignment or order on the docket.[11]

---

6. *Ibid.,* LXII, 72.
7. *Ohio Const. 1851,* Art. IV, sec. 6.
8. *Laws of Ohio,* LXXXI, 168.
9. *Ohio Const. 1851.* Art. IV, sec. 6.
10. *Laws of Ohio.* LXXXI, 168.
11. *Ibid.,* LXXXI, 168.

In 1913 the circuit courts were superseded by the courts of appeals.[12]

The judicial system of Ohio was again slightly changed in 1912 when, by constitutional amendment the circuit courts were renamed courts of appeals. "The court of appeals shall continue the work of the respective circuit courts and all pending cases and proceedings in the circuit courts shall proceed to judgment and be determined by the respective courts of appeals."[13] The judges of the several circuit courts were designated as judges of the courts of appeals, and were directed to perform the duties thereof until the expiration of their terms of office. Vacancies caused by the expiration of terms of office of the judges were to be filled by the electors of the respective appellate districts. The term of office was fixed at six years.

The jurisdiction of the court of appeals remained much the same as that of the district court in 1851. However, the court was assigned original cognizance in writs of prohibition and appellate Jurisdiction in the trial of chancery cases.[14] Certain restrictions were imposed upon the court: "No judgment of a court of common pleas, a superior court or other court of record" shall be reversed except by the concurrence of all the judges of the court of appeals.[15]

At present the court consists of three judges in each of the nine districts into which the state is divided, each of whom shall have been admitted to practice as an attorney-at-law in the state for a period of six years immediately preceding his election. One court of appeals judge is chosen every two years, and he holds office for six years beginning on the ninth day of February next after his election. The salary of the court of appeals judge, fixed at $6,000 per year in 1913, was increased to $8,000 in 1920 and so continues.[16] The judges hold at least one session of court annually in each county in the district.[17]

All records of the district court and of the circuit court prior to 1910 were destroyed in the 1910 fire.

---

12. *Ohio Const. 1851.* Art. IV, sec . 6.
13. *Ibid.*, Art. IV, sec. 6.
14. *Ibid.*, Art. IV, sec. 6.
15. *Ibid.*, Art. IV, sec. 6.
16. *Laws of Ohio.* CIII, 418; CVIII, pt. ii, 1301.
17. G.C. sec. 1517.

104. CIRCUIT AND APPEALS COURT APPEARANCE DOCKET
1911—. 1 vol .

Appearance docket of appeals from common pleas court showing names of parties to suit, case number, kind of action, and remarks. Chronologically arranged. Alphabetical index by names of plaintiffs. Handwritten. 264 pages. 18 x 12 x 2.clerk of courts' vault.

105. CIRCUIT AND APPEALS COURT BAR DOCKET
1911-1924. 1 vol. Discontinued.

Docket of cases appealed from common pleas court to circuit court and court of appeals showing names of parties to suit, case number, kind of action , and orders of court. Chronologically arranged. Alphabetical index by names of plaintiffs. Handwritten. 80 pages. 18 x 12 x .5. Basement vault.

106. CIRCUIT AND APPEALS COURT J0URNAL
1911—. 1 vol.

Journal entry record of all petitions, answers, writs, and court orders of circuit court and court of appeals, showing names of litigants, title of case, case number, and date case appealed. Chronologically arranged. Alphabetical index by names of plaintiffs. Handwritten. 364 pages. 18 x 12 x 3.clerk of courts' vault.

107. CIRCUIT AND APPEALS COURT RECORD
1911—. 2 vols.

Transcripts and records of cases appealed from common pleas court to circuit court and court of appeals showing names of litigants, title of case, case number, and date appealed. Chronologically arranged. Alphabetical index by names of plaintiffs. 1911-1922, handwritten; 1923–, typed. Average 360 pages. 18 x 12 x 3. Clerk of courts' vault.

108. CIRCUIT COURT RECORDS
1911-12. 1 file box.

Original papers filed in cases appealed to circuit court showing names of litigants, title of case, case number, and date filed. Numerically arranged by case Numbers. No index. Handwritten on printed forms. 5 x 10 x 14. Clerk of courts' vault.

109. APPEALS COURT DOCKET
1913—. 2 vols.

Court docket of cases appealed from common pleas court to court of appeals, showing names of litigants, kind of action, names of attorneys, judge's memorandum, and page numbers of Circuit and Appeals Court Journal, entry 106. Chronologically arranged. Alphabetical index by names of plaintiffs. Handwritten. Average 80 pages. 18 x 12 x .5. Clerk of courts' vault.

110. APPEALS COURT RECORDS
1913—. 5 file boxes.

Original papers in cases appealed from common pleas court to court of appeals, showing names of litigants, title of case, case number, date issued, and date filed. Numerically arranged by case numbers. No index. Handwritten. 5 x 10 x 14. Clerk of courts' vault.

The probate court, established by an act of the Northwest Territory on August 30, 1788, consisted of a probate judge with jurisdiction in probate, testamentary, and guardianship matters, and two judges of the court of common pleas, who sat with him and ruled on contested points, definitive sentences, and final judgments.[1]

The judicial system established under the first constitution of Ohio in 1802 did not provide for a probate court but vested the court of common pleas with such powers as had been exercised by the court in the territorial period. The constitution of 1851 re-created the probate court and gave it original jurisdiction in "probate and testamentary matters, the appointment of administrators and guardians, the settlement of the accounts of executors, administrators and guardians, and such jurisdiction in *habeas corpus*, . . . and for the sale of land by executors, administrators and guardians, and such other jurisdiction, . . . as may be provided by law."[2] An amendment to the constitution, adopted in 1912, authorized the common pleas judge, when petitioned by ten percent of the qualified voters in counties having a population less than 60,000 to submit to the voters at any general election the question of combining the probate court and court of common pleas.[3] Accordingly, in Adams County the courts were combined at the general election of 1914.[4]

One of the primary functions of the court, since its inception has been the settlement of estates. The civil code adopted in 1853 gave the court original jurisdiction in taking proof of wills, in granting letters testamentary, and in settling accounts of executors and administrators.[5] Until 1854 the court had jurisdiction in enforcing the payment of debts and legacies of deceased persons. While the court retains the original jurisdiction regarding estates, new duties have been added in recent years. With the development of inheritance tax laws in 1919 as a new means of taxation the probate court has been required to determine and assess the tax after the county auditor has appraised the decedents estate.[6]

---

1. Pease, *op. cit.*, 9.
2. *Ohio Const. 1851*, Art. IV, secs. 7, 8.
3. *Ibid.*, Art. IV, sec. 7. See also p. xxxvi.
4. Separate offices are maintained, however, for the keeping of records which are listed under the appropriate office in the inventory; see also p. xxxvi.
5. *Laws of Ohio*, LI, 167.
6. *Ibid.*, CVIII, pt. I, 561.

By constitutional provision the probate court has original jurisdiction in granting marriage licenses.[7] The court also issues licenses to ministers to solemnize marriages. The former provision was modified by an act adopted in 1931, which requires an elapse of at least five days between the time of application and that of the issuance of marriage licenses. However, power to suspend the operation of the act is vested in the probate judge.[8] Moreover, the probate courts in certain counties, exclusive of Adams, were given concurrent jurisdiction with the court of common pleas in "divorce, alimony, foreclosure, and partition" cases. Thus, in 1894, the legislature conferred such jurisdiction upon the probate courts in Butler, Allen, Richland, Perry, Defiance, and Wood counties.[9] The original act, subject to amendments in 1896, 1900, and 1904, which granted and denied such jurisdiction to the probate courts in certain counties, was repealed in 1911.[10] In 1919 concurrent jurisdiction in such matters was re-established in Pickaway, Licking, Richland, Perry, Defiance, Henry, and Coshocton counties, and established in Fayette County.[11] This jurisdiction was abolished in 1931.[12]

The jurisdiction of the court extends to the state's unfortunates. The constitution of 1851 gave the court jurisdiction in making inquests respecting lunatics, insane persons, and idiots. The constitutional provision in this respect was interpreted by the civil code of 1853. In 1855 the court was granted jurisdiction in the appointment of guardians for minors, idiots, imbeciles, lunatics, and those incompetent by reason of advanced age; a year later the court was authorized to commit persons who were mentally incompetent to state institutions maintained for the care of such persons.[13] In recent years the court has been given jurisdiction in trial cases involving neglected, dependent, and delinquent children.[14]

---

7. *Ohio Const. 1851,* Art, IV, sec. 8.
8. *Laws of Ohio*, CXIV, 93.
9. *Ibid*., XCI, 791, 799-800.
10. *Ibid*., XCII, 643; XCIV, 137-38; XCVII, 113-14; CII, 100.
11. *Ibid*., CVIII, pt. I, 625.
12. *Ibid*., CXIV, 320.
13. *Ibid*., LIII, 81.
14. See p. 27.

Since the middle of the nineteenth century the probate judge has been required to keep a record of vital statistics. In 1867 the duty of keeping a permanent record of births and deaths, which, in 1856, had been conferred upon the clerk of courts, was transferred to the probate judge.[15] When, in 1908, a bureau of vital statistics under the direction of the secretary of state was created the probate judge was relieved temporarily of this task.[16] In 1921 the act of 1908 was amended so as to require the local registrars to transmit to the district health commissioner, who was directed to serve as a state deputy registrar of vital statistics, all certificate of births and deaths received during the preceding month, and a copy of all such certificates to the probate court. Although the General Code still requires the probate judge to keep a permanent record of births and deaths and an index to such records,[17] none has been kept in Adams County since 1908. Records kept prior to that time were destroyed in the courthouse fire of 1910.

Jurisdiction in naturalization proceedings was exercised by the probate court until 1906 when an amendment to the federal statute vested exclusive jurisdiction in naturalization matters in the United State s district courts and all state courts of record having a seal, a clerk, and jurisdiction in actions at law and equity in which the amount in controversy was unlimited.[18] The General Code still requires the probate judge to keep a naturalization record and an index to the records,[19] but jurisdiction was transferred to the courts of common pleas. No naturalization records were found in the inventory.

During the early years of its existence the court was given limited criminal jurisdiction in cases in which the sentence did not impose capital punishment or punishment by imprisonment. By the code of civil procedure adopted in 1853 the judgments and final decrees of the probate court could be reviewed by the court of common pleas on error.[20]

---

15. *Laws of Ohio*, LXIV, 63-64.
16. *Laws of Ohio*. XCIX, 296-307.
17. G.C. sec. 10501-15.
18. *United States Statutes at Large*. XXXIV, pt. I, 596; see also "State of Ohio v. George G. Metzger and Albert L. Irish." 10 N.P. n.s., 97ff.
19. G.C. secs. 10501-15, 10501-16.
20. *Laws of Ohio*. LI, 145.

In 1857 the criminal jurisdiction of the probate court was transferred to the court of common pleas,[21] but later acts retained it in certain counties only. Thus, in 1858 the probate courts of certain counties, exclusive of Adams, were granted jurisdiction in all crimes in which the sentence did not impose capital punishment or imprisonment in a penitentiary.[22] This act was repealed in 1878 and the probate courts of certain counties, exclusive of Adams, were granted concurrent jurisdiction with the court of common pleas in all misdemeanors and proceedings to prevent crime and in 1879 such jurisdiction was extended to Adams County.[23] The last vestige of criminal jurisdiction disappeared with the adoption of the probate code in 1931.[24]

　　　　Miscellaneous duties, remotely related to probate and testamentary matters, have been added by legislative action. Since 1888 the court has been required to file a certified list of all unknown depositors as furnished by institutions or persons engaged in lending money for profit.[25] In 1896 the probate court was given concurrent jurisdiction with the court of common pleas in the matter of changing the names of persons who desired it,[26] a matter in which the court of common pleas had exclusive cognizance from 1842 to 1896.[27] Since 1896 the probate court has been required to file certificates of doctors and surgeons, and since 1916 the certificates of registered nurses which authorize them to practice their professions in the county.[28] Since 1913 the court has been vested with the power to grant injunctions,[29] and since 1915 has had concurrent jurisdiction with the court of common pleas in condemnation proceedings for roads.[30]

---

21. *Ibid.*, LIV, 97.
22. *Ibid.*, LV. 186.
23. *Ibid.*, LXXV, 960; LXXVI, 22.
24. *Ibid.*, CXIV, 475.
25. *Ibid.*, LXXXV, 65.
26. *Ibid.*, XCII, 28.
27. *Ibid.*, XL, 28-29.
28. *Ibid.*, XCII, 46; XCIX, 499; CVI, 193.
29. *Ibid.*, CIII, 427.
30. *Ibid.*, CVI, 583.

In like manner the appointive powers of the probate judge have been expanded. In addition to the authority to appoint administrators and guardians he was authorized by the act of 1891 to appoint the members of the county board of elections; however this appointive power was abrogated by the act of 1892.[31] Then, too, from 1908 to 1913 the probate judge was authorized to appoint a county blind relief commission[32] comprised of three members each of whom served a three-year term.[33] Since 1913 he has had authority to appoint members of the board of county visitors.[34]

The probate judge, like other county officials, has been required by statute to keep a record of the business of his office. The present system, of records, originating for the most part in 1853 and continued by the probate code of 1931, includes a criminal record, an administrative docket, a guardians docket, a marriage record, a record of bonds, a naturalization record, and a permanent record of births and deaths.[35]

The probate judge has the care and custody of the files, papers, books, and records belonging to the probate office and is *ex-officio* clerk of the court. The probate code, adopted in 1931, directed the probate judge to preserve for future reference and examination all pleadings, accounts, vouchers, and other papers in each estate, trust, assignment, guardianship, or other proceedings, such papers to be properly jacketed and tied together; he is required also to make proper entries and indexes omitted by his predecessors.

---

31. *Ibid.*, LXXXVIII, 449; LXXXIX, 455.
32. Sec p . 171.
33. *Laws of Ohio*, XCIX, 56; CIII, 60.
34. *Ibid.*, CIII, 173-4, 853.
35. *Ibid.*, LI, 167; LII, 103; CXIV, 324.

Certificates of marriages, reports of births, and similar papers not a part of a case or proceeding are to be arranged and preserved separately in the order of dates in which they are filed.[36]

In Adams County the judge of the court of common pleas serves also as the judge of the probate court.[37] This combination of offices has not, however, effected the records system as established by law. In those counties in which this combination has not been effected, the probate judge is elected for a four-year term.[38] In recent years there has been an attempt to raise the qualifications of those seeking election to the office. Accordingly, an amendment to the probate code in 1931, restricted eligibility to the office to a practicing attorney or to a person who "shall have previously served as probate judge immediately prior to his election."[40]

All records are in the probate court vault unless otherwise specified.

---

36. *Laws of Ohio*, CXIV, 321-22
37. See pages xxvi, 113.
38. *Laws of Ohio*, CXIV, 320.
39. *Ibid.*, CXVI, 481.
40. *Ibid.*, CXVI, 481.

Calendars and Dockets

111. PROBATE COURT CALENDAR
1888—. 29 vols. Missing: 1902-1909
Record of all cases filed in probate court showing names of litigants, cause of action, date of hearing, case number, and final entry. Chronologically arranged. No index. Handwritten. Average 175 pages. 16 x 13 x 2. 14 volumes, 1888-1901, Basement vault; 15 volumes, 1910—, Probate court vault.

112. COURT DOCKET
1855-1879. 2 vols. Prior records missing; discontinued.
Docket of civil cases heard by probate court showing names of litigants, kind of action, date filed, and motions; also contains docket of criminal cases for the year 1865. Chronologically arranged. Alphabetical index by names of plaintiffs. Handwritten. 450 pages. 15 x 9 x 3.5. Basement vault.

113. CIVIL APPEARANCE DOCKET
1910—. 1 vol. Prior records missing.
Docket of civil cases filed in probate court showing names of litigants, kind of action, date filed, judge's memoranda, and volume and page numbers of Journal, entry 119. Chronologically arranged. Alphabetical index by names of plaintiffs. Handwritten. 480 pages. 18 x 12 x 3.5.

114. CIVIL COURT DOCKET
1907—. 8 vols. (12-19).
Docket of civil cases filed in probate court showing names of litigants, case number, names of attorneys, style of case, judge's memoranda, and volume and page numbers of Journal, entry 119. Chronologically arranged. Alphabetical index by names of plaintiffs. Handwritten. Average 215 pages. 16 x 11 x 1.25.

115. ADMINISTRATION DOCKET
1837—. 7 vols. (B, C, 1-5). Missing: 1881-1909.
Docket of estates settled by administrators or executors showing name of decedent, letters of administration , amount of bond, names of sureties, time of filing each paper, notes of proceedings, names of attorneys, and names of heirs and degree of kinship. Chronologically arranged. Alphabetical index by names of decedents.

Handwritten on printed forms. Average 500 pages. 18 x 12 x 4. 3 volumes, 1837-1880, Basement vault; 4 volumes, 1910—, Probate court vault.

116. GUARDIANS' DOCKET

1910—. 1 vol. Prior records missing.

Record of guardianship cases showing letters of appointment, date, name of ward, case number, names of sureties, amount of bond, and final settlement. Chronologically arranged. Alphabetical index by names of wards. Handwritten on printed forms, 478 pages. 18 x 12 x 3.5.

117. CRIMINAL DOCKET

1853-1914. 3 vols. Missing: 1898-1909.

Docket of criminal cases filed in probate court showing date, names of defendant and attorneys, offense charged, pleadings, writs issued, and volume and page numbers of Journal, entry 119, Chronologically arranged. Alphabetical index by names of defendants. Handwritten. Average 450 pages. 16 x 10 x 3. 2 volumes 1853-1897, Basement vault; 1 volume, 1910-1914, Probate court vault.

Court Proceedings

118. MINUTES

1853-1857. 1 vol. Discontinued.

Minutes of proceedings in criminal cases heard in probate court showing date, case number, names of litigants, title of case, and judge's memoranda of hearing of case, Chronologically arranged. No index. Handwritten. Condition fair. 200 pages. 12 x 8 x 1.5. Basement vault.

119. JOURNAL

1866—. 13 vols. Prior records and 1877-1909, missing.

Journal entry record of proceedings in all cases filed in probate court showing case number, names of litigants, title of case, and date entry filed. Chronologically arranged. Alphabetical index by names of decedents, wards, or principals. Handwritten. Average 640 pages. 18 x 12 x 4. 2 volumes , 1866-1876, Basement vault; 11 volumes, 1910—, Probate court vault.

120. INDEX TO FILES

1910—. 1 vol. Prior records missing.

Index to Civil Records, entry 121, Criminal Records, entry 123, Administrators Records, entry 142, Executors' Records, entry 143, Guardians' Records, entry 144, Inheritance Tax Records, entry 145, Lunacy, Epileptic, and Feeble-minded Records, entry 151, Adoption Records, entry 153, Juvenile Records, entry 172, showing dates, names of decedents, wards, dependents, juveniles, administrators, executors, and guardians, case number, and file box locations. Alphabetically arranged by names of principals. Handwritten. 250 pages. 20 x 14 x 2.5.

121. CIVIL RECORDS

1910—. 4 file boxes. Prior records missing.

Original papers issued in civil cases filed in probate court showing names of litigants, title of case, case number, date issued, and date filed. Chronologically arranged. For index, see entry 120. Handwritten on printed forms, 5 x 10 x 14.

122. CIVIL RECORD

1910—. 17 vols, (1-17). Prior records missing.

Complete record of proceedings in civil cases filed in probate court showing names of litigants, title of case, date case filed, and case number. Chronologically arranged. Alphabetical index by names of decedents, wards, or principals. Handwritten. Average 530 pages. 18 x 12 x 3.75.

123. CRIMINAL RECORDS

1910—. 1 file box (labeled by subjects). Prior records missing.

Original papers issued in criminal cases filed in probate court showing name of defendant, offense charged, case number, date of issue, and date filed. Chronologically arranged. For index, see entry 120. Handwritten on printed forms. 5 x 10 x 14.

124. CRIMINAL RECORD

1853-1887. 2 vols.

Complete record of proceedings in criminal cases heard in probate court showing name of defendant, offense charged, date filed, and case number. Chronologically arranged. Alphabetical index by names of defendants. Handwritten. Average 400 pages. 18 x 12 x 3.

125. COURT RECORDS

1852-1910. Approx. 500 bundles in 4 boxes.

Original papers issued in cases filed in probate court, salvaged from courthouse fire of 1910, showing names of litigants, title of case, case number, date issued, and date filed. Papers tied in bundles; only a few bundles marked as to contents. No systematic arrangement. No index. Handwritten on printed forms. Bundles 3.5 x 3 x 8; boxes, 15 x 15 x 22. Basement vault.

126. GENERAL RECORD

1911—. 1 vol.

Miscellaneous and unclassified records including applications for release of sureties on bonds, showing names of sureties, name of principal, case number, amount of bond, date, and reason for asking release; also special letters of administration showing name of decedent, date of death, and name of applicant; petitions to file special accounts in cases of trustees and guardians, petitions for removal of administrators, and petitions to file amended inventories by trustees. Chronologically arranged. Alphabetical index by names of principals. Handwritten. 600 pages. 18 x 12 x 4.

Wills

127. WILL RECORD

1910—. 7 vols. Prior records missing.

Record copies of wills signed and acknowledged by testators as their last will and testament showing signatures of two witnesses, affidavits of witnesses, date of probate, and signature of judge. Chronologically arranged by dates of probation. Alphabetical index by names of testators. 1910-November 1933, handwritten. November 1933— typed. Average 575 pages. 18 x 12 x 3.

Estates

Appointments., Bonds, and Letters

128. NOTICE OF APPOINTMENT

1910—. 2 vols. Prior records missing.

Record copies of notices of appointment of administrators, executors, and guardians showing date and name of decedent or ward; also clipped copy of newspaper notice of appointment. Chronologically arranged. Alphabetical index by names of decedents or wards. 1910-1924, handwritten; 1925—, handwritten on printed forms. Average 470 pages. 16 x 12 x 3.5.

129. BONDS, LETTERS, AND RECORDS OF FIDUCIARIES AND ESTATES WITH RECORD OF WILLS
1849—. 8 vols. Missing: 1861-1909.

Record of bonds and letters of fiduciaries and copies of wills filed for probate in the settlement of estates, showing date filed, names of decedents and witnesses, names and addresses of beneficiaries, and distribution of estate. 1849–1860, chronologically arranged. 1910—, alphabetically arranged by names of decedents and chronologically thereunder. No index, Handwritten. Average 575 pages. 18 x 12 x 4.

For related records, see entries 130-135.

130. ADMINISTRATOR'S AND EXECUTOR'S BONDS
1855-1887. 4 vols.

Record copies of bonds given by administrators and executors of estates showing name of decedent, names of sureties, amount of bond, and date filed. Chronologically arranged. Alphabetical index by names of decedents. Handwritten. Condition fair, Average 450 pages. 14 x 9 x 3. Basement vault.

For related records, see entries 129, 131, 133-135.

131. ADMINISTRATORS', EXECUTORS', AND GUARDIANS' BONDS, 1863-1867. 1 vol .

Record copies of bonds filed by administrators, executors, and guardians showing date, name of decedent or ward, names of sureties, and amount of bond. Chronologically arranged. Alphabetical index by names of decedents or wards. Handwritten on printed forms. 770 pages. 15 x 9 x 4.5. Basement vault.

For related records, see entries 129, 130, 132-135.

132. GUARDIANS' BONDS
1867—. 3 vols, missing: 1878-1909.

Record copies of bonds filed by guardians showing date, name of ward, names of sureties, and amount of bond. Chronologically arranged. Alphabetical index by

names of wards. 1867-1877, handwritten; 1910—, handwritten on printed forms.
Average 500 pages. 15 x 11 x 4.

 For related records, see entries 129, 131.

133. ADMINISTRATORS' BONDS AND LETTERS
1910—. 6 vols.

Copies of letters granted to administrators to settle estates of deceased persons
showing name of decedent, date, and name of administrator; also copies of bonds
filed by administrators showing name of decedent, names of sureties, and amount
of bond. Chronologically arranged. Alphabetical index by names of decedents.
Handwritten on printed forms. Average 480 pages. 16 x 12 x 3.5.

 For related records, see entries 129-131.

134. EXECUTORS' BONDS
1866-1879. 1 vol .

Record copies of bonds given by executors showing date, names of testator and
sureties, and amount of bond. Chronologically arranged. Alphabetical index by
names of decedents. Handwritten on printed forms. 540 pages. 14 x 9 x 3. Basement
vault.

 For related records, see entries 129-131, 135.

135. EXECUTORS' BONDS AND LETTERS
1910—. 3 vols.

Record copies of letters testamentary and bonds of executors of wills showing date,
name of testator, names of sureties, and amount of bond. Chronologically arranged.
Alphabetical index by names of decedents. Handwritten on printed forms. Average
430 pages. 16 x 13 x 3.5.

 For related records, see entries 129-131, 134.

Inventories and Sale Bills

136. INVENTORY AND APPRAISEMENT RECORD
1810—. 13 vols. Missing: 1817–1834, 1870-1909.

Record of appraisements and inventories of estates showing date, name of decedent,
name of administrator or executor, case number, and itemized list of property with
appraisal value. Chronologically arranged. Alphabetical index by names of

decedents. 1810-1855, handwritten; 1856-1933, handwritten on printed forms; 1933—, typed on printed forms. Average 500 pages. 17 x 11 x 3.5. 3 volumes 1810-1816, 1835-1869, Basement vault; 10 volumes 1910—, Probate court vault.

137. INVENTORY AND SALE BILL RECORD
1825—. 11 vols. Missing: 1836-1846, 1856-1909.
Inventories and sales record of estates settled through courts showing names of decedents and of administrators or executors, case number, and itemized inventory and sale record of assets. Chronologically arranged. Alphabetical index by names of decedents. 1825-1855, handwritten; 1910—, handwritten on printed forms, 1825-1855, condition fair. 1825-1855, average 300 pages. 15 x 9 x 2.5. 1910—, average 64 pages. 18 x 12 x 4.5. 5 volumes, 1825-1835, 1847-1855, Basement vault. 6 volumes. 1910—, Probate court vault.

138. RECORD OF SALES
1910—. 5 vols. Prior records missing.
Record of sales of real estate in settlement of estates where personal property will not satisfy outstanding debts showing date, names of decedents and administrators, case number, and description of real estate. Chronologically arranged. Alphabetical index by names of decedents. Handwritten. Average 580 pages. 13 x 12 x 3.5.

Cost Bills and Settlements

139. COST BILL RECORDS, ESTATES
1863—. 15 vols. Missing: 1895-1909.
Itemized record of costs taxed in settlement of estates showing date, name of decedent, name of administrator or executor, and case number. Chronologically arranged. Alphabetical index by names of decedents. Handwritten on printed forms. Average 560 pages. 18 x 12 x 4. 7 volumes. 1868-1894, Basement vault. 8 volumes 1910—. Probate court vault.

140. COST BILL RECORD, GUARDIAN AND MISCELLANEOUS
1910—. 1 vol. Prior records missing.
Itemized record of costs assessed in guardianship and trusteeship cases showing date, name of ward, decedent, guardian, or trustee and case number. Contains Cost Bills, Assignees, entry 149. Chronologically arranged. Alphabetical index by names

of wards or decedents. Handwritten on printed forms. 570 pages. 18 x 12 x 4.

141. SETTLEMENT RECORD
1853—. 10 vols,. Missing: 1856-1909.
Record of settlements with probate court by guardians, administrators, executors, and assignees, showing date, inventory, receipts and disbursements, and amount turned into probate court for distribution. Contains Settlement Record, Assignees, entry 150. Chronologically arranged. Alphabetical index by names of decedents or wards. 1853-1933, handwritten; 1934—, typed. Average 590 pages. 18 x 12 x 4 . 2 volumes 1853-1865, Basement vault. 8 volumes. 1910—, Probate court vault.

Original Papers

142. ADMINISTRATORS' RECORDS
1910—. 68 file boxes (labeled by subjects). Prior records missing.
Original estate papers filed by administrators showing name of decedent, name of administrator, case number, and date filed. Chronologically arranged. For index, see entry 120. Handwritten on printed forms, 5 x 10 x 14.

143. EXECUTORS' RECORDS
1910—. 71 file boxes (labeled by subjects). Prior records missing.
Original estate papers filed by executors showing names of testator and executor, case number, and date filed. Chronologically arranged. For index, see entry 120. Handwritten on printed forms. 5 x 10 x 14.

144. GUARDIANS' RECORDS
1910—. 28 file boxes (labeled by Subjects).
Original papers issued in guardianships showing names of guardian and ward, case number, and date filed. Chronologically arranged. For index, see entry 120. Handwritten on printed forms. 5 x 10 x 14.

Inheritance Taxes
(See also entries 200, 236)

145. INHERITANCE TAX RECORDS
1919—. 1 file box.
Original papers issued in inheritance tax cases showing names of decedent and of administrator or executor, case number, and date filed. Numerically arranged by case numbers. For index, see entry 120. Handwritten on printed forms. 5 x 10 x 14.

146. INHERITANCE TAX RECORD
1919—. 1 vol.
Record of estates subject to inheritance tax showing name of decedent, date of death, name of administrator or executor, estimated value of property, value as fixed by court, indebtedness, administration cost, exemption, amount taxable, amount of tax, and names and relationship of heirs-at-law. Chronologically arranged. Alphabetical index by names of decedents. Handwritten on printed forms. 500 pages. 18 x14 x 4.

147. ESTATES NOT SUBJECT TO INHERITANCE TAX
1919—. 1 vol.
Record of estates exempt from inheritance tax showing case number, name of decedent, date, name of administrator or executer, estimated value of estate, and value as fixed by court. Chronologically arranged. Alphabetical index by names of decedents. Handwritten on printed forms. 330 pages. 18 x 14 x 3.5.

Assignments

148. ASSIGNEES BONDS
1883—. 1 vol.
Record copies of assignees bonds showing date, names of assignee and assigner, amount of bond, and names of sureties. Chronologically arranged. Alphabetical index by names of assignees. Handwritten on printed forms. 330 pages. 14 x 8 x 3.

149. [COST BILLS, ASSIGNEES]
1910—. In Cost Bill Record, Guardian and Miscellaneous, entry 140.
Itemized record of costs showing names of assignor and assignee, case number, and amount.

150. [SETTLEMENT RECORD, ASSIGNEES]
1853—. In Settlement Record, entry 141.
Record of settlements with probate court showing names of assignor and assignees, inventory, credits, debits, and amount for final distribution.

Record of Dependents

151. LUNACY, EPILEPTIC, AND FEEBLE-MINDED RECORDS
1910—. 8 file boxes. Prior records missing.
Original papers issued in lunacy, epileptic, and feeble-minded cases filed in probate court showing name of dependent, case number, date issued, and date filed, Chronologically arranged. For index, see entry 120. Handwritten on printed forms. 5 x 10 x 14.

152. LUNACY RECORD
1880—. 4 vols. Missing: 1888-1909.
Record of lunacy, epileptic, and feeble-minded cases filed in probate court showing affidavit of complaint, warrant to arrest, inquest and physician's certificate, warrant to convey, case history, final disposition of case, sheriff's returns on writs, date filed, and names of patient and complainant. Chronologically arranged. Alphabetical index by names of patients. Handwritten on printed forms. Average 300 pages 18 x 12 x 2.

153. ADOPTION RECORDS
1910—. 1 file box. Prior records missing.
Original papers issued in adoption cases by probate court showing case number, names of child and applicant, date of issue, and date filed, Chronologically arranged. For index, see entry 120. Handwritten on printed forms. 5 x 10 x 14.

154. ADOPTION RECORDS
1910—. 2 vols. Prior records missing.
Records of adoption of minor children showing date, name of child, investigation of persons applying, and adoption agreement. Chronologically arranged. Alphabetical index by names of children. 1910-1922, handwritten; 1923—, handwritten on printed forms. Average 475 pages. 16 x 11 x 3.5.

Vital Statistics

155. MARRIAGE LICENSE RECORD
1803—. 10 vols. Missing: 1834-1909.
Record of marriage licenses Issued showing names of applicants and date of application. Marriage banns are recorded in back of volumes, 1910—. 3 volumes, 1803-1833, are original records salvaged from courthouse fire of 1910. Chronologically arranged. Alphabetical index by names of contracting parties. 1803-1833, handwritten; 1910—, handwritten on printed forms. 3 volumes, 1803-1833, average 180 pages 14 x 8 x 1. 7 volumes, 1910—. Average 415 pages. 18 x 12 x 3.

156. MARRIAGE LICENSE RETURNS
1910—. 3 file boxes. Prior records missing.
Ministers' and magistrates' returns on marriage licenses certifying the solemnizing of marriages showing names of contracting parties, date of marriages, name of minister or magistrate, and date filed. Chronologically arranged. No index. Handwritten on printed forms. 5 x 10 x 14.

Licenses

157. MINISTERS' LICENSES
1910—. 1 vol. Prior records missing.
Record of licenses issued to ordained ministers to perform marriage ceremonies showing name of licensee, church denomination, and date of issue. Chronologically arranged. Alphabetical index by names of ministers. Handwritten on printed forms. 304 pages. 14 x 9 x 3.

158. NURSES' AND LIMITED PRACTITIONERS' LICENSES
1910—. 1 vol. Prior records missing.
Record of licenses issued to nurses and limited practitioners showing names of licensees, graduate of what training school, date of graduation, date of license, and date recorded. Chronologically arranged. Alphabetical index by names of nurses or practitioners. Handwritten on printed forms. 280 pages. 16 x 11 x 1.75.

159. PHYSICIANS' LICENSES
1910—. 1 vol. Prior records missing.
Record of licenses issued to practice medicine and surgery showing name of licensee, graduate of what school, date of graduation, date of license, and date recorded. Chronologically arranged. Alphabetical index by names of physicians. Handwritten on printed forms. 288 pages. 16 x 11 x 1.75.

160. WATERCRAFT RECORD, 1920—. 1 vol.
Record of licenses issued to operate watercraft on Ohio River showing name of licensee, date, and kind of craft. Chronologically arranged. No index. Handwritten on printed forms. 100 pages 15 x 9 x .75.

Fiscal Accounts

161. COST BILL RECORD
1882-1894. 1 vol. Discontinued.
Itemized account of costs assessed in filing of election of widow, lunacy proceedings, commitment to boys' or girls' industrial school, petition to sell real estate, and petition to sell chattels, showing name of payee, date, and amount charged for each service. Chronologically arranged. Alphabetical index by names of principals. Handwritten on printed forms. 585 pages. 18 x 12 x 4. Basement vault.

162. FEE BOOK
1852-1878. 2 vols. Discontinued.
Record of fees due in probate court natters showing date, for what, to when charged, by whom paid, amount, and date paid. Chronologically arranged. No index. Handwritten. Average 250 pages. 16 x 11 x 3. Basement vault.

163. RECORD OF ACCRUED FEES
1910—. 3 vols.
Record of fees accrued in probate court cases showing date, case number, for what, to whom charged, amount, and date paid Chronologically arranged. No index. Handwritten. Average 500 pages. 16 x 14 x 3.5.

164. CASH BOOK

1910—. 9 vols. Prior records missing.

Daily record of money paid into probate court showing date, from what source, by whom paid, to whom due, amount, and how distributed. Chronologically arranged. No index. Handwritten. Average 400 pages. 18 x 12 x 3.

Miscellaneous

165. EXAMINER'S REPORTS

1910-1931. 1 file box. Prior records missing; discontinued.

Record copies of examiners reports on condition of accounts in county treasurer's office showing dates and signatures of examiners. Chronologically arranged. No index. Handwritten on printed forms. 5 x 10 x 14.

For related records, see entry 261.

166. UNCLAIMED DEPOSITS

1911—. 1 vol. Prior records missing.

Record of unclaimed deposits in banking institutions reported to probate court by bank officials showing name of depositor, amount, interest, dividend, total, and date of last credit or debit. Chronologically arranged. Alphabetical index by names of banks. Handwritten. 402 pages. 18 x 12 x 3.

167. RECEIPTS

1930—. 1 vol.

Record of papers and documents removed from files showing date, case number, kind of case, by whom removed, date returned, and by whom returned. Chronologically arranged. No index. Handwritten. 280 pages. 15 x 9 x 1.75.

168. RECORD OF CORONER'S INQUESTS

1910—. 1 vol.

Record of inquests and autopsies held in cases of accidental, sudden, or homicidal deaths, showing date and findings in each case by coroner or coroner's jury; also an inventory of effects found on body. Chronologically arranged. Alphabetical index by names of decedents. Handwritten. 447 pages. 16 x 11 x 3.5.

For related records, see entries 81, 180.

The juvenile court, though of uncertain origin, has been generally recognized as an American contribution to the administration of social justice. The establishment of such courts was the logical outcome of the practical philosophy of enlightened public men that child offenders against the law, or conventional social standards, should not be treated as criminals, but as unfortunates needing the help, supervision, and protection of the state.[1] Although the first separate court in the United States for the trial of juvenile offenders was established in 1899, in Cook County, Chicago, Illinois, by an act of the legislature of that state, the juvenile court was an institution of gradual growth. The Illinois experiment gave impetus to the children's movement in the middle west.[2]

The Ohio legislature was not slow in seeing the advantage of the Illinois experiment, and accordingly, in 1902, an act was passed creating the juvenile court in Cuyahoga County. Under this act all counties having a population of over 380,000 and an insolvency court were authorized, under an extension of the jurisdiction of this court to establish children's courts. The stipulations of this act excluded Adams County. It gave the court jurisdiction of the trial of cases involving delinquent and neglected children; defined the terms "delinquent, dependent, and neglected;" authorized the appointment of a probation officer, and made it his duty to investigate the facts of cases coming before the court, and to take charge of the offender before and after trial. The clerk of the juvenile court was directed to keep a journal in which were to be recorded the minutes of the case.[3] The judge of the insolvency court serving as juvenile judge served for a period of five years, and from 1935 the common pleas judge serving in such a capacity was to serve for six years.[4]

Two years after the establishment of the Cuyahoga County juvenile court, the assembly provided by statute for the establishment of juvenile courts in the rural counties of the state which, because of their lack of population, were unable to create the newer agencies under the provisions of the act of 1902.

---

1. Miriam Van Waters, *Youth in Conflict* (New York, 1925), 147, 159, 161.
2. Edwin H, Sutherland, *Principles of Criminology* (Chicago, 1934) 270-72.
3. *Laws of Ohio*. XCV, 785.
4. *Ibid.,* XCI, 845; CXVI, pt. ii, 157.

Under the act of 1904 the judges of the court of common pleas, probate court, and where established, the insolvency courts, wherein three or more judges held court concurrently, were authorized to appoint one of their members a "juvenile judge." The court was given original jurisdiction in all cases involving neglected, dependent, and delinquent children under the age of sixteen years; and all children, who had been scheduled in the past for trial in a justice of the peace or police court were in the future to be tried before a juvenile judge. As under the act of 1902, the judge was authorized to appoint a probation officer, and the clerk of courts was directed to keep a journal of the minutes of each case.[5] In 1908 the court was given jurisdiction in cases involving minors under seventeen years of age, and such children as were brought before the juvenile judge were to become wards of the court until they had attained the age of twenty-one years. The county commissioners were authorized to provide by lease or purchase, a "detention home" where neglected or dependent children might be detained pending the final disposition of their cases. The clerk of courts was directed to keep not only a journal, but also an appearance docket containing all orders, judgment, and findings of the court. It provided also for case studies to be made by the probation officer.[6] In 1937 a cash book was required to be kept. Records of the juvenile court are open only by order of the court to persons having a legitimate interest in them.[7] The age jurisdiction of the court was increased to eighteen in 1913.[8]

While provisions were being made for the establishment of juvenile courts, the legislature gave the court jurisdiction in cases involving adults who committed crimes against children or contributed to the delinquency of dependent children. Thus in 1906 it was made a misdemeanor to contribute to the delinquency of a child under seventeen years of age.[9] Two years later the "lack of parental care" was defined and it was made a misdemeanor to fail to support a minor, or to cause him to engage in begging.[10] In 1913 "proper parental care" was defined by statute.[11]

---

5. *Ibid.,* XCVII, 561.
6. *Laws of Ohio,* XCIX, 192.
7. *Ibid.,* CXVII, Am. s.b. 268.
8. *Ibid.,* CIII, 869.
9. *Ibid.,* XCVIII, 314.
10. *Ibid.,* XCIX, 193.
11. *Ibid.,* CIII, 870.

Marked progress has been made in the medical treatment of juveniles. While the act of 1913 authorized the juvenile judge to submit any child sentenced to an institution for correction to a mental test, the act of 1929 authorized him to submit any child coming before the court to a mental and physical test to be made by a physician or psychiatric.[12] To further the scientific handling of children, the county commissioners were authorized, in the same year, to lease or construct a separate building to be known as the "juvenile court" which should be appropriately constructed, arranged, furnished, and maintained for the convenient and effective transaction of the business of the court, including adequate facilities to be used as laboratories, dispensaries, or clinics for the scientific use of specialists attached to the court.[13]

One of the guiding principles of the court has been to make its "custody and discipline" of children approximate as nearly as possible that which should be given by their parents. In the cases involving neglected or dependent children, not sentenced to state institutions, it has been the policy of judges to assign children to private homes, and make arrangements for their adoption. Many other functions have been taken over by the juvenile court such as administering mothers' pensions.[14]

The juvenile court of Cuyahoga County is the only independent juvenile court in the state. There are seven other juvenile courts in Ohio attached to courts of domestic relations. In nearly all other counties the probate judge serves as judge of the juvenile court under the provisions of the act of April 29, 1937 which repealed the act of 1904 providing for the appointment of the juvenile judge.[15] In Adams County, where there is neither an independent juvenile court nor a court of domestic relations and the probate court has been merged with the court of common pleas, a judge of the court of common pleas serves as judge of the juvenile court.

---

12. *Ibid.,* CIII, 872; CXIII, 471.
13. *Ibid.,* CXIII. 470.
14. *Ibid.,* CIII, 877.
15. G.C. sec. 1639-7.

169. JUVENILE APPEARANCE DOCKET
1910—. 2 vols.
Docket of cases filed in juvenile division of probate court showing name, cause, date, and court orders. Chronologically arranged. Alphabetical index by names of juveniles. Handwritten. Average 450 pages. 16 x 12 x 3.5. Probate court vault.

170. JUVENILE JOURNAL
1910-1917. 2 vols. Discontinued.
Journal entries of all cases coming before juvenile division of probate court showing date, name of defendant, cause, findings in case, and final disposition of case. Chronologically arranged. Alphabetical index by names of juveniles. Handwritten. Average 420 pages. 16 x 12 x 3. Probate court vault.

For subsequent records, see entry 171.

171. JUVENILE RECORD
1918—. 2 vols.
Complete record of all cases coming before juvenile division of probate court showing date, name, cause, findings in case, and final disposition of case. Chronologically arranged. Alphabetical index by names of juveniles. Handwritten. Average 460 pages. 16 x 12 x 3.5. Probate court vault.

For prior records, see entry 170.

172. JUVENILE RECORDS
1910—. 8 file boxes.
Original papers issued in juvenile cases including affidavits of information and complaint, medical certificates, investigation reports of family history and home, warrants to arrest, warrants to convey to correctional institution, and journal entries, showing case number, name of juvenile or offender, date filed, offense charged, and volume and page numbers of Juvenile Journal, 1910-1917, entry 170, or Juvenile Record, 1918—, entry 171. Chronologically arranged. For index, see entry 120. Handwritten on printed forms. 14 x 10 x 5. Probate court vault.

In 1891 the judges of the court of common pleas in counties having a population of not less than 33,000 nor more than 50,000 were authorized to appoint four residents of the county to serve as a jury commission for a term of one year. The limitations of this act excluded Adams County. It was the duty of this commission to determine the qualifications and fitness of persons to be selected as jurors.[1] Three years later, in 1894, the provisions of the act were extended to Adams County and all other counties in the state except Cuyahoga, Franklin, Hamilton, Lucas, Montgomery, and Mahoning.[2] In 1902 the statute was amended to include all counties.[3] In 1913 the number of jury commissioners in each county was reduced to two.[4]

The jury code, which became effective August 2, 1931, provided for a jury commission of the same number and same qualifications previously provided for, to hold office at the pleasure of the court, and to meet and select prospective jurors both grand and petit, for the ensuing year from a list provided by the board of elections.[5] At the beginning of each jury year the commissioners are required to make up a new and complete jury list, known as the annual jury list, arranged alphabetically by precincts, districts, and townships, recording the name, occupation, business address, and residence of each prospective juror, and to prepare an index to this list. A duplicate list is certified by the commissioners and filed in the office of the clerk of the court of common pleas.[6]

The jury commissioners select prospective jurors for civil and criminal cases as well as for the grand jury. It selects jurors for the probate court, juvenile court, and other minor courts.

---

1. *Laws of Ohio,* LXXXVIII, 200.
2. *Ibid.,* XCI, 176.
3. *Ibid.,* XCVI, 3.
4. *Ibid.,* CIII, 513; CVI, 106.
5. *Ibid.,* CXIV, 193-213.
6. *Ibid.,* CXIV, 205.

173. RECORD [Jury Commission Minutes]

1932—. 1 vol. Prior records missing.

Minutes of meetings of jury commission showing date, certifications of exemption from jury duty, venires drawn for jury duty, and grand jury panels. Chronologically arranged. by dates of court terms. No index. Handwritten. 400 pages. 20 x 14 x 3.5. Clerk of courts' vault.

174. ANNUAL JURY LIST

1932—. 2 vols.

Annual records of electors certified by jury commission to clerk of courts as eligible for duty. Alphabetically arranged. by names of townships and alphabetical thereunder by names of electors. Alphabetical index by names of townships. Handwritten. Average 100 pages. 12 x 22 x 1.25. Clerk of courts' vault.

The grand jury, sometimes called the palladium of English liberty, has as its function the preliminary examination of persons charged with a capital or other infamous crime. The right, guaranteed by the federal constitution, to an examination by a grand jury, is recognized in the provisions of the Ohio constitution of 1802 and 1851 and in the amendments of 1912.[1]

Under the present system, which does not differ in detail from that inaugurated in the early days of the state's history, the grand jury is composed of fifteen members, resident electors of the county having "the qualifications of jurors."[2] It is the duty of the grand jury to inquire of and present all offenses committed in the county in and for which it was empaneled and sworn.[3] The proceedings of the grand jury are secret and each juror is required to take an oath to preserve such secrecy. Moreover, no grand juror may be required to reveal the way he or other grand jurors voted.[4]

The grand jurors are aided in their investigations by the county prosecuting attorney who since 1869 has been authorized by statute to present evidence before this body and compel the attendance of witnesses against whom he may institute contempt proceedings if they refuse to testify.[5] The prosecuting attorney must leave the room before the jurors begin the expression of their views or before a poll is taken. The courts have decreed, however, that the mere presence of the prosecuting attorney in the room during the deliberations is "not sufficient to sustain a plea in abatement."[6] Since 1902 the official court stenographer of the county, may take shorthand notes of the testimony, and furnish a transcript to the prosecuting attorney, at his request. This reporter, like the prosecuting attorney and his assistants, is required to retire from the jury room before the grand jury begins its deliberations.[7]

1. *Ohio Const. 1851*, Art. I, sec. 10.
2. G.C. sec. 13436-2.
3. *Ibid.,* sec. 13436-5.
4. *Ibid.,* sec. 13436-16.
5. See p. 82.
6. See State of Ohio v. William Stichtenoth, 8 N.P. n.s. 297-339.
7. G.C. sec. 13436-8.

At least twelve of the fifteen jurors must concur in finding an indictment.[8] Indictments found by the grand jury are presented by the foreman to the court and are filed with the clerk of courts.[9] No grand juror or officer of the court is permitted to disclose that a person has been indicted before such indictment is filed and the case docketed.[10] Any incarcerated person charged with an indictable offense who has not been indicted during the term of court at which he is held to answer is discharged.[11]

Since 1869 it has been the duty of the grand jury to visit the county jail once at each term of court at which they may be in attendance, examine its state and condition and inquire into the discipline and treatment of prisoners, and return a written report to the court.[12]

The majority of contemporary opinion holds that the grand jury, although still defended as a safeguard against oppressive prosecution, seems to be of little usefulness in the administration of modern criminal justice. It is argued that the grand jury not only delays the prosecution of criminal offenses but makes it impossible to place responsibility for neglect of duty, and is, in many instances, a rubber stamp for the opinions of the county prosecuting attorney.

The grand jury keeps no permanent records.

For records in other offices, see entries 96, 97, 174, 175, 177.

---

8. *Ibid.*, sec. 13436-17.
9. *Ibid.*, sec. 13436-21.
10. *Ibid.*, sec . 13436-15.
11. G. C. sec. 13436-23.
12. *Ibid.*, sec. 13436-20.

The petit jury, like the grand jury, had its origin in England during the reign of Henry II.[1] The right of trial by jury, guaranteed by the federal constitution, was included in each of the Ohio constitutions. At any trial, in any court, for the violation of a statute of the state of Ohio, or any ordinance of any municipality, except in cases where the penalty involved does not exceed a fine of fifty dollars, the accused is entitled to a trial by jury.[2]

Except in the method of selecting prospective jurors, the petit jury has remained unchanged for over 134 years. At each session of the court the jury commissioners[3] select not less than fifty nor more than seventy-five names for jury service. A venire is issued to the county sheriff for persons whose names are so drawn to appear on the day fixed for the trial.[4] From the person so summoned a jury of twelve is empaneled. The county prosecuting attorney and the defense counsel may, in capital cases, peremptorily challenge six of the jurors. In other cases, four peremptory challenges are allowed.[5] Other challenges, alternately made, may be made for reasons prescribed by statute.[6]

When the case is submitted, the jury may decide the question before it in court, or retire to deliberate. Upon retiring the jury members, in charge of an officer at a convenient place, must be kept together until they agree upon a verdict or are discharged by the court. The court may permit them to separate at night.[7] If the jurors disagree as to testimony, or desire to be further instructed on the law in the case, they may request the officer in charge to conduct them to the court for additional information.[8]

1. Adams, *op. cit.,* 116.
2. G.C. sec. 13443.
3. See p. 80.
4. G.C. sec. 13443-1.
5. *Ibid.,* secs. 13443-4, 13443-6.
6. *Ibid.,* sec. 13443-8.
7. *Ibid.,* sec. 11420-3.
8. *Ibid.,* sec. 11420-6.

In civil actions a jury renders a verdict upon the concurrence of three fourths or more of its members. This verdict, in writing, is signed by each juror concurring therein.[9]

Under the criminal code adopted in 1929 the accused may waive his right to a jury trial in favor of a trial by a judge. This procedure, although criticized by some, is considered by others to be a logical step in the administration of criminal justice in a modern state.

No separate records are kept by the petit jury.

For records in other offices, see entries 96, 97, 174.

---

9. *Ibid.*, sec. 11420-9.

The office of county prosecuting attorney, unlike the sheriff and coroner, is relatively one of the newer agencies in the administration of criminal justice. Established in America by the English during the colonial period, it offers a striking difference in the development of American criminal procedure as contrasted with English procedure where criminal prosecutions were usually instituted by private persons. As developed in recent years, the office of the prosecuting attorney has become one of the state's most important agencies in its defense against modern crime.

The acts of the Northwest Territory placed the responsibility for criminal prosecutions upon the attorney general, who, in turn, appointed and commissioned persons to prosecute cases in their respective counties.

While the acts of the Northwest Territory outlined the local institutions for the newer states, the constitution of Ohio contained no provision for a prosecutor, leaving its creation to the discretion of the legislature. In 1803, during the first session of the legislature, an act was passed authorizing the supreme court to appoint in each county an attorney to prosecute cases in behalf of the state.[1] Two years later, the appointing power was vested in the court of common pleas.[2] The office remained an appointive one until 1833 when the electorate of the county was directed to choose a prosecutor in each county for a two-year term.[3] The act of 1852 left the office elective and the term unchanged, but in 1881 the term of office was set at three years, and in 1906 it was reduced to two years and in 1936 increased to four years.[4]

Under the present system the prosecuting attorney is elected for a four-year term.[5] He is required to give bond of not less than one thousand dollars conditioned for the faithful performance of the duties of his office. If the office becomes vacant the court of common pleas is authorized to appoint a successor.[6]

---

1. *Laws of Ohio*, I, 50.
2. *Ibid.,* III , 47.
3. *Ibid.,* XXXI, 13-14; Chase, *op. cit,*. III, 1935.
4. *Laws of Ohio*, LXXVIII, 260; XCVIII, 271-72; CXVI, pt. ii , 184.
5. G.C. sec. 2909.
6. *Ibid.,* sec. 2909.

The county prosecuting attorney is authorized to appoint clerks, assistants, and stenographers and to fix their salaries subject to the approval of the county commissioners. Since 1911 he has been authorized to appoint a secret service agent or officer whose duty it is to aid him in the collection of evidence to be used in the trial of criminal cases and in matters of a criminal nature. The compensation of such an officer is determined by the court of common pleas.[7]

Most important among the duties of the prosecuting attorney are those connected with criminal prosecutions. Differing little from those of the early days of the office, these duties include the prosecution on behalf of the state of all complaints, suits, and controversies in which the state is a party, and such other suits, matters, and controversies as he is directed by law to prosecute within or without his county, in the probate court, court of common pleas, and court of appeals. In conjunction with the attorney general, he prosecutes cases in the supreme court which originated in his county.[8]

In felony cases, when a complaint is made to the prosecuting attorney, he is required to examine the evidence and determine if it is sufficient for prosecution. If he decides in the affirmative, he prepares the evidence for presentation to the grand jury.[9] If this body returns an indictment the prosecutor prepares to present the evidence in trial court. The court of common pleas may appoint an attorney to assist the prosecuting attorney in criminal cases.[10] In the case of conviction, the prosecutor causes execution to be issued for the fines or costs and pays into the county treasury all moneys so received.[11] Without reference to the grand jury, the county prosecutor may initiate prosecutions in misdemeanor cases in the court of common pleas by information.[12] After prosecution is inaugurated, he may eliminate the case without trial by means of the *nolle prosequi*. Although he is prohibited from enlisting the *nolle prosequi* without leave of the court on good cause shown, his requests are usually granted.[13]

---

7. *Ibid.,* secs. 2914, 2915-1.
8. *Ibid.,* sec. 2916.
9. See p. 82.
10. G.C. sec. 2918.
11. *Ibid.,* sec. 2916.
12. *Ibid.,* sec. 13437-34.
13. *Ibid.,* sec. 13437-32.

After prosecution has begun, it remains with the prosecuting attorney whether the case shall be pressed and steps taken that will lead to conviction.

Besides prosecution in criminal cases, the prosecuting attorney also acts in civil matters. He may bring suit in the name of the state when he is convinced that public money is being misapplied or is being illegally withheld or withdrawn from the county treasury. Moreover, he may bring suit against persons violating the obligations of contracts of which the county is a party, or when county property is being used or occupied illegally.[14]

In addition to these, other duties have been prescribed by statute. On the request of the judge having jurisdiction over juvenile cases, he must prosecute individuals for committing crimes against children.[15] Furthermore, when directed by the court of common pleas, he must prosecute persons for keeping a house of prostitution.[16] At the instigation of the secretary of state, he must prosecute any officer who refuses to furnish gratuitously statistical information for the use of that office.[17]

The prosecuting attorney has also served in an advisory capacity since 1906.[18] He acts as an adviser to all county boards and officials and to township officers who may require his opinion in writing on matters connected with their official duties.[19] In addition, he prepares official bonds for all county officers.[20]

The prosecuting attorney is required to make annually a report to the county commissioners stating the number of criminal prosecutions completed, the name or names of the party or parties to each, and the amount collected in fines and costs, and the amount forfeited.[21] Moreover, on the demand of the attorney general he must make an annual report on forms provided by the state on all criminal action s prosecuted by indictments in his county.[22]

---

14. *Ibid.,* sec. 2921.
15. *Ibid.,* sec. 1664.
16. G.C. secs. 6212-5, 6212-7.
17. *Ibid.,* sec. 174.
18. *Laws of Ohio*, XCVIII, 160-61.
19. *Ibid.,* LXXVIII, 120; G.C. sec, 2917.
20. G.C. sec. 2920.
21. *Laws of Ohio*, LXXVIII, 120; G.C. sec. 2926.
22. G.C. sec. 2925; *Laws of Ohio*, XC, 225.

175. DOCKET [Prosecuting Attorney's]
1910-1927. 16 vols. Discontinued.
Docket of cases of indictments by grand jury for trial in common pleas court
showing name of accused, date, nature of offense, defendant's plea, verdict, and
sentence. Chronologically arranged. Alphabetical index by names of defendants,
Handwritten. Average 120 pages. 18 x 12 x .75. Basement vault

176. RECORDS [of Criminal Cases]
1912—. 7 file boxes.
Prosecutor's record of criminal cases prosecuted showing date, name of defendant,
case number, nature of offense, and findings. Chronologically arranged. No index.
Handwritten on printed forms, 5 x 10 x 14. Clerk of courts' vault.

177. GRAND JURY RECORDS
1910—. 10 file boxes.
Records of cases before grand jury showing date, name of accused, nature of
offense, and findings. Chronologically arranged. No index. Handwritten on printed
forms, 5 x 10 x 14. Clerk of courts' vault.

178. PROBATION RECORDS
1910—. 5 file boxes.
Records of and reports on persons placed on probation by courts showing date,
name of probationer, offense, case number, and terns of probation. Chronologically
arranged. No index. Reports, handwritten; records, handwritten on printed forms.
5 x 10 x 14. Clerk of courts' vault.

179. REPORTS [on Investigations]
1910—. 9 file boxes.
Reports by county prosecutor on cases investigated, showing nature of investigation
and findings, also contains copy of annual report to commissioners of cases
prosecuted. Chronologically arranged. No index. Handwritten on printed forms. 5
x 10 x 14. Clerk of courts' vault.
For commissioners' copies, see entry 4.

The office of coroner, next to that of sheriff the oldest county office in America, had its inception in England during the latter part of the twelfth century when the coroner kept a record of the activities in the county, especially in regard to the administration of criminal justice. At the end of the thirteenth century it was his duty to make inquests whenever there was a sudden death in the shire, and the results were recorded in the coroners rolls and presented to the justices when they made their eye.[1]

This office, transplanted to America during the colonial period, was continued by the states, and was adopted by the territory of which the state of Ohio was then a part. An ordinance of the Northwest Territory published in 1788 authorized the governor to appoint a coroner in each county within the Territory. This act, together with a supplementary act of 1795 adopted from the Massachusetts code, fixed the power and duties of the coroner. He was empowered to do any act which, by previous legislation had been delegated to the sheriff; and was given the ancient duty of English coroners in holding preliminary investigations over the bodies of all persons found within his county, who were believed to have died by violence or casualty.[2]

The Ohio Constitution of 1802 continued the historic office, making it elective for a two-year term.[3] A statute of 1805 defined the duties and authority of the coroner which, in the main were comparable with those prescribed in the territorial code, except that he was denied the privilege of concurrent jurisdiction with the sheriff.[4] The act further provided that the coroner should receive his remuneration from fees; and that if the office of sheriff were to become vacant the coroner was to execute temporarily the duties of the sheriff.[5] The latter provision remained active until its abrogation in 1887.[6]

---

1. Pollock and Maitland, *op. cit.,*. I, 519, 571; II , 641.
2. Pease, *op. cit.*, 24-25, 272-75.
3. *Ohio Const. 1802*, Art. VI, sec. 1.
4. *Laws of Ohio*, III, 156-61.
5. *Ibid.*, III, 158-61.
6. *Ibid.*, LXXXIV, 208-10.

The constitution of 1851 and the constitutional amendments of 1912 left the duties of the coroner unchanged and it was not until recent years when he became an aid in the scientific detection of crime that laws have been passed which materially affected his office. By the legislative act of 1921 in all counties having a population of 100,000 or more only licensed physicians were eligible to the office, and at the same time the coroner was made official custodian of the morgue, and in 1937 such restrictions were extended to all counties.[7] In 1927 an act was passed, apparently designed to attract more highly trained physicians, which set the salary of the coroner at $6,000 per year in all counties having a population of 400,000 or more, and authorized him to appoint one stenographer, a secretary, and three assistant custodians of the morgue.[8] By an act of the legislature in 1937 coroners of counties having a population of 400,000 or more may appoint an assistant coroner who shall be a licensed physician, and a pathologist. By the same act coroners of counties having a population of 100,000 or more were authorized to appoint an official stenographer-secretary.[9]

In 1936 the tenure of office of the coroner was extended from two to four years.[10]

---

7. *Laws of Ohio*, CIX, 543-44; CXVII, Am. H. 67.
8. *Ibid.,* CXII, 204-5. In Adams County however, the coroner receives his remuneration in fees.
9. *Ibid.,* CXVII, Am. s.b . 75.
10. G.C. sec. 2823.

180. CORONER'S RECORD
1927—. 1 vol.

Record of all cases investigated by coroner showing name, age, color, and sex of decedent, date of death, and cause of death. Chronologically arranged. Alphabetical index by names of cases. Handwritten on printed forms. 300 pages. 16.25 x 11.25 x 1.5. Office of Dr. E. T. Gibboney, West Main St., West Union, on desk.

For related records, see entries 81, 168.

The office of sheriff antedates the Norman Conquest. This official was enjoying great power and importance centuries ago, and was probably brought into the English system after a model which existed in the Roman law. The name comes from the Saxon "shire-reeve" softened to "shireve," "shyrife," and finally to "sheriff." In ancient times he received his commission directly from the king and specifically represented the sovereign. Originally the sheriff in England was a judicial as well as a ministerial officer. He once held court in the shire and exercised no inconsiderable jurisdiction . By the time of Lord Coke (1560-1634), the functions of the English sheriff had become standardized under three general heads: (1) to serve process by which a suit was begun; (2) to execute the decrees of the court; (3) to act as conservator of peace within the county.[1]

The office appeared in America in modified form among the earliest colonial institutions, being created in Virginia in 1634, and in Massachusetts in 1654. This ancient office was continued by the states created after independence.[2] The office assumed a new significance in the latter part of the eighteenth century when a flood of colonists swept across the ineffective Allegheny barrier to establish homes in the Northwest Territory organized by Congress in 1787. In the remote West the pioneers, far removed from the orderly legal processes and courts of the East, were subjected to the machinations of the lawless element prevalent in every new community.

In 1792 the governor and judges of the territory adopted an act providing for the appointment by the governor of a sheriff in each county and defining his duties.[3] This pioneer law clearly established three of the four major duties of the sheriff as they remain today namely: attendance upon the court; execution of writs, warrants, and the like and policing and the arrest of criminals.

---

1. George Burton Adams, *Constitutional History of England* (New York, 1921), 17-19; William A. Morris, "The Office of Sheriff in the Anglo-Saxon Period." *English Historical Review.* XXXI (1916), 20-40; Raymond Moley, *The Sheriff and the Coroner in The Missouri Crime Survey* (New York, 1926), pt. ii, 59-60.

2. For a comparative study of the sheriff in England and the Chesapeake colonies, see Cyrus Herreld Karraker, *The Seventeenth-Century Sheriff*, (Chapel Hill, 1930).

3. Pease, *op. cit.*, 8.

When Ohio entered the Union as a state in 1803, the office of sheriff was continued by constitutional provision, and was made elective for a two-year term.[4] Since that time relatively few changes have been made in the structural organization of the office. When a new county was erected the associate judges appointed a day on which the qualified voters met at the temporary seat of justice and elected a sheriff who served until the next general election.[5] Although the constitution of 1851 did not specifically provide for this office, it did declare that no person should be eligible to the office for more than four in any period of six years.[6] No county officer was to have a longer term than three years,[7] but the matter of removal from office was left to legislative action.[8] The limitation upon the consecutive terms which a sheriff might serve remained in force until 1933, when it was repealed by an amendment authorizing any county to adopt a charter form of government. The term of office remained at two years until 1936 when it was extended to four years.[9] The sheriff received his remuneration from fees until 1906 when a definite salary was specified by the legislature.[10] The salary for each sheriff was based upon the population of his county according to the last federal census next preceding his election.[11] In 1831, due to the increasing complexity of the duties of the office, the sheriff was authorized to appoint, with the consent of the court of common pleas, one or more deputies. These men, like their superior, were required to give bond for the faithful performance of the duties of their office, and the sheriff was made responsible for their neglect of duty or misconduct in office.[12]

4. *Ohio Const. 1802*, Art. IV, sec. 1.
5. A. E. Gwynne, *A Practical Treatise On the Law of Sheriff and Coroner* (Cincinnati, 1849), 3.
6. *Ohio Const. 1851*, Art. X, sec. 3.
7. *Ibid.,* Art. X, sec, 2.
8. *Ibid.,* Art, X, sec. 6.
9. *Laws of Ohio,* CXVI, pt. ii.184.
10. *Ibid.,* III, 49-51; XXXIII, 18; XXXV, 53; LII, 86.
11. *Ibid.,* XCVIII, 89.
12. *Ibid.,* XXIX, 410.

The present organization of the office may be briefly summarized: The sheriff is elected for a four-year term,[13] can hold no other elective office at the same time, and may not practice law while in office.[14] He is required to give bond, the cost of which is paid by the county commissioners[15] who are also required to provide an office for the sheriff at the county seat, equipment, supplies, and other essentials of the office.[16] The commissioners also appropriate funds for the expenses incurred by the sheriff in carrying out the various duties of his office.[17] The sheriff may appoint a deputy or deputies, but all appointees must be endorsed by the local judge of the common pleas court, be electors of the county, and are not permitted to be a justice of peace or mayor.[18] Deputies are also forbidden to practice law while in office.[19] The sheriff fixes the salaries of the deputies, subject to the budget limitations of the county commissioners,[20] and shares with his deputies certain civil and criminal liabilities.[21] The salary of the sheriff is based on a graded scale according to population with a $6,000 per year maximum.[22] The office may be vacated by failure to give proper bond, nonacceptance, or death,[23] Vacancies in the office are filled by the county commissioners.[24]

---

13. G.C. sec. 2823.
14. *Ibid.,* secs. 11, 1706, 2565, 2783, 2910.
15. *Ibid.,* sec. 2824.
16. *Ibid.,* sec. 2832.
17. *Ibid.,* sec. 2997.
18. *Ibid.,* secs. 1706, 2830.
19. *Ibid.,* sec. 1706.
20. *Ibid.,* sec. 2981.
21. Willis A. Estrich, ed., *Ohio Jurisprudence* (Rochester. 1934), XXXVI. 660-72. 699-701.
22. G.C. secs. 2994, 2996, 2997; Estrich, *op. cit.,* 94-95.
23. G.C. secs 2827, 12196.
24. *Ibid.,* sec. 2828.

The sheriff may be removed for various financial defalcations,[25] for willfully refusing or neglecting his duty in criminal cases,[26] for malfeasance in office,[27] or for permitting the lynching of a person in his custody.[28] In the latter case the governor conducts the hearing and may remove the sheriff. If for some reason the sheriff is unable to serve a court order the judge of the common pleas court is authorized to make a temporary appointment for the post.[29] The retiring sheriff is required to deliver to his successor all moneys, papers, books, and the like, as well as the custody of all the prisoners.[30]

Aside from his power to appoint deputies, the sheriff has other special powers which are largely the products of historical development. From earliest years the sheriff has been empowered to call to his aid such persons as he deemed necessary to perform his lawful duty in the apprehension of criminals.[31] Thus the *posse comitatus* was at his disposal as it is today.[32]

The specific duties of the sheriff were and are prescribed by statute and may be classified under four main divisions: (1) attendance upon the courts; (2) executions of summons, warrants, processes, and other writs; (3) control and responsibility in the care of the jail and courthouse; (4) policing and the arrest of criminals.

The territorial law of 1792 required the sheriff to attend upon the court of common pleas and the court of appeals during their sessions,[33] and this requirement has been carried over into the laws of Ohio;[34] the present duties of the sheriff in this respect being survivals from the provisions of this act.

---

25. *Ibid.,* secs. 3036, 3049.
26. *Ibid.,* secs. 12850, 12851.
27. *Ohio Const. 1851* (Amendment, 1912), Art. II , sec. 38.
28. *Laws of Ohio*, CI. 109.
29. G.C. sec . 2828.
30. *Ibid.,* secs. 2842, 2843.
31. *Laws of Ohio*, III, 156-58; XXIX, 112-13.
32. G.C. sec. 2833.
33. Pease *op. cit.,* I, 8.
34. *Laws of Ohio*, III, 156-58; XXIX, 112; LXXXII, 26.

He is required to attend the county court of common pleas,[35] the appellate court,[36] and the probate court if required by the judge of that division.[37] The sheriff may adjourn the court of common pleas from day to day upon failure of the judge to appear at regularly scheduled sessions.[38]

The duty of the sheriff to execute all warrants, writs, and processes directed to him by the proper and lawful authority has also been operative since the territorial period.[39] At present he executes every summons, order or other process, and makes return thereof as required by law.[40] He executes processes from the probate, juvenile, common pleas, and appellate courts. Although the jury commission has supplanted the clerk of courts in the matter of selecting names of prospective jurors from the jury wheel, the sheriff's duties in this respect remain much as they were in the earlier years of his office. He also executes warrants issued by the governor of the state,[41] and serves writs and subpoenas issued by various state officers and boards.[42] In other words, the sheriff serves all the papers which concern the county as a unit of government and some for the state as well.

As early as 1805 the sheriff was made official custodian of the county jail.[43] Although the early statutes directed the county commissioners to provide dungeons for the incarceration of prisoners, the act of 1847 directed the sheriff to exercise reasonable care for the preservation of the life, health, and welfare of those committed to his care. He was and is authorized to transport prisoners to other counties for safekeeping.[44] Under the direction and control of the county commissioners the sheriff is also given charge of the courthouse.[45]

---

35. G.C. sec. 2833.
36. *Ibid.,* secs. 1530, 2833.
37. *Ibid.,* sec. 2833.
38. *Ibid.,* sec. 2855.
39. Pease, *op. cit.,* I, 6; *Laws of Ohio.* III, 156-58; XXIX, 112; LXXXII, 26 .
40. G.C. sec. 2834.
41. *Ibid.,* sec. 118.
42. *Ibid.,* secs. 285, 346, 2709, et al .
43. *Laws of Ohio.* III, 157.
44. *Ibid.,* III, 157; XXIX, 112-13; XCIII, 131, For general provisions as to jail duties see G.C. secs. 3157-3176, *passim.*
45. G.C. sec. 2833.

The sheriff has had extensive and important police powers since 1792 when the territorial act authorized him to keep and preserve the peace, and suppress affrays, routs, riots, unlawful assemblies, and insurrections; to apprehend, and confine in jail all felons and traitors; and to return persons who, having committed a crime in his county, had taken refuge in another.[46] During the legislative session of 1805 the general assembly passed an act defining the duties of the sheriff which were in all respects similar to the provisions inherited from the territorial code.[47] In the same year the sheriff was designated as the county's executioner, and was bound to carry out sentences of death by hanging when imposed by the courts upon those convicted of murder.[48] Public executions, the general rule during the earlier years, were abolished in 1844.[49] In 1886 the sheriff's duties in this respect were delegated to the warden of the Ohio Penitentiary.[50]

An act of 1831, repealing the act of 1805 redefined the duties of the sheriff as a conservator of the peace in his county,[51] and his present duties in this respect are survivals from the provisions of this act.[52] Although the sheriff is still regarded as the chief peace officer in the county, many of his earlier duties in this respect have been abolished by the development of other agencies of law enforcement, notably the state highway patrol. On the other hand, the powers of the sheriff to suppress affrays, riots, and unlawful assemblies become especially important in times of strikes or threatened riots. On a properly issued warrant he may arrest any person charged with the probability of doing injury to another person or the property of another.[53] Moreover, since 1921 the sheriff has forwarded to the bureau of criminal identification all fingerprints of persons arrested for a felony,[54] and since 1913 has been authorized to arrest any person violating his parole.[55]

---

46. Pease, *op. cit.*, I, 8.
47. *Laws of Ohio*, III, 156-58.
48. Chase, *op. cit.*, 97-101, 142-43.
49. *Laws of Ohio*, XLII, 71.
50. *Ibid.*, LXXXIII, 145.
51. *Ibid.*, XXIX, 112-13.
52. *Ibid.*, LXXXII, 26.
53. G.C. sec. 13428-1.
54. *Laws of Ohio*, CX, 5; CIX, 584.
55. *Ibid.*, CIII, 404.

The present police powers of the sheriff are quite comprehensive. His jurisdiction is coextensive with the county, including all municipalities and townships, and he is the chief law enforcement officer of the county. In municipalities the sheriff and mayor stand on an equality as law enforcement officers so far as state laws are concerned, and neither is permitted to cast the burden of action upon the other.[56]

The sheriff has possessed and still possesses many powers and duties which are miscellaneous in nature. As in England the sheriff, during the earlier years of his office, was required to notify the electors of his county of the time and place of holding elections. He was enjoined to furnish ballot boxes at the expense of the county, hold special elections when so directed by the governor, and deliver the poll books to the secretary of state.[57] Since 1891 these duties have been taken over by the board of elections.[58] The sheriff also has many heterogeneous powers and duties regarding elections,[59] executive orders of the secretary of agriculture,[60] fish and game laws,[61] probation officers,[62] military census,[63] traffic rules and regulations,[64] funds and deposits in court,[65] shanty boats,[66] and executive orders of the governor.[67]

The multiplicate duties of the sheriff have made it necessary to require many records to be kept of the business of the office. The present practice of keeping a foreign execution docket began in 1838.[68] Since 1842 the sheriff has kept a cash book,[69] and since 1843 a jail register.[70]

---

56. Estrich, *op. cit.* 645, For most important police powers see, G.C. secs 2833, 3545, 4112, 12811.
57. *Laws of Ohio*, II, 88-90; III, 331-32.
58. See p. 137.
59. G.C. secs. 4785-124, 4829.
60. *Ibid.,* sec. 1110.
61. *Ibid.,* secs, 1434, 1441, 1444, 1451.
62. *Ibid.,* sec. 1639-19.
63. *Ibid.,* sec. 5188-5.
64. *Ibid.,* sec. 7251-1.
65. *Ibid.,* sec. 11900.
66. *Ibid.,* sec. 13403-1.
67. *Ibid.,* sec. 118,
68. *Laws of Ohio,* XXXVI, 18; LVII, 6; LXXXIV, 208-9.
69. *Ibid.,* XL, 25; LXV, 115; LXXXIV, 208; LXXXVI, 239.
70. *Ibid.,* XLI, 74.

Indexes, direct and reverse, to the foreign execution docket were prescribed by the legislature in 1925.[71] Since 1843 he has been required annually to transmit the jail register, in certified copies, to the clerk of courts, the county auditor, and the secretary of state.[72] Since 1850 he has been required, on the first Monday of September in each year, to submit to the county commissioners a certified statement of all fines and costs collected during the year, and the amount of fees collected and paid to the clerk of courts of common pleas.[73]

   Thus the modern sheriff keeps the following records: (1) a cash book which is a record of all moneys handled; (2) a foreign summons docket which is a record of all summons from counties other than his own; (3) a foreign execution docket which is a record of executions from counties other than his own; (4) a service record which includes all probate and divorce papers served; (6) an execution register which records all executions handled; (7) an accrued fee record which lists fees received; (8) a commission register which records the commissions of all special deputies; (9) a jail register which records all prisoners brought in, the charge, how long detained, and when released.[74] By statute the sheriff is also required to make an annual financial report to the county commissioners.[75]

---

71. *Ibid.,* CXI, 31.
72. *Ibid.,* XLI, 74.
73. G.C. sec. 2844; *Laws of Ohio.* XLVIII, 66.
74. G.C. secs. 2837, 2839, 2979, 3045, 3046.
75. *Ibid.,* sec. 2844. See entry 4.

Dockets

181. FOREIGN SUMMONS DOCKET

1911—. 1 vol. Prior records missing.

Record of summonses from outside courts which were served in Adams County showing names of litigants, what county, what court, case number, title of case, date writ received, on whom issued, copy of sheriff's return on writ, and itemized account of costs. Chronologically arranged. Alphabetical index by names of plaintiffs. Handwritten. 176 pages. 16.25 x ll.75 x 1.5. Sheriff's office.

182. FOREIGN EXECUTION DOCKET

1911—. 1 vol. Prior records missing.

Sheriff's record of execution orders received from courts outside of Adams County showing names of litigants, kind of action, and date received; also copies of sheriff's returns on writs and record of sheriff's sales of property to satisfy judgments. Chronologically arranged. Alphabetical index by names of plaintiffs. Handwritten. 180 pages. 15 x 11 x 1.5. Sheriff's office.

Fiscal Accounts

183. CASH BOOK

1910—. 4 vols. Prior records missing.

Daily record of money received by sheriff showing from whom, for what, amount, and to whom due. Chronologically arranged. No index, Handwritten. Average 150 pages. 17.5 x 16 x 1.75. 1 volume, 1910-1913, Basement vault; 3 volumes, 1914—, Sheriff's office.

184. SHERIFF'S RECEIPTS

1915—. 3 vols. Missing: 1919-1920, 1920-1928.

Original receipts for fees turned into county treasury by sheriff showing date, case number, title of case, amount, and for what service. Chronologically arranged. No index. Handwritten on printed forms. Average 150 pages. 15 x 10.5 x 1.75. 2 volumes 1915-1924, Basement vault; 1 volume 1929—, Sheriff's office.

185. RECORD OF ACCRUED FEES
1910—. 4 vols.

Record of accrued fees in all civil and criminal cases showing to whom charged, for what, and date paid. Chronologically arranged. No index. Handwritten. Average 238 pages. 18.5 x 12.5 x 1.75. 3 vols, 1910-1924, Basement vault; 1 volume 1925—, Sheriff's office.

186. SHERIFF'S EXPENSE BOOK
1929—. 1 vol. Record initiated 1929.

Record of expenses of sheriff or deputies in serving warrants and subpoenas or in the performance of official duties showing date and amount. Chronologically arranged. No index. Handwritten. 161 pages. 14.25 x 9.5 x 1.5. Sheriff's office.

187. JAIL COST BOOK
1911-1923. 1 vol. Discontinued.

Record of inmates confined in county jail showing name of prisoner, nativity, color, date committed, cause, by what authority, date discharged, manner of discharge, description of prisoner, number of days sentenced, and amount of sheriff's fees, Alphabetically arranged by names of prisoners. No index. Handwritten. 128 pages. 18 x 12 x 1. Basement vault.

Miscellaneous

188. JAIL REGISTER
1862—. 4 vols. Prior records missing.

Record of inmates confined in county jail, held for grand jury or trial by common pleas court in default of bail, or to serve fines and costs imposed by courts, showing date committed, for what, by what authority, date released, manner of release, and description of prisoner. Alphabetically arranged by names of prisoners. No index. Handwritten. Average 270 pages. 18 x 12 x 2. County Jail Office, corner Mulberry and Cherry Streets, West Union, Ohio.

The office of county treasurer was established by an act of the Northwest Territory in 1792 and continued by the state of Ohio.[1] Although the constitution of 1802 made no provision for the office of county treasurer, it was created by the legislative act of 1803.[2] The treasurer, appointed by the associate judges in 1803 and by the county commissioners in 1804, was required to take an oath and give bond for the faithful performance of the duties of his office, and was subject to removal by the appointing power.[3] The treasurer remained an appointive official until 1827 when the office became an elective one by popular vote in the county.[4] Although it did not specifically create the office, the constitution of 1851 stated that no person should hold the office of treasurer for more than four years in any six.[5] This provision was repealed in 1933 by an amendment authorizing any county to adopt a charter form of government. Interpreting the constitutional provision, the legislature fixed the term of office at two years in 1859.[6] The term of office continued at two years until 1936 when it was extended to four years.[7] Until 1906 the county treasurer received his remuneration from fees; since that date his salary has been determined by law according to the population of the county.[8]

The duties of the treasurer were defined by statute in the earlier period and specified in detail by the acts of 1827 and 1831 repealing previous acts. The provisions of the latter act, although subject to amendment and repeal, furnished the basis for subsequent legislation and laid the basis for the present duties of the treasurer, which do not differ greatly from those prescribed by the earlier statutes.

---

1. Pease, *op. cit.,* 68-69.
2. *Laws of Ohio,* I, 97.
3. *Ibid.,* I , 97-98; II, 154.
4. *Ibid.,* XXV, 25-32.
5. *Ohio Const. 1851,* Art. X, sec . 3.
6. *Laws of Ohio,* LVI, 105.
7. *Ibid.,* CXVI, pt. ii, 184.
8. *Ibid.,* XCVIII, 89.

In 1803 the treasurer was given his present duty of giving public notice of the tax duplicate. On receiving from the county auditor a duplicate of the taxes assessed upon the property of the county, the treasurer prepares and posts notices in three places in each township including the place in which elections are held and inserts the notice for six consecutive weeks in the newspaper having the greatest circulation in the county.[9] He receives money in payment of taxes levied for the county, for the state, and for other purposes, and gives the payer a receipt.[10] In the earlier years of the office the treasurer was required to give announcement of the time he would be in the respective townships of the county and in his office at the seat of justice to receive tax collections. Since 1858 the treasurer has been authorized to prescribe the semiannual payment of taxes or assessments levied upon real estate or upon delinquent real estate taxes or assignments.[11] Moreover, since 1908, the commissioners have been authorized to extend the time for paying taxes for not more than thirty days after the time fixed by law.[12]

After each semiannual collection of taxes, the treasurer is required to report to the auditor showing the amount of taxes received in each taxing district in the county since the last settlement. Since 1904 the semiannual settlements have been made under the heads of liquor, cigarette, inheritance, delinquent personal, road, and general taxes. The treasurer keeps his accounts in books which enable him to compile such reports.[13]

After the taxes are collected and immediately after each settlement with the county auditor, the county treasurer, upon the presentation of the proper warrant from the auditor, pays to the township treasurer, city or village treasurer, the treasurer of the school district, or treasurer of any legally constituted board authorized by law to receive the funds or proceeds of any special tax levy, or other officer delegated with authority to receive such funds, all money in the county belonging to such boards and subdivisions.[14]

---

9. *Ibid.,* I. 98; XXIX, 291; LII, 124.
10. G.C. sec. 2650; *Laws of Ohio.* XXIX, 292; LXXVI, 70; LXXXV, 327.
11. *Laws of Ohio,* LV, 62; LVI, 101.
12. *Ibid.,* XCIX, 435; CXIV, 730; CXV, pt. ii, 226.
13. G.C. sec. 2643; *Laws of Ohio,* XXIX, 296; XCVII, 458.
14. G.C. sec. 2689; R.S. 1122; *Laws of Ohio,* LVI. 101.

In addition, after the treasurer has made each settlement with the county auditor, he is required to pay to the state treasurer, on warrant from the state auditor, the full amount of all sums found by the latter to belong to the state.[15]

Another function of the county treasurer, which had its inception in the earlier years of the office, is the collection of delinquent taxes. It was and is his duty to assess a penalty on the tax duplicate for nonpayment of taxes which penalty when collected, is paid to the treasurer's fund. If the treasurer is unable to collect the delinquent taxes, he is authorized to apply to the clerk of court of common pleas who serves notice to show cause why such taxes were not paid. The court may enter a rule against the delinquent taxpayer for the payment and costs and enforce it by attachment.[16]

During the last decade provision has been made whereby delinquent taxes, assessments, and penalties charged on the tax duplicate against any entry of real estate may be paid in installments during the five consecutive semiannual taxpaying periods, whether such real estate has been certified as delinquent or not.[17] The Whittemore Act, passed as an emergency measure in 1933, provided for the collection by installments, without interest or penalty, of delinquent real estate taxes and assessments, personal property, and classified property taxes. Anyone electing to pay such delinquent real property taxes and assessments in installments pursuant to this act may, at any installment period, pay the entire unpaid balance of the principal sum of such delinquent taxes and assessments, in which event no interest shall be charged or collected on the amount so paid.[18] In February 1937 an act was passed providing for the settlement of taxes delinquent prior to 1936 without interest or penalties in one payment or in ten annual installments.[19] In some counties more populous than Adams the treasurer maintains a separate bureau for the collection of delinquent taxes.

---

15. *Laws of Ohio*, LVI, 101; CXIV, 732.
16. G.C. sec. 2660; *Laws of Ohio*, LVI. 175; XCIX, 435.
17. G.C. sec. 2672; *Laws of Ohio*, CXIV, 827.
18. *Laws of Ohio*, CXV, 161-64; CXVI, pt. ii, 14-21; CXVI, 199, 468.
19. *Ibid.,* CXVII, Am. substitute s .b. 87.

The county treasurer has charge of the funds collected by taxes, and also of other funds belonging to the county. Although earlier acts made provision for storage vaults in the county treasury for county deposits, the commissioners have been authorized, since 1894, to receive sealed bids for the deposit of county funds; and the banks or trust companies offering the highest rates of interest are selected as the county depositories.[20]

The treasurer is required to keep an account current with the county auditor - a practice which originated in 1831. Each day the treasurer makes a statement to the county auditor for the previous day's business showing the amount of taxes received on auditor's drafts, the amount received from other sources, together with the amount of money deposited in the depository, the total amount paid out by check and by cash, and the balance in the treasury.[21]

The treasurer, as well as the sheriff, the prosecuting attorney, and the clerk of courts, is required to report annually to the county commissioners.[22] Since 1874 the county auditor and county commissioners have been required to make a thorough examination of all books, vouchers, accounts, moneys, bonds, securities, and other property in the treasury at least every six months.[23] Besides being under the supervision of the county commissioners and county auditor, the treasurer is subject to the supervision of the state auditor. In 1902 an act was passed providing for a uniform system of accounting and auditing for all public offices in the state, under the direction of a bureau of inspection in the office of the state auditor, and for the annual examination of the finances of all public offices.[24] The treasurer is a member of the budget commission, the county board of revision, and serves as a trustee of the sinking fund.[25]

---

20. *Ibid.,* XCI, 403; CII, 59; CXV. pt. ii, 215.
21. G.C. sec. 2642; *Laws of Ohio*, XCVII, 457.
22. G.C. sec. 2504.
23. *Ibid.,* sec. 2699; R.S. 1129; *Laws of Ohio*, LXXI, 137.
24. G.C. sec. 2641; *Laws of Ohio*, CXIV, 726; R.S. 1084.
25. G.C. secs. 5625-19, 2976-18, 5580. See also pages 131, 133, 134.

Since the early days of the office the treasurer has been the official custodian of the bonds furnished to the state by the county auditor, county commissioners, and other officials. Since 1869 he has been required to record and preserve a record of the deputies appointed and removed by the county auditor,[26] but such record was not found in Adams County.

Like other county officials, the treasurer is required at the expiration of his term to turn over to his successor all books, papers, moneys, and records appertaining to his office.[27]

---

26. *Ibid.*, sec. 2563; *Laws of Ohio*, LXVI, 35 .
27. G.C. sec. 2639.

Tax Records
(See also entries 213-35)

Tax Duplicates

189. TREASURER'S TAX DUPLICATE
1909—. 395 vols, (labeled by years and names of taxing districts). Prior records missing.

Treasurer's duplicate of real property taxes assessed showing name of taxing district, name of property owner, town or township survey number, entry number, description of tract or lot, acreage, lot number, original quantity, original proprietor, watercourse, land value, building value, and total value; value of personal property and amount of tax assessed, 1909-1921; and amount delinquent and penalty, 1909-1928, Alphabetically arranged by names of taxing districts and alphabetical thereunder by names of property owners. No index. Handwritten. Average 50 pages. 19 x 14.5 x .5. 211 volumes 1909-1924, Basement vault; 154 volumes 1925-1934, Treasurer's vault 30 volumes. 1935—, Treasurer's main office.

190. TREASURER'S PERSONAL DUPLICATE
1910—. 27 vols. (labeled by years). Prior records missing.
Tax duplicate on personal property showing name of taxing district, name of property owner, town or township, property value, tax assessed, years delinquent, amount delinquent, and total due. Alphabetically arranged under tabs by names of

taxing districts and alphabetical thereunder by names of property owners. No index. Typed. Average 200 pages. 16.5 x 18.5 x 1.5. 25 volumes. 1910-1934, Basement vault; 2 volumes 1935—, Treasurer's main office

191. TREASURER'S CLASSIFIED DUPLICATE
1935—. 1 vol. Record initiated 1935. First entry 1935.
Tax duplicate on classified personal tax showing name of taxing district, name of taxpayer, town or township, value of tangible chattels, value of intangibles other than money and notes, value of moneys and bank credits, total value, and tax assessed. Alphabetically arranged under tabs by names of taxing districts and alphabetical thereunder by names of property owners. No index. Typed. 200 pages. 16.25 x 18.5. x 1.5. Treasurer's main office

192. DOG TAX DUPLICATE
1878-79. 1 vol. Discontinued.
Duplicate of taxes assessed on dogs showing name of taxing district, name of owner, description of dog, and amount assessed. Alphabetically arranged by names of owners. No index. 150 pages. 16.25 x 11.25 x 1.25. Basement vault.

Delinquent Taxes

193. LAND DELINQUENT RECORD
1901—. 7 vols. Prior records missing.
Record of real estate taxes returned to auditor as delinquent showing name of taxing district, name of taxpayer, property value, years delinquent, total tax, and penalty due. Alphabetically arranged by names of taxing districts and alphabetical thereunder by names of property owners. No index. Handwritten. Average 320 pages. 16 x 12 x 3. 1 volume 1901-1908, Basement vault; 6 volumes 1909—, Treasurer's vault.

194. DUPLICATE DELINQUENT PERSONAL TAXES
1905—. 18 vols. Missing: 1909-1911.
Record of personal property taxes unpaid at yearly settlement with county auditor showing name of taxing district, name of taxpayer, property value, years delinquent, total tax, and penalty due. Alphabetically arranged by names of taxing districts and alphabetical thereunder by names of property owners. No index. Handwritten on

printed forms. Average 160 pages. 16 x 11 x 2. 9 volumes, 1905-1921, Treasurer's vault 9 volumes; 1922—. Treasurer's main office.

Tax Receipts and Collections

195. TREASURER'S TAX RECEIPTS
1910—. 389 vols. Prior records missing.
Receipts for payment of taxes showing name of taxpayer, description, of property, amount, and date of payment. Alphabetically arranged by names of taxing districts and alphabetical thereunder by names of property owners. No index. Handwritten. Average 250 pages. 18 x 12.5 x 2 . 195 volumes. 1910-1924, Basement vault; 145 volumes. 1925-1934, Treasurer's vault; 49 vols.1935—, Treasurer's main office.

196. RECORD OF TAX COLLECTIONS
1916—. 11 vols. Prior records missing.
General record of tax collections in county showing name of taxing district, name of taxpayer, amount paid, and date paid. Alphabetically arranged by names of taxing districts and alphabetical thereunder by names of taxpayers. No index. Handwritten on printed forms. Average 600 pages. 18 x 13 x 3. Treasurer's vault.

Tax Stamps

197. EXCISE TAX STAMPS
1933-1934. 1 vol. Discontinued.
Record of cosmetic excise tax stamps sold showing date, name of purchaser, number of each denomination, and total amount of sale. Chronologically arranged No index. Handwritten on printed forms. 300 pages. 12 x 9 x 2. Treasurer's vault.

198. RECORD OF CIGARETTE TAX AND STAMPS
1915—. 2 vols.
Record of cigarette tax stamps received and sold, 1915—; and of beverage and malt stamps, 1933-1935; showing date and amount. Chronologically arranged No index. Handwritten. Average 200 pages. 14.75 x 12 x 1.25. 1 volume 1915-1930, Basement vault; 1 volume 1931—, Treasurer's main office.

199. DAILY RECORD AND INVENTORY OF SALES, SALES TAX STAMPS

1935—. 1 vol.

Treasurer's inventory record of sales tax stamps sold showing date, number on hand, and number received. Chronologically arranged. No index. Handwritten on printed forms. 300 pages. 10 x 12 x 2. Treasurer's main office.

Inheritance Tax
(See also entries 145-47, 236)

200. INHERITANCE TAX CHARGES

1923—. 1 vol.

Record of inheritance tax due from estates and heirs showing name of decedent, date of death, name of administrator or executor, taxing district, names and relationship of heirs-at-law or legatees or devisees, value of estate subject to taxation, to whom charged, amount of tax, and date paid. Alphabetically arranged by names of estates. No index. Handwritten on printed forms. 200 pages. 14 x 20 x 1.5. Treasurer's vault.

Business Administration of Office

201. [Treasurer's] LEDGERS

1904—. 6 vols.

Record of receipts and disbursements showing date and monthly balances in each fund in county treasury. Alphabetically arranged under tabs by names of funds and chronologically thereunder. No index. Handwritten on printed forms. Average 480 pages. 15 x 13 x 3. Treasurer's vault.

202. CASH BOOKS

1904—. 2 vols.

Treasurer's daily record of cash receipts showing date, amount, name of payer, for what, and to what fund credited. Chronologically arranged No index. Handwritten. Average 159 pages. 18 x 12.5 x 1.5. Treasurer's vault.

203. PAY-IN ORDERS, RECEIPTS
1910—. 24 vols.

Orders issued by county auditor to payer for all money to be paid into treasury showing name of payer, for what, amount, and date. Chronologically arranged. No index, Handwritten on printed forms. Average 200 pages. 13 x 9.5 x 2. 11 volumes 1910-1922, Basement vault;.12 volumes. 1923-1934, Treasurer's vault. 1 volume 1935—, Treasurer's main office.

204. JOURNAL OF WARRANTS REDEEMED, JOURNAL OF RECEIPTS
1908—. 9 vols. Prior records missing.

Record of auditor's redeemed warrants on treasury showing warrant number, date, name of payee, for what, and amount; also record of cash receipts into treasury showing from what source, amount, and to what fund credited. Numerically arranged by warrant numbers. No index. Handwritten. Average 235 pages. 20 x 18 x 3. Treasurer's vault.

205. COURT WARRANTS REDEEMED
1904—. 2 vols.

Daily record of warrants issued by clerk of courts and probate judge countersigned by auditor, and paid by treasurer from court funds, showing date, what court, warrant number, name of payee, for what, and amount. Chronologically arranged. No index. Handwritten on printed forms. Average 320 pages. 18 x 13 x 2. Treasurer's vault.

206. RECORD OF FEES
1910—. 4 vols.

Record of county's share of cigarette fees, 1910—, and sales tax fees, 1935—, collected by county treasurer, showing dates and amounts. Chronologically arranged. No index. Average 160 pages. 14.5 x 9.5 x 1. 3 volumes; 1910-1928, Basement vault; 1 volume 1929—, Treasurer's main office.

Bonds

207. OFFICIAL BOND REGISTER
1908—. 2 vols. Prior records missing.
Record copies of bonds given by county officials for the faithful performance of their duties showing name of official, what office, amount of bond, names of sureties or of bonding company, and date filed. Alphabetically arranged under tabs by names of officials and chronologically thereunder. No index. Handwritten. Average290 pages. 18 x 13 x 2. Treasurer's vault.
For related records, see entries 208, 258, 259.

208. RECORD, OFFICIAL BONDS, TOWNSHIP
1924—. 1 vol. Prior records missing.
Record copies of bonds of all township officials in Adams County showing name of official, what office, township, amount of bond, names of sureties, and date filed. Alphabetically arranged under tabs by names of officials and chronologically thereunder. No index. Handwritten on printed forms. 220 pages. 18.25 x 12.5 x 1.75. Treasurer's main office.
For related records, see entries 207, 258, 259.

The first Ohio constitution, adopted in 1802, did not provide for the office of county auditor and it was not until 1820 that the general assembly by joint resolution appointed an auditor in each county for a one-year term.[1] In 1821 the office became elective and the term was fixed at one year.[2] In 1831 the term was set at two years, in 1877 at three years, in 1906 reduced to two years, and in 1919 extended to four years.[3]

The county auditor is required to take oath and give bond for faithful performance of the duties of his office; to preserve all copies of entries, surveys, extracts, and other documents transmitted to his office from the state auditor; and to transfer to his successor all books, records, maps, and other papers pertaining to his office.[4] With the approval of the county commissioners he is authorized to appoint deputies, for whose official acts he and his sureties are held liable; the record of these appointments which has been required to be filed with the county treasurer since 1869[5] was not located in the inventory of the Adams County treasurer's office. If the office of county auditor falls vacant the county commissioners are authorized to appoint a successor.[6]

The first auditor in each county was required to list all lands in his county subject to taxation. From this list and one submitted to him by the county commissioners and one from the state auditor the county auditor was directed to make a tax duplicate to be kept in a book for that purpose, and to give a copy of the list to the tax collector.[7] The auditor was also directed to compile from the treasurer's duplicate a list of lands on which taxes were delinquent, and if such lands were sold for taxes to grant a deed to the purchaser.[8]

---

1. *Laws of Ohio*, XVIII, 71.
2. *Ibid.*, XIX, 116.
3. *Ibid.*, XXIX. 280; LXXIV, 381; XCVIII, 271; CVIII, pt. ii. 1294.
4. *Ibid.*, XIX, 116; R.S. 1033; G.C. secs. 2559, 25.
5. *Laws of Ohio*, LV, 20; LXVI, 35; G.C. sec. 2563.
6. *Laws of Ohio*, XXIX, 260-91; LXVII, 103.
7. *Ibid.*, XVIII, 79.
8. *Ibid.*, XVIII, 82; XIX, 115.

Subsequent legislation expanded and itemized the duties of the auditor regarding taxation; with modifications to meet modern requirements these duties have continued much as they were during the earlier years of his office. During the 1840s the office of county assessor was abolished and provision was made for township assessors whose duty it was to list all taxable property and make a return to the auditor.[9] Since 1874 the auditor is required by statute to keep a book in which he lists additions to and deductions from the amount of tax assessment.[10] In 1915 he was made chief assessing officer of the county.[11]

The county auditor has served as a member and the secretary of the county budget commission since its beginning in 1911, his duties including keeping full and accurate records of the proceedings of that body. For the purpose of adjusting the tax rates and fixing the amount to be levied each year the commissioners are governed by the amount of taxable property as shown on the auditors tax list for the current year. He submits to the commissioners the annual tax budget given him by each taxing authority of each subdivision, together with an estimate of any state levy prepared by the state auditor, and such other information as the budget commission may request or the state tax commission require.[12]

Tax settlements had been made annually until 1859 when the auditor was required to make semiannual settlement with the treasurer to ascertain the amount of taxes the treasurer is to stand charged.[13] Since 1904 liquor, cigarette, and inheritance taxes have constituted separate funds. All other taxes are credited to the general fund.[14]

Since 1831 the county auditor has kept an account current with the county treasurer showing the payments of moneys into the treasury, listing the date, by whom paid, and on what fund. On receiving the treasurer's daily statement the auditor enters on his account current the amount shown as a charge to the treasurer.[15]

---

9. *Ibid.,* XXXIX, 22-25.
10. *Ibid.,* LXXI, 30.
11. *Ibid.,* CVI, 246.
12. G.C. sec . 5625-19; *Laws of Ohio.* CXI I, 402.
13. G.C. sec. 2596; *Laws of* Ohio, LVI, 132; LXXVIII, 226.
14. *Laws of Ohio*, XCVII, 457..
15. *Ibid.,* XXIX, 280-91; LXVII, 103.

Another important function of the county auditor is the approval before payment of bills and other claims against the county. Since 1831 he is authorized to issue, on presentation of the proper voucher, all warrants on the county treasurer for moneys payable from the county treasury; and to preserve all warrants, showing the number, date of issue, amount for which drawn, in whose favor, and from what fund.[16] County money due the state is paid on warrant of the state auditor. Since 1904 a bill or voucher for payment from any fund controlled by the county commissioners or board of county infirmary directors is filed with the county auditor and entered in a book for that purpose at least five days before its approval for payment by the commissioners, and when approved the date is entered opposite the claim.[17]

Besides approving bills and claims against the county, the auditor in 1835 was given the duty of certifying all moneys, except collections on the tax duplicate, into the county treasury, specifying by whom paid and the fund to which such payment is credited. Such moneys he charges to the treasurer and keeps a duplicate copy of the statement in his office. Since 1835 all costs collected in penitentiary cases which have been or are to be paid to the state have been certified into the treasury as belonging to the state.[18]

In 1902 the legislature provided for a system of uniform accounting and auditing of all public offices, and for the annual examination of their finances, under the director of a bureau of inspection in the office of the state auditor.[19] Since 1904 the county auditor has been required to report to the commissioners on the state of county finances; on the first business day of each month he prepares in duplicate a statement of the county finances for the preceding month, compares it with the treasurer's balance, and submits it to the commissioners who post one copy of it in the auditor's office for thirty days for public inspection.[20]

---

16. G.C. sec. 2570; R.S. 1024; *Laws of Ohio*, XXIX,- 280-91; LXVII, 103.

17. *Laws of Ohio*, XCVII, 25; CVIII, pt. ii. 272.

18. *Ibid.*, XXXIII, 44; LXVII, 103.

19. *Ibid.*, XCV, 511-15.

20. *Ibid.*, XXXIII, 44; LXVII, 103.

During the development of the office additional duties and great diversity have been delegated to the county auditor. Since 1833 he has been authorized to discharge prisoners jailed for nonpayment of any fine or amercement due to the county when it in his opinion payment is not collectible.[21] In 1838 an act was passed making him county superintendent of schools. He was relieved of this duty in 1848 when a county superintendent of schools was authorized in each county.[22] Since 1846 he has served as the sealer of weights and measures, is responsible for the preservation of the copies of the original standards delivered to his office, and enforces in his county all state laws regulating weights and measures.[23] In 1861 he was authorized to report to the state auditor statistic a concerning the deaf, dumb, blind, insane, and idiots in his county, with the names and addresses of their parents or guardians.[24] Eight years later, in 1869, he was authorized to report, to the same officer statistics concerning livestock in his county as returned to his office by assessors, and an abstract of the funded indebtedness of his county, and of each township, city, village, and school district.[25] In 1862 he was authorized to issue peddlers licenses to persons who filed a statement of stock in trade in conformity with the law requiring the listing of such stock for taxation, and since 1917 he issues dog licenses.[26]

---

21. G.C. sec. 2576, *Laws of Ohio*, XXXI, 18; LXVII, 103.
22. *Ibid.*, XCVII, 457.
22. see p. 141.
23. G.C. sec. 2615; *Laws of Ohio*, XLIV, 55; LVIII, 78; CI. 234.
24. *Laws of Ohio*; LVIII, 40.
25. G.C. sec. 2604.
26. *Laws of Ohio*, LIX, 67; LXXIX, 96; CVII, 534.

Since 1850 he has been official custodian of the reports submitted to the commissioners by the prosecuting attorney, the clerk of courts, the sheriff, and the treasurer; these reports are recorded by the auditor in books kept specially for the purpose.[28] The volume record has apparently not been kept in Adams County but the original records are extant from 1910 to date.[29]

The county auditor is a member of the county board of revision established in 1825, secretary of the budget commission, and serves as a trustee and the secretary of the board of trustees of the sinking fund established in 1919.[30]

In recent years there has been increasing criticism of the office of county auditor. The chief complaint Is the duplication of the work of the office of the county treasurer, the daily registers of the two offices being similar in all respects.

27. G.C. sec. 2566; *Laws of Ohio*. XIX, 147.
28. G.C. sec. 2504; R.S. 686; *Laws of Ohio*, XLVIII, 66.
29. see entry 4.
30. see pages. 131, 133, 134.

Property Transfers
(See also entries 25-48)

209. AUDITOR'S RECORD OF TRANSFERS
1853—. 20 vols.
Transfers of real estate as recorded for taxation purposes showing date, names of grantor and grantee, survey and entry numbers, name of taxing district, name of original proprietor, acreage or size of lot, and value. Alphabetically arranged under tabs by names of taxing districts and chronologically thereunder. No index. Handwritten. Average 320 pages. 18 x 12 x 2.5. Auditor's vault.

210. AUDITOR'S DEEDS
1823—. 2 vols.
Memoranda of deeds given by auditor for lands sold for taxes showing date, name of owner, acreage, location, and amount of delinquent taxes and penalty, amount of sale, and name of grantee. Chronologically arranged No index. Handwritten. Average 420 pages. 16 x 12 x 3. Auditor's vault.

Maps and Plats
(See also entries 46-48)

211. PLAT BOOK
n.d. 1 vol.
Plat book showing the surveys of the five original townships and of Manchester, the first settlement in the county. Prepared by county surveyor. Alphabetically arranged by names of surveys. No index. Hand drawn. Condition poor. Scale, 1 inch equals 1,000 feet. 50 pages. 17 x.15 x .5. Basement vault.

212. PLAT BOOKS
1827—. 5 vols.
Plats showing townships, villages, additions, and farm areas, with highways, streams, railroads, and boundary line landmarks. Prepared by county engineer. Chronologically arranged. Alphabetical index by names of townships and villages. Hand drawn. Scale, 1 inch equals 1,000 feet. Average 160 pages. 26 x 20 x .75. Auditor's vault.

Tax Records
(See also entries 189-99)

Tax Appraisements and Assessments

213. APPRAISEMENT RECORD [Railroads]
1891-1910. 1 vol. Discontinued.
Auditor's record of railroad appraisals for taxation as certified by the board of appraisers and assessors showing date, amount of trackage, value per mile of rolling stock, value of buildings, tools and machinery, and total value; also minutes of meetings of board of appraisers and assessors. Chronologically arranged. No index. Handwritten. 140 pages. 12 x 18 x 1. Basement vault.

214. QUADRENNIAL LAND APPRAISEMENT
1913—. 5 vols. Last appraisal 1929.
Record of land appraisements for taxation showing name of owner, name of taxing district, location, description, quantity, and value, Alphabetically arranged by names of taxing districts and alphabetical thereunder by names of property owners. No index. Handwritten. Average 250 pages. 14 x 20 x 1.75. Auditor's vault.

215. INTER-COUNTY ROAD ASSESSMENTS
1926—. 2 vols.
Record of special assessments against abutting and adjacent property for highway construction showing name of taxing district, name, of owner, acreage, frontage, and amount assessed. Alphabetically arranged by names of taxing, districts and alphabetical thereunder by names of property owners. No index. Handwritten. Average 350 pages. 14 x 12 x 3. Auditor's vault.

Tax Lists

216. AUDITOR'S TAX LIST
1911—. 26 vols. Prior records missing.
Record of real estate valuations for taxation showing name of owner, name of taxing district, location, description, auditor's valuation, tax commission's valuation, board of equalization's valuation, and amount of tax. Alphabetically arranged under tabs by names of taxing districts and alphabetical thereunder by

names of property owners. No index. Handwritten. Average 300 pages. 20 x 14 x
2.5. 15 volumes, 1911-1925, Basement vault; 11 volumes 1926—. Auditor's vault.

217. AUDITOR'S CLASSIFIED LIST
1928—. 3 vols.
List of classified personal property showing assessment certificate, name of
property owner, name of taxing district, investment, credits, money and other
taxable intangibles, total tax for year, advance payment, and balance. Alphabetically
arranged under tabs by names of taxing districts and alphabetical thereunder by
names of property owners. No index. Handwritten. Average 340 pp, 17 x 14 x 2.5.
Auditor's vault.

Tax Duplicates

218. AUDITOR'S DUPLICATE
1893—. 47 vols. (labeled by years and tax districts). Prior records missing.
Tax duplicates of real estate showing name of owner, survey and entry numbers,
name of original proprietor, acreage or size of lot, value of land and buildings, and
amount of tax. Alphabetically arranged by names of taxing districts and alphabetical
thereunder by names of property owners. No index. 1893-1920, handwritten;
1921—, typed. Average 430 pages. 18 x 15 x 3.25. Auditor's vault.

219. AUDITOR'S PERSONAL DUPLICATE
1897—. 36 vols.
Tax duplicates of personal property showing name of taxing district, name and
address of owner, taxable value, and amount assessed. Alphabetically arranged by
names of taxing districts and alphabetical thereunder by names of property owners.
No index. 1897-1920, handwritten; 1921—, typed. Average 250 pages. 14 x 18 x
2. Auditor's vault.

220. DOG TAX DUPLICATE
1878-79. 1 vol. Discontinued.
Dog tax duplicates showing name of owner, name of taxing district, number and
value of dogs, special tax, and total tax. We arranged by names of taxing districts
and alphabetical thereunder by names of dog owners. No index. Handwritten. 200
pages. 16 x12 x 1.5. Basement vault.

221. CIGARETTE TAX DUPLICATES

1915-1932. 1 vol. Discontinued.

Auditor's cigarette tax assessment duplicates showing name of licensee, business address, name of property owner, date, and amount of tax. Chronologically arranged No index. Handwritten. 250 pages. 16 x 18 x 1.75. Auditor's vault.

For subsequent records, see entry 254.

Tax Returns

222. PERSONAL PROPERTY RETURNS

1923—. 171 vols. 5 bundles.

Returns on personal property for taxation by individuals showing name of owner, name of taxing district, itemized list of chattels, value of each item, and total value. Alphabetically arranged by names of property owners. No index. Handwritten on printed forms. Volumes average 500 pages. 14 x 9 x 5; bundles, approximately 14 x 9 x 4. Basement vault.

Additions and Deductions

223. ADDITIONS AND DEDUCTIONS

1877-1878. 1 vol. Prior records missing.

Record of additions and deductions to tax duplicates showing name of taxing district, name of property owner, description, acreage, value of real estate, value of property, amount of addition, amount of deduction, and remarks. Alphabetically arranged by names of taxing districts and alphabetical thereunder by names of property owners. No index. Handwritten. 310 pages. 9 x 15 x 2.5. Basement vault.

For subsequent records, see entries 224, 225.

224. ADDITIONS

1910—. 4 vols. Missing: 1879-1909.

Record of additions to tax duplicates by reason of improvements to property or error on previous duplicates showing name of taxing district, name of property owner, description of property, and amount of addition. Alphabetically arranged by names of taxing districts and alphabetical thereunder by names of property owners. No index. Handwritten on printed forms. Average 200 pages. 16 x 11 x 1.5. 1 volume

1910-1915, Basement vault; 3 volumes 1916—, Auditor's vault.
  For prior records, see entry 223.

225. DEDUCTIONS
1910—. 3 vols. Missing: 1879-1909.
Record of deductions from tax duplicates by reason of error on previous duplicates or buildings destroyed showing name of taxing district, name of property owner, description of property, and amount of deduction. Alphabetically arranged by names of taxing districts and alphabetical thereunder by names of property owners. No index. And written on printed forms. Average 200 pages. 16 x 11 x 1.5. 1 volume 1910-1916, Basement vault; 2 volumes 1917—. Auditor's vault.
  For prior records, see entry 223.

Delinquent Taxes

226. DELINQUENT LAND LIST
1876—. 9 vols. Missing: 1918-1920.
Record of delinquent taxes on lands showing name of owner, name of taxing district, original acreage, survey number, watercourse, name of original proprietor, acreage, value, special assessments, penalty, and total amount due. Alphabetically arranged by names of taxing districts and alphabetical thereunder by names of property owners. No index. Handwritten. Average 520 pages. 18 x 14 x 4. 4 volumes 1878-1917, Basement vault; 5 volumes, 1921—. Auditor's vault.

227. DELINQUENT PERSONAL DUPLICATE
1897—. 8 vols.
Record of delinquent personal taxes showing name of taxpayer, name of taxing district, valuation, amount of tax due, penalty, and total due. Alphabetically arranged by names of taxing districts and alphabetical thereunder by names of taxpayers. No index. Handwritten. Average 480 pages. 18 x 12 x 3.5. 4 volumes, 1897-1920, Basement vault; 4 volumes, 1921—, Auditor's vault.

228. AUDITOR'S DELINQUENT LAND TAX CERTIFICATE
1918—. 2 vols.
Record of certifications of delinquent taxes on real estate showing name of taxing district, name of owner, description and value of property, amount of taxes due,

penalty, date sold, and date redeemed. Alphabetically arranged under tabs by names of taxing districts and alphabetical thereunder by names of property owners. No index, Handwritten. Average 200 pages. 14 x 20 x 2. 1 volume, 1918-1931, Basement vault; 1 volume, 1932—. Auditor's vault.

229. QUADRENNIAL DELINQUENT UND CERTIFICATES
1922-1931. 1 vol.

Certified copies of delinquent land assessments showing number of years delinquent, amount of taxes, penalty and interest , name of taxing district, name of owner, location, description of property, advertising fee, certificate fee, and total due. Alphabetically arranged under tabs by names of taxing districts and alphabetical thereunder by names of property owners. No index. Handwritten. 430 pages. 18 x 14 x 3.5. Auditor's vault.

230. FORFEITED LISTS
1919—. 5 vols.

Record of lands forfeited for taxes showing name of township, name of taxing district, name of owner, original quantity, entry number, watercourse, name of original proprietor, acreage, value, delinquent tax due, and remarks. Alphabetically arranged under tabs by names of taxing districts and alphabetical thereunder by names of property owners. No index. Handwritten. Average 460 pages. 18 x 12 x 3.5. Auditor's vault.

Settlements

231. AUDITOR'S SCHOOL SETTLEMENT RECORD
1904—, 4 vols. Prior records missing.

Record of settlements with school districts showing name of school district, date of settlement, amount allotted to each fund and total amount, Alphabetically arranged under tabs by names of school districts and chronologically thereunder. No index. Handwritten. Average 400 pages. 18 x 12 x 3. Auditor's vault

232. SETTLEMENT RECORD
1911—. 4 vols. Prior records missing.

Auditor's record of settlements with townships and villages showing amount allotted; also the amount allotted to each fund. Alphabetically arranged under tabs by names of townships and villages and chronologically thereunder. No index. Handwritten. Average 500 pages. 15 x 20 x 4. Auditor's vault.

233. SEMIANNUAL TAX SETTLEMENT
1859–. 154 sheets.
Records amount, of taxes collected in Adams County showing amount due the state, and date of settlement by auditor. Chronologically arranged by dates of settlements. No index. Handwritten. Sheets (unbound), 20x 14. 147 sheets, 1859-1934, Auditor's basement storage room, 7 sheets, 1935—. Auditor's office.

234. SETTLEMENT RECORD
1928-1932. 1 vol. Discontinued.
Record of distribution of motor vehicle license fees showing amount due each taxing district. Alphabetically arranged by names of taxing districts. No index. Handwritten 350 pages. 17 x 11 x 2.5 Auditor's vault.
For other records, see entry 261.

Inheritance Tax
(See also entries 145-147, 200)

235. AUDITOR'S INHERITANCE TAX CHANGES
1923—. 1 vol. Prior records missing.
Auditor's record of inheritance tax charges as certified by probate judge, showing date, name of decedent, value of estate, names of heirs-at-law, and amount of tax. Chronologically arranged. Alphabetical index by names of decedents. Handwritten on printed forms. 200 pages. 12 x 12 x 2. Auditor's vault

Business Administration of Office

General Accounts

236. APPROPRIATION LEDGER
1911—. 10 vols.
Record of appropriations made by county commissioners showing, date, name of fund, and amount appropriated to each fund. Alphabetically arranged under tabs by

names of funds and chronologically thereunder. No index. Handwritten. Average
450 pages. 15 x 12 x 3.5. Auditor's vault.

237. FEE RECORD
1907—. 4 vols.

Daily record of fees received showing date, for what, amount, and name of payer.
Chronologically arranged by dates of payment. No index. Handwritten. Average
410 pages. 16 x 12 x 3. 1 volume 1907-1915, Basement vault; 3 volumes 1916—,
Auditor's vault.

238. AUDITOR'S LEDGER
1904—. 6 vols. Missing 1918-1922.

Record of credits, debits and balance or deficit of each fund showing date, name of
fund, name of township, and amount. Arranged under tabs by names of funds and
townships and chronologically thereunder by dates of entry. No index. Handwritten.
Average 470 pages. 18 x 12 x 3.5. 1 volume, 1904-1909, Basement vault; 5
volumes, 1910—. Auditor's vault.

Special Accounts

239. SHEEP CLAIM RECORD
1892—. 1 vol.

Record of claims allowed for sheep killed and injured by dogs showing name of
claimant, number of sheep killed or injured, value per head, total amount of claim,
amount allowed, date paid, and warrant number. Chronologically arranged.
Alphabetical index by names of claimants. Handwritten. 400 pages. 16 x 12 x 3.
Auditor's vault.

240. MOTHERS' PENSION RECORD
1914—. 1 vol.

Record of aid to mothers with dependent children showing date, names, number of
dependents, ages of minor children, amount of grant, record of payments made, and
warrant number. Chronologically arranged. Alphabetical index by names of
mothers. Handwritten. 202 pages. 16 x 11 x 1.5. Auditor's vault.

For other records, see entries 308, 309.

Road and Bridge Accounts (See also entries 7-10)

241. PIKE DIRECTORS' JOURNAL
1894-1906. 1 vol. Discontinued.
Auditor's record of expenditures authorized by board of turnpike directors showing turnpike name or section number, date, amount of expenditure, to whom, and voucher number. Chronologically arranged. No index. Handwritten. 400 pages. 16 x 12 x 5.5. Basement vault.

242. BRIDGE RECORD
1911—. 3 vols.
Records bridge fund receipts and expenditures showing from what source, expenditures for what, name of bridge, name of payee, date, amount, and voucher number. Receipts are recorded in front of each volume and expenditures in back of each volume. Chronologically arranged. Receipts. No index. Expenditures, Alphabetical index by names of bridges. Handwritten. Average 260 pages. 18 x 14 x 2. Auditor's vault.

243. ROAD RECORD
1912 . 5 vols.
Record of road appropriations and expenditures showing date, amount of appropriations, and amount of expenditures for construction and maintenance of public roads. Chronologically arranged. Alphabetical index by names of roads. Handwritten. Average 300 pages. 18 x 12 x 2.5. Auditor's vault.

Bills, Warrants, and Vouchers

244. AUDITOR'S DOCKET, COMMISSIONERS' BILLS
1904—. 5 vols.
Auditor's record of bills filed with commissioners showing date, name of creditor, for what, amount, date approved, date paid, and warrant number. Chronologically arranged. No index. Handwritten. Average 300 pages. 19 x 13 x 3. Auditor's vault.

245. AUDITOR'S JOURNAL OF WARRANTS ISSUED AND PAYMENTS INTO TREASURY
1904—. 9 vols. Missing 1910-1915.

Auditor's record of warrants issued on county treasurer for payment from county funds showing date, to whom issued, for what, which fund, amount, and warrant number; also record of payments into county treasury showing name of payer, for what, amount, pay-in order number, and to what fund credited. Chronologically arranged. No index. Handwritten. Average 280 pages. 20 x 17 x 2. 1 vol. 1904-1909, Basement vault; 8 volumes 1916—, Auditor's vault.

246. AUDITOR'S JOURNAL OF COURT WARRANTS
1911—. 5 vols.

Record of warrants issued for jury and witness fees showing date, to whom issued, for what, amount, and warrant number. Chronologically arranged. No index. Handwritten. Average 260 pages. 20 x 17 x 2. Auditor's vault .

247. COURT WARRANTS [Cancelled]
1910—. 21 file boxes (labeled chron.)

Cancelled warrants which were issued by clerk of courts or probate judge for payment of witness, jury, and other court fees, showing date, warrant number, name of payee, amount, and for what. Numerically arranged by warrant numbers. No index. Handwritten on printed forms. 5 x 10 x 14. Auditor's vault.

248. WARRANTS [Cancelled]
1910—. 19 bundles, 44 file boxes.

Warrants issued by auditor for payment of bills and claims from county funds showing date, warrant number, name of payee, for what, amount, from what fund, and date paid. Chronologically arranged by dates of payments. No index. Handwritten on printed forms. Bundles, 3.5 x 5 x 8; file boxes, 5 x 10 x 14. 19 bundles, 1910-1914, Basement vault ; 44 file boxes, 1915—. Auditor's vault.

249. VOUCHERS
1911—. 1 file box. Prior records missing.

Stubs of vouchers issued for payment of blind relief grants showing name of payee, date, and amount. Chronologically arranged. No index. Handwritten on printed forms, 5 x 10 x 14. Auditor's vault.

For related records, see entries 13, 302.

250. VOUCHERS

1910—. 59 file boxes (labeled chron.)

Cancelled vouchers issued on auditor by county officials certifying that amount specified is due person named for services or materials showing date, voucher number, name of creditor, for what, and amount. Numerically arranged by voucher numbers. No index. Handwritten on printed forms. 5 x 10 x 14. Auditor's vault.

Licenses

251. DOG AND KENNEL LICENSES

1917—. 6 vols. Missing: 1920-1925.

Record of licenses issued to dog owners showing name and address of licensee, age and description of dog, fee, and tag number. Alphabetically arranged by names of owners. No index. Handwritten. Average 50 pages. 18 x 14 x 1. 3 volumes, 1917-1930, Basement vault; 3 volumes. 1931–. Auditor's vault.

252. DOG TAG APPLICATIONS

1932—. 3 file boxes.

Applications for dog tags showing application number, name of applicant, description of dog, and fee. Numerically arranged by application numbers. No index. Handwritten on printed forms. 5 x 10 x 14. Auditor's vault.

253. VENDOR'S LICENSES

1935—. 1 vol.

Record copies of licenses issued to retail merchants in compliance with sales tax stamp regulations showing license number, date issued, name and business address of licensee, and kind of business. Chronologically arranged. No index. Handwritten on printed forms. 500 pages. 9 x 12 x 5. Auditor's vault.

254. CIGARETTE LICENSE APPLICATIONS

1932—. 2 file boxes.

Applications for licensee to retail cigarettes showing application number, name and address of applicant, name of property owner, and amount of fee. Numerically arranged by application numbers. No index. Handwritten on printed forms. 5 x 10 x 14. Auditor's vault.

For prior records, see entry 221.

255. RECORD, COSMETIC AND BEVERAGE LICENSES
1933-1935. 1 vol. Discontinued,

Record of licenses issued to dealers in cosmetics, 1933-1934, and nonintoxicating beverages, 1933-1935, showing date issued, name and business address of licensee, kind of business, and license fee. Beverage licenses recorded in front half of volume and cosmetic licenses in back half of volume. Chronologically arranged by dates of issue. No index. Handwritten on printed forms. 140 pages. 10 x 14 x 1. Auditor's office.

Bonds

256. BOND REGISTER
1892—. 2 vols.

Register of bonds issued for construction of county highways, public buildings, or other public improvements showing date of issue, for what purpose, authority for issue, amount of issue, and date of retirement. Chronologically arranged. No index. Handwritten. Average 120 pages. 18 x 12 x 1. Auditor's vault.

257. REGISTER, FREE TURNPIKE BONDS
1878-1909. 1 vol. Discontinued.

Record of bonds issued for construction of free turnpikes showing date of issue, amount of issue, and date of retirement. Chronologically arranged. No index. Handwritten. 196 pages. 16 x 12 x 1.25. Basement vault.

258. RECORD OF 0FFICIAL BONDS
1913—. 2 vols.

Record of surety bonds given by county officials showing date, name of principal, amount, names of sureties, and title of office. Chronologically arranged. Alphabetical index by names of principals. Handwritten on printed forms. Average150 pages. 16 x 12 x 1. Auditor's vault.

For related records, see entries 207, 208, 259.

259. BONDS
1915-1931. 2 vols. Discontinued.
Record of township assessors' bonds showing date. amount of bond, and names of sureties. Chronologically arranged. Alphabetical index by names of assessors. Handwritten on printed forms. Average 105 pages. 18 x 11 x .75. 1 volume 1915-1925, Basement vault; 1 volume, 1926——. Auditor's vault.
For related records, see entries 207, 208, 258.

260. RECORD OF FORFEITED RECOGNIZANCES
1877-1922. 1 vol. Discontinued.
Recognizance bonds certified by county prosecutor to county auditor as forfeited, showing which court, nature of offense, date, amount, names of principals, and names of sureties. Chronologically arranged. No index. Handwritten on printed forms. 170 pages. 14 x 8 x 1. Basement vault.

Reports

261. EXAMINERS' REPORTS
1911——. 2 file boxes. Prior records missing.
Copies of examiners' reports on examinations of various county offices showing date, record of findings, and signatures of examiners. Chronologically arranged. No index. Typed on printed forms. 5 x 10 x 14. Auditor's vault.
For related records, see entry 165.

262. AUDITOR'S DAILY AND MONTHLY STATEMENT, MOTOR VEHICLE LICENSE
1921-1932. 2 vols. Discontinued.
Record showing name of motor vehicles registered in each subdivision, amount of fees collected, and amount of fees apportioned to each subdivision. Alphabetically arranged by names of subdivisions and chronologically thereunder by dates of distribution. No index. Handwritten. Average 400 pages. 14 x 18 x 2.5. Auditor's vault.
For other records, see entry 235.

Miscellaneous

263. MISCELLANEOUS RECORDS
1803-1910. Approx. 600 bundles in 3 boxes.
Records including orders, vouchers, and reports salvaged from courthouse fire of
1910. No systematic arrangement No index, 1803-1845, handwritten; 1846-1910,
handwritten on printed forms. Condition fair. 15 x 15 x 22. Basement vault.

264. TOWNSHIP AND MUNICIPAL ROSTER
1922—. 1 vol.
Record of all township and municipal officials elected showing date, name of
elected or appointed official, title of office, town or township, and term of office,
Alphabetically arranged under tabs by names of townships and villages and
chronologically thereunder. No index. Handwritten. 652 pages. 15 x 9 x 4.5.
Auditor's vault.

A budget commission was established in Adams County under the act of 1911 which made provision for the establishment of a budget commission in each county to be composed of the county auditor, the mayor of the largest municipality, and the prosecuting attorney.[1] It was not until after the World War, when county expenditures steadily increased, that the importance of improved methods of finance were forcibly brought to the attention of the legislature. This new need was met in 1927 by the establishment of a budget commission in each county. This commission, consisting of the county auditor, the county treasurer, and the county prosecuting attorney, receives and examines the annual budget of county, municipal, township, and school authorities, with an estimate of the amount to be raised for state purposes in each subdivision.[2] If the total amount exceeds the sum authorized to be raised, the commission adjusts the amount to be raised and may change and revise the estimates. The commission may reduce all items in the budget, but it is prohibited from increasing the total of any budget or any item.

The adjusted budget is certified to the taxing authority in each subdivision. If the work of the commission is satisfactory, each taxing authority by ordinance or resolution authorizes the necessary tax levies and certifies them to the county auditor. On the other hand, the taxing authority in any subdivision may appeal, through its fiscal officer, from the decision of the budget commission to the state tax commission of Ohio, which is empowered to adjust the estimates of revenues and balances in fixing the tax rates.[3]

The county auditor, as secretary to the commission, is required to keep a full and accurate record of the proceedings of the commission.

---

1. *Laws of Ohio*, CII, 271.
2. *Ibid.,* CXII, 399.
3. G.C. secs. 5625-25, 5625-28.

265. JOURNAL
1911—. 1 vol .

Record of minutes of meetings of budget commission showing the anticipated operating expenses for the various taxing and school districts Chronologically arranged. No index, Handwritten. 368 pages. 18 x 12 x 2.5. Auditor's vault.

The county board of revision, the object of which was to correct some of the defects and inequalities of tax assessments, was established by the legislature in 1825. The first board of revision, or equalization as it was sometimes called, was composed of the county commissioners, the county auditor, and the assessor. The board was authorized to meet at the seat of justice on the first Monday in June annually to hear and determine the complaint of any owner of property listed and valued by the assessor, and shall correct any list or valuation made by the assessor, either by adding to or deducting from his valuation.[1] The act of 1831, repealing the act of 1825, left the duties and personnel of the board unchanged.[2]

In 1859 the legislature made provision for two county boards of equalization. One board, composed of the county auditor and the county commissioners, was directed to meet annually for the purpose of equalizing real and personal property and moneys and credits in the county. The other board, composed of the county auditor, the county surveyor, and the county commissioners, was authorized to meet sexennially for the same purpose.[3]

The act of 1863, amending the act of 1859, left the personnel and duties of the annual county board unchanged. The second county board, although continuing without alteration in composition or duties, was directed to meet decennially, rather than sexennially.[4] The legislative act of 1868, amending the act of 1863, left the membership of the annual and special boards, as well as their duties, practically unchanged.[5]

The annual and special boards of equalization were abolished, when, in 1913, the state tax commission of Ohio was given the task of supervising the assessment of real and personal property in the state. Under this arrangement each county constituted a district. In each district containing less than 60,000 inhabitants by which stipulation Adams County was included, there was to be appointed by the governor one state tax commission. In all other districts there was appointed, in the same manner, two state deputy tax commissioners. In each district there was appointed a district board of complaints.

---

1. *Laws of Ohio*, XXIII, 64.
2. *Ibid.*, XXIX, 278.
3. *Ibid.*, LVI, 193-94.
4. *Ibid.*, LX, 57, 59.
5. *Ibid.*, LXV, 168-70.

This board, appointed by the state tax commission with the consent of the governor, took over the duties and powers formerly vested in the boards of equalization. The county auditor, made secretary to the board of complaints, was required to be present at each meeting in person or by deputy, and keep an accurate record of their proceedings to be kept in a book for that purpose.[6] Moreover, the board was directed to take full minutes of all evidence given before it and might have such evidence taken in shorthand and extended into typewritten form. The auditor was required to preserve in his office separate records of all minutes and documentary evidence offered in each complaint.[7]

This arrangement, after being in operation for two years, was abrogated by the legislature in 1915. In that year the county auditor, under the supervision of the tax commission of Ohio, became the chief assessing officer in the county. The county treasurer, the county prosecutor, the probate judge, and the president of the county commissioners were to constitute a board for the purpose of appointing three members to constitute a board of revision. Again the county auditor was made secretary to the board and was directed to keep a record of their proceedings and to preserve in his office a separate record of all minutes and documentary evidence offered in each complaint.[8]

Under the present system, inaugurated in 1917, the county treasurer, the county auditor, and the president of the county commissioners constitute a board of revision. This board organizes annually, on the second Monday in June, by electing a chairman for the ensuing year. The county auditor serves as secretary to the board.[9] The county board of revision may, with the consent and approval of the tax commission of Ohio, employ experts, clerk, and other employees.[10]

The duties of the board, not differing in detail from those prescribed in 1825, include the hearing of all complaints relating to valuation or assessments of real property as it appears upon the tax duplicate of the "then current year."

---

6. *Laws of Ohio*, CIII, 791.
7. *Ibid.*, CIII, 794.
8. *Ibid.*, CVI, 254-58.
9. G.C. sec. 5580.
10. *Ibid.*, sec. 5587.

However, no valuation is increased without giving notice to the person in whose name the property affected is listed.[12] The board of revision, in all respects, is governed by the laws respecting the valuation of real property and makes no change of any valuation "except in accordance with such laws."[13]

On the second Monday in June, annually, the county auditor lays before the board of revision the returns of assessments of any real property for the current year, and the board proceeds to review the assessment. The board of revision certifies its action to the county auditor, who corrects the tax list and duplicate according to the additions and deductions ordered by the board. The auditor is prohibited by statute from making up his tax list and duplicate, until the board has completed its work and has returned to him all the returns laid before it with revisions.[14] But in the event the tax duplicate has been delivered to the county treasurer, the auditor is required to certify such corrections to him and enter such corrections in his tax duplicate.[15]

In its investigations the board may examine, under oath, persons as to their or others real property. In the event witnesses fail to appear or refuse to testify, the board by its chairman is authorized to make a complaint in writing to the probate judge, who, by statute, is directed to institute proceedings against them.[16]
The decisions of the board are subject to appeal, within thirty days after a decision is served, to the tax commission of Ohio.[17]

The secretary of the board is required to keep an accurate record of the proceedings of the board in a book to be kept for that purpose.[18] The county auditor, as in 1913, is required to preserve in his office separate records of all minutes and documentary evidence offered in each complaint.[19] The records of the board are open to the inspection of the public.[20]

The board of revision keeps no permanent records.

---

11. *Ibid.*, sec. 5597
12. *Ibid.*, sec. 5599.
13. *Ibid.*, sec. 5596.
14. *Ibid.*, sec. 5605.
15. *Ibid.*, sec. 5602.
16. *Ibid.*, sec. 5596.
17. *Ibid.*, sec. 5610.
18. *Ibid.*, sec. 5592.
19. *Ibid.*, sec. 5603.
20. *Ibid.*, sec. 5591.

The board of trustees of the sinking fund, composed of the prosecuting attorney, auditor, and treasurer, was organized in 1919 in each county owing a bonded debt. The records of Adams County are extant from 1924. The county prosecuting attorney serves as president of the board and the auditor as secretary. It is the duty of the trustees to provide for the payment of all bonds issued by the county and the interest maturing thereon.[1]

From 1919 all bonds issued by the county were required to be recorded in the office of the trustees of the sinking fund, and to bear a stamp containing the words "Recorded in the office of the sinking fund trustees" and be signed by the secretary before they became valid in the hands of any purchaser. In 1921 the act was amended to allow such recording and authenticating to be performed by the county treasurer and in 1935 such provisions were abrogated by the legislature.[2]

On or before the first Monday in May of each year, the trustees certify to the county commissioners the rate of tax necessary to provide a sinking fund both for the payment at maturity of bonds heretofore issued by the county and for the payment of interest on the bonded indebtedness. The amount certified by the trustees is set forth without diminution in the annual budget of the commissioners.[3] Then, after each semiannual settlement of taxes and assessments, the county auditor reports to the trustees the amount of money in the treasury of the county charged to the credit of the sinking fund. Money drawn from the county treasury for investment or disbursement is by the issuance of a voucher signed by all the members of the board and directed to the county auditor. The trustees are directed, by statute, to invest all moneys subject to their control in United States bonds, Ohio bonds, or bonds of a municipal corporation, school district, township, or county in the state.

The board members are required to keep a full and complete record of their transactions, a complete record of the funded debt of the county specifying the dates, purposes, amounts, numbers, maturities, and rates and maturities of interest and installments thereof, and where payable, and an account exhibiting the amount held in the sinking fund for the payment thereof.[4]

---

1. G.C. secs. 2976-18, 2976-19.
2. *Laws of Ohio.* CXIX, 16; CXVI, 442.
3. G.C. sec. 2976-26.
4. *Ibid.,* sec. 2976-24.

The meeting of the trustees are open to the public. All questions relating to the purchase or sale of securities or the payment of bonds or interest are decided by a yea and nay vote, which is recorded in their journal.

266. JOURNAL, SINKING FUND TRUSTEES
1924—. 1 vol . Prior records missing.
Record copies of minutes of meetings of sinking fund trustees and record of bonds authorized and issued by county commissioners showing for what purpose issued, amount of issue, number of bonds in the issue, amount of each bond, rate of interest, maturity dates, interest due dates, rate of taxation necessary to retire each issue, amount of funds available for retirement, and interest payments. Chronologically arranged. No index. Handwritten. 200 pages. 15 x 10 x 1.25. Auditor's vault.

The responsibility for supervising and conducting elections in the county is delegated to state deputy supervisors of elections, the county board of elections. This board, created by the legislature in 1891 and consisting of four qualified voters in the county, is appointed for a four-year term by the secretary of state, who, by virtue of his office, is the chief election official of the state.[1] On the first day of March in the even-numbered years, the secretary of the state appoints two board members, one of whom is from the political party which cast the highest number of votes in the state for the office of governor at the last preceding state election, and the other from the political party which cast the next highest vote at such election.[2] The board members may be removed by the secretary of state for the neglect of duty, malfeasance, misfeasance in office; for willful violation of the election laws; or for other good and sufficient causes.[3] The compensation of the members is determined on the basis of population of the county and is paid by the county.[4] Similarly the expenses of the county board are paid from the county treasury, in pursuance of appropriations by the county commissioners, in the same manner as other expenses are paid.[5]

The persons so appointed by the secretary, meeting five days after their appointment, select one of their members as chairman and a resident elector of the county who is not a member of the board as clerk.[6] The board is vested with authority to establish, define, and provide election precincts; fix places of registration; provide for the purchase, preservation, and maintenance of voting booths, ballot boxes, books, maps, flags, blanks, cards of instruction, and other equipment used in registration and to issue rules, regulations, and instructions not inconsistent with the law or contrary to the rules and regulations as established by the chief election official.[7]

---

1. *Laws of Ohio*, LXXXVIII, 449.
2. G.C. sec. 4785-8. For the method of appointment when the term of each of the four members of the board expires on the same date see G.C. sec. 4735-8a.
3. G.C. sec. 4785-11.
4. *Ibid.*, sec. 4785-18.
5. *Ibid.*, sec. 4785-20.
6. *Ibid.*, sec. 4785-10.
7. G.C. sec. 4785-13.

Besides providing places of voting and equipment, the board is authorized to appoint clerks and other officers of elections. On or before the first day of September before each November election the board by a majority vote is authorized, after careful examination and investigation as to their qualifications, to appoint for each precinct six "competent persons, four as judges and two as clerks, who shall constitute the election officers of such precinct. Not more than two of the judges and one of the clerks, states the law, shall be members of the same political party." Precinct election officers, appointed for a one-year term, may be removed by the board for neglect of duty, malfeasance, or misconduct in office.[8]

The county board of elections is authorized to receive and examine and certify the sufficiency and validity of nominating petitions. They receive the election returns, canvass the returns, then make abstracts therefrom and transmit them to the proper authorities. They issue certificates of elections on forms prescribed by the secretary of state and report annually to the same official, on forms prescribed by him, the number of voters registered, elections held, votes cast, and such other information as the secretary of state may require. Moreover, the board prepares and submits to the proper authorities a budget estimating the cost of elections for the ensuing year.[9]

Finally the board is empowered to investigate irregularities, non-performance of duty, or violation of election laws by election officials. For the purpose of conducting investigations they may administer oaths, issue subpoenas, summon witnesses, and compel the presentation of books, papers, and records in connection with any investigation and report the facts to the prosecuting attorney.[10]

The secretary of state, in 1930, ruled that the members of the various boards of elections were to be considered as state officers. This had reference to appointments made under sec. 4785-8a of the General Code.[11]

All records are located in the office of the board of elections unless otherwise specified.

---

8. *Ibid.,* sec. 4785-25.
9. *Ibid.,* sec. 4785-13.
10. *Ibid.,* sec. 4785-13.
11. *Ibid.,* See George C. Trautwein, ed. *Supplement to Page's Annotated General Code 1926-1935* (Cincinnati, 1935), note on p. 688.

Journals

267. RECORD OF BOARD OF ELECTIONS
1891—. 2 vols.

Record of minutes of county board of elections showing business transactions and financial record including source and amount of receipts with itemized account of expenditures. Chronologically arranged. No index. Handwritten. Average 640 pages. 18.5 x 12.25 x 3. 1 volume, 1891-1909, Auditor's vault; 1 volume, 1910—, Board of Elections office.

Records of Electors

268. POLL BOOKS AND TALLY SHEETS
1922—. 760.vols. (labeled by years, names of subdivisions, precinct nos.).

Record showing names and addresses, also signatures of voters casting ballots at regular elections. Tally sheets show tabulated summary of votes cast for each candidate or proposal. Alphabetically arranged by names of voters. No index. Handwritten. Average 28 pages. 26 x 14 x .25.

269. POLL BOOKS AND TALLY SHEETS
1925—. 673 Vols. (labeled by years, subdivisions, precinct nos.).

List of voters casting ballots at primary elections. Tally sheets show tabulated summary of votes cast for each candidate. Alphabetically arranged by names of voters. No index. Handwritten. Average 30 pages. 26 x 14 x .25.

270. REGISTER OF ABSENT VOTERS
1926—. 2 vols.

List showing names of voters casting votes by absent voters ballot. Chronologically arranged. No index. Handwritten on printed forms. Average 99 pages. 14.25 x 8.75 x .75.

271. CASH LEDGER, FISCAL ACCOUNTS

1926—. 1 vol .

Record of fees paid by candidates showing date, office desired, amount of salary of desired office, and name of candidate. Chronologically arranged. No index. Handwritten. 108 pages. 9.5 x 6 x .5.

272. ORDER OF WARRANTS

1930—. 2 vols.

Stubs of warrants issued for payment of bills and accounts from election funds showing warrant number, date, name of payee, for what, and amount. Chronologically arranged. No index. Handwritten on printed forms. Average 1,000 pages. 12 x 8 x 3.

The county board of education, a modern administrative and supervisory agency developed during the last two decades, supplanted the smaller educational units, which, established during the early period of Ohio history, became inefficient and unable to meet the modern requirements as demanded by rural communities.

During the earlier period of Ohio history, educational administration, because of the newness of the state, the sparseness of the population, and the undeveloped means of transportation was, by necessity, local in character. For 14 years after the accession of Ohio to statehood, though the constitution stated that means of education should be encouraged by the general assembly no legislation was enacted for public schools.[1] It was not until 1817 that the legislature authorized six or more people to form associations to build schoolhouses and to be incorporated for educational purposes.[2] This was a beginning, but as yet the values of an educational system were not readily perceived by those engaged in subduing a stubborn wilderness.

The first permanent law for the organization of schools in Ohio was passed in 1821. Under the provisions of this act, the electors of the township were authorized to vote on the proposition of dividing the townships into school districts. If the proposal carried, there were to be elected three school commissioners, who, in turn, were authorized to select a clerk and a collector who should act as a treasurer; They were instructed also, to levy taxes for the support of schools and to hire teachers.[3]

As education began to advance in the early years of the nineteenth century, some kind of state control was needed. Accordingly, in 1837, the office of state superintendent of schools was established. A year later an act was passed making the county auditor also the county superintendent of schools; and in each township the clerk became superintendent of the smaller unit. The county superintendent was made responsible to the state superintendent in all educational affairs. In the same year each incorporated city, town, or borough not regulated by a charter was made a separate school district.

---

1. *Ohio Const. 1802*, Art. VIII, secs. 3, 25, 27.
2. *Laws of Ohio*, XV, 107.
3. *Ibid.*, XIX, 52.

The voters in each division were authorized to elect three directors.[4] The effectiveness of this organization, however, was destroyed in 1840, when the legislature abolished the office of state superintendent and the secretary of state took over his functions of tabulating and transmitting school statistics.[5] Seven years later, twenty-five counties exclusive of Adams were allowed to have county superintendents,[6] and in 1848 the provision s of the previous act were extended to all other counties in the state.[7]

Although marked changes were made in the curriculum of the schools, the history of education in Ohio from 1850 to the early part of the twentieth century was largely one of the gradual transference of powers from districts to townships, and from townships to county in the interest of a better system of education. It was not, however, until within the last three decades that the county became the unit for educational administration.[8]

Although the county superintendent was known as early as 1838, the first permanent law for the establishment of a county board of education was enacted in 1914. Under this act the school districts were classified, and provision was made for a county school district, exclusive of the territory embraced in any city or village having a population of three thousand or more desiring exemption. The county district was to be under the supervision of five board members elected by the presidents of the village and rural school boards. The members were to hold office for one, two, three, four, and five years respectively, and each year thereafter one member was to be selected to serve for a five-year term.

The county board of education was authorized to change school district lines; afford transportation for children living more than two miles from a schoolhouse; appoint a county superintendent; and certify annually to the county auditor the number of teachers and superintendents employed, their salaries, and the amount apportioned to each school district for the payment of the salaries of the county and district superintendents.

---

4. *Ibid.,* XXXI, 24
5. *Ibid.,* XXXVIII, 130.
6. *Ibid.,* XLV, 32.
7. *Ibid.,* XLVI, 86.
8. *Ibid.,* LXX, 195, 242; XCVII, 354.

The county superintendent, acting as secretary of the board, was required to keep in a book provided for the purpose a full record of the proceedings of the board properly indexed. Each motion, together with the name of the person making it and the vote thereon, was to be entered on the record.[9]

The county was divided into administrative divisions containing one or more villages or rural school districts. Each district was to be under the supervision of a district superintendent, who was required to visit the schools in his charge, direct and assist teachers in the performance of their duties, and classify and control promotion of pupils, Moreover, he was required to report annually to the county superintendent on matters under his charge, and assemble teachers for the purpose of conferring on curricular matters, discipline, and school management.[10]

Significant changes were made by the act of 1921, under which the board members became elective by popular vote. They were authorized to appoint one or more assistant county superintendents for a term of three years. Adams County, however, has no assistant. The board was authorized to publish, with the advice and consent of the county superintendent, a minimum course of study to serve as a guide to local board members. The same act abolished the office of district superintendent.[11]

The county organization has placed the rural schools on a plane of equality with the city schools. The consolidation of the smaller units has eliminated the small, ill-equipped schools, and provides under one roof facilities and instruction suited to the needs of the rural children under the supervision of educational specialists.

All records are located in the board of education office.

9. *Ibid.,* CIV, 133; CVIII, pt. I. 704.
10. *Ibid.,* CIV, 133-45.
11. G.C. secs. 4728-1, 4729; *Laws of Ohio*, CIX, 242.

273. MINUTE RECORD OF SUPERINTENDENT OF SCHOOLS AND BOARD OF EDUCATION
1914—. 2 vols.

Record of minutes of meetings of county board of education, with record of receipts for schools and itemized account of expenditures, showing date, name of payee, for what, and amount. Chronologically arranged. No index. 1914-1935, handwritten; 1936—, handwritten and typed. Average 478 pages. 16.25 x11.75 x 2.75.

274. SCHOOL EXAMINERS' RECORD
1888-1935. 2 vols. Discontinued.

Record of applicants for teachers certificates on examination in Adams County showing name and address of applicant, date of examination, grades received, and kind and term of certificate granted. Chronologically arranged. Alphabetical index by names of applicants. Handwritten. Average 457 pages. 16.25 x 12 x 2.25.

275. ATTENDANCE OFFICER'S RECORD
1924-1930. 1 vol. Discontinued.

Record showing date and names of children in county cited for truancy. Chronologically arranged. Alphabetical index by names of truants. Handwritten. 200 pages. 14 x 8.75 x 1.75.

276. EXAMINATION FOR HIGH SCHOOL
1893-1914. 1 vol. Discontinued.

Records showing date, names and grades of students taking Boxwell-Patterson examinations for entrance to high school. Chronologically arranged. No index, Handwritten. 190 pages. 16.5 x 11.25 x 2.75.

277. REPORTS [County Superintendent's]
1930-1932. 1 vol. Discontinued.

Record copies of financial statements by county superintendent of schools to state department of education of the twenty school districts in Adams County showing receipts and expenditures of each district. Alphabetically arranged by names of school districts. No index. Handwritten. 76 pages. 14 x 11 x .75.

For subsequent records, see entry 278.

278. [Annual] REPORTS [County Superintendent's]
1933—. 1 file box.
Record copies of annual financial reports by county superintendent of schools to state department of education showing source and amount of all receipts for school purposes; also expenditures showing amount for teachers, supervision, janitors, and incidental expenses. Chronologically arranged by years. No index. Typed on printed forms. 12 x 12 x 22.
For prior records, see entry 277.

279. REPORTS, STATISTICAL
1924—. 1 file box. Prior records missing.
Record copies of county superintendent's annual statistical reports to state department of education showing number of school districts, buildings, rooms, teachers and principals, number pupils enrolled in each district, number in each grade, number of graduates from high school, number of weeks of school, and average daily attendance. Chronologically arranged by years. No index. Typed on printed forms, 12 x 12 x 22.

The general health district, or county health department, is one of the recent developments in county health administration, An act of the legislature in 1919 provided that townships and municipalities in each county, exclusive of any city with 25,000 or more population, should constitute a general health district; cities with 25,000 or more population a municipal health district; and municipalities of not less than 10,000 nor more than 25,000 population, and maintaining a board of health meeting the qualifications of the legislative act, were authorized after examination by the state health department to continue operation as separate health districts.[1]

An amendment in December 1919 made each city a health district; the townships and villages in each county were combined into a general health district; and a city and general health district might combine for administrative purposes.[2] The mayor of each municipality not constituting a city health district, and the chairman of the trustees of each township, are authorized to meet at the seat of justice and by selecting a chairman and a secretary organize a district advisory council which selects and appoints a district board of health composed of five members, one of whom must be a physician, who serve without compensation.[3]

Within thirty days after their appointment the members of the district board of health—the county board of health—organize by appointing one of their members president and another president *pro tempore*. The board is authorized to appoint an district health commissioner a licensed physician who is designated deputy state registrar of vital statistics and is required to report monthly to the state registrar of vital statistics, and who serves as secretary to the board.[4]

---

1. *Laws of Ohio*, CVIII, pt. I. 238.
2. *Ibid.,* CVIII, pt. ii, 1085.
3. *Ibid.,* CVIII, pt. ii, 1085.
4. G.C. sec.1261-32; *Laws of Ohio*, CVIII, pt. I. 238-42.

On recommendation of the district health commissioner the board appoints a whole-time public health nurse, a clerk, and such additional public health nurses, physicians, and others as may be necessary for the proper conduct of its work. The board studies the prevalence of disease, especially communicable diseases, provides treatment for venereal diseases, and is authorized to make any and all regulations it deems necessary for the prevention or restriction of disease, and the prevention, abolition, or suppression of nuisances. It provides for inspection of public charitable, benevolent, correctional, and penal institutions; and may provide inspection of dairies, stores, restaurants, hotels, and other places where food is manufactured, handled, stored, sold, or offered for sale. The board is authorized to carry on necessary laboratory tests by establishing a laboratory or contracting with existing laboratories, and all state institutions supported in whole or in part by public funds must furnish such laboratory service to a county board of health under the terms agreed upon.[5]

The health department is financed by public taxation. The district board of health annually estimates in itemized form the amount needed for the fiscal year, and these estimates are certified to the county auditor and submitted by him to the county budget commissioners who may reduce any item but cannot increase any item or the aggregate of all items. The total amount fixed by the budget commissioners is apportioned by the county health department on the basis of taxable valuations in the townships and municipalities composing the district.[6]

All records are located in the board of health office, southeast corner Mulberry and Market Streets, West Union, Ohio.

---

5. *Laws of Ohio*, CVIII, pt. ii, 1088-89.
6. *Ibid.,* CVIII. pt. ii, 1091.

280. MINUTE BOOK

1925—. 1 vol. Prior records missing.

Record copies of minutes of meetings of board of health with financial record showing date, amount of appropriations, and itemized account of expenditures. Chronically arranged. No index. Handwritten. 125 pages. 12 x 16 x 1.

281. GENERAL [Health] REPORT OF ADAMS COUNTY

1926—. 1 file box.

General health report to state beard of health from county health district including sanitation, contagious and communicable diseases, tuberculosis, child health, vaccinations, and immunizations. Chronologically arranged. No index. Handwritten. 10 x 6 x 12.

282. BIRTHS

1921—. 70 vols. (1-70). Prior records missing.

Record copies of birth certificates sent in by local registrars showing name of child, date and place of birth, sex, color, residence of parents, name of father, and maiden name of mother. Chronologically arranged. No index. Handwritten on printed forms. Average 88 pages. 8.5 x 7 x .5.

283. DEATHS

1921—. 43 vols. (1-43). Prior records missing.

Record copies of death certificates as sent in by local registrars showing name of decedent, date of death, residence, place of death, date of birth, age, color, sex, cause of death, and names of parents. Chronologically arranged. No index. Handwritten on printed forms. Average 100 pages. 9 x 7.7 x.5.

The Adams County poorhouse, now called the county home, was established in 1837 under the provisions of the legislative act of 1831 which supplemented the initial legislation of 1816. Under this act the commissioners, as in 1816, were authorized to purchase land and construct poorhouses in which to care for the county's indigent. In 1837 the commissioners, taking advantage of the legislation, purchased 211 acres of land from G.L. Compton, located on Beasley's Run in the southern part of the county, improved the log cabin located thereon and prepared to give institutional relief to those who were unable to care for themselves. This site continued to serve as the location for the county home until 1859 when the commissioners sold the original tract and purchased sixty-six acres of land located one and one-half miles south of West Union and constructed a building on the new grounds. This structure, enlarged in 1897 and remodeled in 1926, continues to house the county's indigent.

By the act of 1831, the commissioners again, as in 1816, were also authorized to appoint a board of directors who were empowered to make all necessary rules and regulations necessary for the management of the institution. Paupers not having the residence requirements necessary to obtain institutional care could be removed to their legal place of residence by the directors. Furthermore the directors, or a committee of that body, were required to visit the institution monthly and report to the commissioners on such matters as the treatment of inmates, their clothing, and food. Each year the board was required to report to the commissioners on the state of the institution together with a full and accurate account of their proceedings including a record of receipts and disbursements.[1]

Besides appointing a board of directors, the commissioners were directed to appoint a superintendent who was required to keep a record of the name, age, and the date each patient was admitted. Furthermore he was directed to discharge from the institution any person who had been received because of illness when he had sufficiently recovered, any "pauper" rejected by the board of directors could be turned over to the township overseers to be cared for by contracting with the lowest bidder.[2]

----

1. *Laws of Ohio*, XXIX, 319-22.
2. *Laws of Ohio*, XXIX. 321-22.

In 1850 the name county poorhouse was changed to that of county infirmary Fifteen years later, in 1865, the board of infirmary directors, consisting of three resident electors, were to be elected by the voters of the county for a three-year term. The board was still authorized to appoint a superintendent, and was still required to make inspection visits, and report their findings to the county commissioners.[3]

Although reports had been required in previous years, it was not until the decade of the 1870s that the legislature enacted measures looking forward to some business-like management of this ancient institution. Accordingly, in 1872, an act was passed which required each infirmary director, as well as the superintendent, to give bond conditioned for the faithful performance of the duties of his office.[4] Under this act the directors were required to report semiannually to the county commissioners the condition of the infirmary, the number of inmates, and such other information as the county commissioners believed proper. Furthermore, the board of directors was required to file a full account "of all moneys received and paid out, together with the vouchers . . . from whence received, to whom and for what paid out" with the county commissioners, who, after examining it, entered the report in the minutes of their proceedings. This report, as well as the vouchers, was filed in the auditor's office, and was to be "safely preserved" by that officer.[5]

The county infirmary served also as a place for the confinement of children, the mentally ill, and persons afflicted with epilepsy. Although the state assumed responsibility for the mentally ill in the early years of the nineteenth century, it was not until 1898 that it was made unlawful to confine adult insane and epileptics in the county home.[6] Previously, in 1884, the legislature prohibited the housing of children in the county infirmary who were eligible to a county children's home or to some other charitable institution unless separated from adults.[7] However exceptions were made in the case of insane, idiotic, and epileptic children.[8] The latter provision is still effective in Ohio.[9]

---

3. *Ibid.,* LXII, 24-25.
4. *Ibid.,* LXIX, 120-21.
5. *Ibid.,* LXIX, 121-22.
6. *Ibid.,* XCIII. 274.
7. *Ibid.,* LXXXI. 92.
8. *Ibid.,* CIII, 890.
9. G.C. sec. 3091.

By an act of May 31, 1911, effective January 1, 1913, the board of infirmary directors was abolished and the powers formerly exercised by this body were transferred to the county commissioners and the infirmary superintendent.[10] The superintendent is still required to keep a record of the inmates, as prescribed by statute, and to report annually to the county commissioners. This report, the acceptance of which is evidenced by an entry in the minutes of the commissioners journal, is filed with the county auditor and by him preserved.[11] In 1919 the name county infirmary was changed to that of county home.[12]

The county commissioners still make provision for the establishment and maintenance of the county home, appoint a superintendent, and make regular inspection visits. The superintendent is appointed from a list of names of persons eligible under civil service regulations. Moreover, since 1882, they have been authorized to appoint an infirmary physician, who, like the superintendent, is required by statute to report to the county commissioners. This report, made quarterly, includes such information as the nature and extent of medical services rendered, to whom, and the character of the disease treated.[13]

Whenever the buildings of the county home become unsuitable for habitation or whenever the population is too small for economical operation, the commissioners are authorized to abandon the county home and provide for the care of inmates and others afterward accepted by placing them with another county home or in private homes or rest homes within the county.[14]

Although corrective measures have been passed, the county home has remained one of the most unprogressive institutions of the county. There is no uniform system of administration of indigent relief. The state department of public welfare is authorized to inspect the county home, but is powerless to enforce its recommendations.

All records are located in the office of the superintendent of the county home.

---

10. *Laws of Ohio*, CII, 433.
11. G.C. sec. 2535.
12. *Laws of Ohio* CVIII. pt. I. 68.
13. G.C. sec. 2546; *Laws of Ohio*, LXXIII, 233; LXXIX. 90; CII, 436; CVIII, pt. I. 269.
14. G.C. sec. 2557; *Laws of Ohio*, CXVII, Am. H. 91.

284. ENROLLMENT RECORD
1880——. 2 vols.

Record of enrollments at the county home showing name, sex, nativity, date admitted, length of time in county, from that township, physical condition, reason and date of discharge, date of death, and cause of death. Chronologically arranged. No index. Handwritten. Average 500 pages. 16 x 12 x 3.

285. DAILY RECORD
1913——. 324 vols.

Daily record of admissions, discharges, and deaths at the county home, showing date and names of inmates registered. Chronologically arranged. No index. Handwritten. Average 60 pages. 9 x 12 x .25.

286. RECEIPTS AND EXPENDITURES RECORD
1913——. 4 vols.

Record of receipts and expenditures at the county home showing date, from what source received, and for what expended. Receipts are in front of volumes and expenditures are in back of volumes. Chronologically arranged. No index. Handwritten. Average 200 pages. 18 x 18 x 1.5.

287. REPORTS
1917——. 2 file boxes.

Record copies of monthly and annual reports by county home superintendent to state division of charities showing date, number of inmates in home, number admitted, number discharged, and number of deaths. Chronologically arranged. No index. Handwritten on printed forms. 12 x 12 x 24.

Although the legislature made provision for the institutional care of the county's indigent as early as 1916, it was not until after the middle of the nineteenth century, when hundreds of Ohio children were left homeless by the scourge of civil war, that the legislature enacted measures for the care of dependent children. Previous to this time the Ohio statutes relative to the care of children had been taken from the territorial code which authorized the overseers of the poor, and later the trustees of the "poor house," to apprentice the children of the indigent, boys until twenty-one and girls until eighteen years of age.[1] The fact that this system was not only inhuman, but entirely unsatisfactory, is evidenced by the innumerable advertisements for run-away apprentices appearing in the press.

In 1865 the legislature authorized the county commissioners to receive bequests for orphans' asylums, and, when funds accumulated in sufficient quantities to construct such a home, and appoint a board of directors consisting of six persons who were given the task of managing the institution, subject to the rules and regulations of the county commissioners. This board, electing a president and a treasurer from its own number, was required annually to make a report of the receipts and disbursements of the asylum, together with the number of orphans received into and discharged from the institution. This report was to be published by the commissioners in a newspaper having a general circulation.[2]

A year later, in 1866, the commissioners were authorized, when in their judgment the best interests of the wards of the county would be served, to establish children's homes, and to provide by means of taxation, funds to be used for the purchase of a site, to construct buildings, and to maintain such charitable institutions.[3] Then, in 1876, an act, repealing all previous legislation was passed, which established the present duties of the county commissioners, trustees, superintendent, and matron in respect to children's homes. The act authorized the county commissioners to appoint a board of trustees and a superintendent of each children's home.[4]

---

1. Pease *op. cit.,* 219; *Laws of Ohio,* III, 276; VIII, 223-24; XXIX, 318.
2. *Laws of Ohio,* LXII, 97.
3. *Ibid.,* LXIII, 45.
4. *Ibid.,* LXXIII, 64.

The Wilson Children's Home of Adams County was established in 1885 and the expense of construction was defrayed from a sum of $50,000 given to the county for that purpose by J.T. Wilson in 1882, The home is situated one-half mile east of the courthouse, in West Union.[5]

The board of trustees consists of five members appointed for a five-year term. The trustees, besides appointing a superintendent, hold monthly meetings at which time they examine all accounts presented for payment, examine into the condition of the property and the manner of care offered to the wards. Annually, or oftener, they are required to file with the state board of charities a detailed account giving the whereabouts of each child and the physical condition of each ward, under their care.[6]

The superintendent, operating under the rules and regulations of the trustees, has entire charge and control of the home and its inmates. He may appoint a matron, assistant matron, and other necessary employees, subject to the approval of the board of trustees. It is the duty of such employees to care for the inmates in the home, direct their employment and give suitable physical, mental, and moral training. Under the direction of the superintendent, the matron has general management and supervision of the household duties of the home. The matron, like other employees, receives such salary as the trustees may direct and may be removed by the superintendent or at the pleasure of a majority of the trustees.[7]

The county children's home serve as an asylum for children under eighteen years of age who have resided in the county one year and who are, in the opinion of the trustees, eligible to admission by reason of orphanage, abandonment, or neglect by parents, or the inability of parents to provide for them.[8] Children are admitted to the home on order of the juvenile court or upon the order of a majority of the board of trustees.

------

5. Evans and Stivers, *op. cit.,* 137.

6. G.C. sec. 3082-1.

7. *Ibid.,* sec. 3085.

8. *Ibid.,* sec. 3089.

Since 1876 each child committed to the children's home must be accompanied by a statement of the facts setting forth his name, his age, his birthplace, and his condition. These facts, recorded by the superintendent in a book kept for that purpose, are confidential and open to inspection only at the discretion of the board of trustees.[9] All wards of the children's home who have been committed to the institution by the juvenile court because of abandonment, neglect, or dependency or who have been voluntarily surrendered by their parents are under the exclusive jurisdiction, guardianship, and control of the trustees until they have become of lawful age.[10]

The county commissioners may, subject to the approval of the board of state charities, after an opportunity has been given to the electorate to demand a referendum on the proposition, abandon the children's home. If the home is discontinued, they may sell the site and buildings and use the funds for care of neglected and dependent children, providing that the wards in the children's home who are placed in foster homes and those who are under the guardianship of the trustees are legally committed to the guardianship of the board of state charities.[11]

All records are located in the office of the superintendent of the children's home.

---

9. *Ibid.,* sec. 3089; *Laws of Ohio*, LXXIII, 64; LXXXIII, 196; XCIX, 187; CIII, 889.
10. G.C. sec. 3093.
11. *Laws of Ohio*, CIX, 533.

288. [Case] HISTORY
1885—. 2 vols.
Family history of children admitted to home showing age, birth date (if known), nativity, color, sex, physical condition, date admitted, date discharged, and adopted or otherwise. Chronologically arranged. Alphabetical index by names of children. Handwritten. Average 390 16 x 12 x 3.

289. CASE REC0RD
1913—. 2 file boxes.
Case history, court orders, and medical record of each child of the children's home. Each case is in a separate folder. Alphabetically arranged by names of children. No index. Handwritten on printed forms. 12 x 10 x 30.

290. CARD INDEX

1933—. 1 file box.

Record of dismissals from children's home showing date, names of children discharged from home, placed in private homes, or adopted. Alphabetically arranged by names of children. No index. Handwritten on printed forms. 5.5 x 7 x 12.

291. RECEIPTS AND EXPENDITURES

1917—. 2 vols. Prior records, missing.

Classified record of receipts and expenditures showing date, from what source received, and for what purpose expended. Chronologically arranged. No index. Handwritten. Average 320 pages. 18 x 12 x 3.

292. BILL BOOKS

1885—. 5 vols.

Record of expenditures for children's home supplies showing date of purchase, item, and cost. Chronologically arranged. No index. Handwritten. Average 510 pages. 18 x 12 x 3.5.

293, REPORTS

1917—, 20 folders in 1 file box.

Record copies of monthly and annual reports by superintendent of children's home to state division of charities showing date of report, number of children in home, number placed in private homes, adopted, admitted, discharged, why discharged, and number of deaths. Chronologically arranged by dates of reports. No index. Handwritten on printed forms. Folders, 12 x 10; file box, 12 x 12 x 24.

The board of county visitors, an agency for the examination and inspection of county institutions supported wholly or in part by county or municipal taxation, was created by an act of the general assembly in 1882. Under this act, the judge of the court of common pleas was authorized to appoint five persons, three of whom were to be women, who were to visit periodically such county institution s as the county infirmary, county jail, municipal prisons, and children's home, and file annually a report of their proceedings and recommendations for changes with the clerk of courts, and to forward a copy to the state board of charities. The members, appointed for an indefinite period, were t o serve without compensation.[1]

By the act of 1892 the personnel of the board was increased to six persons, three of whom were to be women, and not more than three to have the same political affiliations. Furthermore the act made it the duty of the probate judge, whenever proceedings were instituted in his court to commit a child under sixteen years of age to the boys industrial home or to the girls industrial home, to have notice given to the board of such proceedings; and it was made the duty of the board of visitors to attend the meetings of the court, as a body or as a committee, to protect the interests of the child.[2]

While the provisions of the act of 1892 were redefined by the acts of 1898 and 1900, these acts did not, in the main, affect the duties of the board.[4] The latter act, however, made the board a continuous body with two members serving for one year, two members serving for two years, and two members serving for three years. In addition to this, the board was allowed a minimum expense schedule for their services.[4] Six years later the board was authorized to recommend to the county commissioners measures for the more economical administration of county institutions. Their report, together with their recommendations, was to be filed each year with the judge of the probate court and with the county prosecuting attorney.[5]

---

1. *Laws of Ohio*, LXXIX, 107.
2. *Ibid.,* LXXXIX, 161.
3. *Ibid.,* XCIII, 57; XCIV, 70.
4. *Ibid.,* XCIV, 70.
5. *Ibid.,* XCVIII, 29.

In 1913 the power of appointment of board members was transferred to the probate judge. Under this act the juvenile judge, like the probate judge under the act of 1892, was authorized to notify the visitors when any proceedings were instituted in his court for the commitment of any child to a state institution for correction.[6] The practice of annually filing reports of the board with the probate judge, prosecuting attorney, and state board of charities has been continued.[7]

Although the statute requires reports from the board of county visitors, none were listed in the Adams County inventory.

---

6. *Ibid.,* CIII, 173-74, 888.
7. G.C. sec. 2976

County relief for the indigent, one of the most pressing problems of the twentieth century, was met in frontier Ohio. As early as 1805 there was passed an act, modeled from the territorial law, which was similar in all respects to the poor laws of seventeenth century England.[1] Under the early enactments the township trustees were authorized to appoint overseers of the poor. In 1816 the county commissioners were authorized to construct "poor houses" for the care of the county's indigent. As the system developed in succeeding decades the county was made responsible for those who had become permanently disabled, and for paupers who could not be satisfactorily cared for except at the county infirmary, now called the county home. The township trustees and officials of municipal corporations were made responsible for providing temporary relief to needy residents of the state, or the county, township, or city. In the event any person became chargeable to a township in which he had not gained legal residence, it was the duty of the overseers, later the township trustees, to remove him to the township where he was legally settled. With slight alterations, the principles of this system continued until the twentieth century.[2]

The unprecedented depression in the third decade of the twentieth century proved the antiquated un-centralized system was entirely inadequate. As a result of the abnormal employment conditions and the crop failures following the drought of 1930, many local subdivisions of the county charged by law to administer support and medical relief to the indigent were unable to discharge their obligations. Accordingly, in 1931, the legislature passed an emergency act authorizing the county, township, and municipal taxing authorities to borrow money and issue bonds for poor relief, providing the state tax commission found that no other funds were available.[3]

During the early months of 1932 the governor, aware of the wide-spread suffering in the state, called the legislature into special session.[4]

---

1. *Laws of Ohio*, III, 272,

2. For an excellent study, but biting criticism, of the administration of relief in Ohio prior to 1934 see Aileen Elizabeth Kennedy, *The Ohio Poor Law and its Administration.* Sophonisba P. Breckinridge, ed. "Social Service Monographs," 22, University of Chicago Press, Chicago,- 1934.

3. *Laws of Ohio*, CXIV. 11-12.

4. See message of the governor to the Eighty-ninth General Assembly in *Laws of Ohio*. CXIV, pt. ii. 6-8.

At this session the legislature authorized him to appoint a state relief commission composed of five members to study the relief situation. The commission was permitted to cooperate with the national, state, or local relief commission, which, in many counties, had been established and was already functioning.[5] Since the county and township treasuries were depleted, on account of the excessive drain caused by the mounting relief load and the steady decline of tax collections, the legislature authorized an excise tax on utilities, for the years 1932-1937, to be used for relief purposes. This state tax was to be allocated to the counties on the basis of population, the tax duplicate, and the value of the utilities property in the county as of 1930. The funds allocated to each county under this act were to be credited to the "county poor relief excise fund."[6]

The county commissioners were authorized to borrow money for emergency relief and evidence such indebtedness by the issuance of negotiable bonds and notes. Upon submission of such resolution to the state tax commission, the commission was directed to estimate the amount which would probably be allocated to the county from the public utility excise taxes, and was directed to calculate the total amount of bonds, the principal and interest on which might be paid out of such estimated allocation. The date of maximum maturity of such bonds was to be on or before March 15, 1938, If, in the year 1932, additional funds were needed for poor relief, the county commissioners were authorized, after the state tax commission found that no other funds were available, to issue additional bonds in the amount not exceeding one tenth of one percent of the general tax list and duplicate of the county. The maturity date of such additional bonds was to be on or before September 15, 1940.[7]

The proceeds of the sale of such bonds were to be placed in a special fund, denominated the "emergency relief fund." No expenditures were to be made from this fund except in accordance with the method and under the uniform regulations prescribed by the state relief commission, and in no case after December 31, 1933.

---

5. *Laws of Ohio*, CXIV, pt. ii. 11-12.
6. *Ibid.,* CXIV, pt. ii. 19-20
7. *Ibid.,* CXIV, pt. ii. 18-21.

The county commissioners were authorized to distribute, prior to the first of March 1933, portions of the fund to the political subdivisions of the county, according to their needs for poor relief determined by the county and set forth in such approved budget. The money distributed to the subdivisions was to be expended in them for poor relief, including tho renting of lands and the purchase of seeds for gardening by the unemployed.[8] County poor relief included mothers' pensions, soldiers' relief, temporary assistance to nonresidents, maintenance of a county and children's home, and work and direct relief. In the townships and municipalities relief was interpreted to be the support of the poor and burial of the indigent dead. Each subdivision administering funds under the act was expected to require labor in exchange for relief given to any family where there resided an able-bodied wage earner.[9]

In February 1933, the tenure of the state relief commission was extended to March 1, 1935.[10] In the same year, the legislature levied an additional stamp tax on the sale of bottled and bulk beer, malt, cosmetics, and toilet preparations to furnish additional funds for emergency relief.[11] The state treasurer was authorized to appoint the county treasurer as his deputy for the purpose of selling tax stamps to be affixed to such articles.[12]

When, in 1935, the state relief commission ceased to exist by reason of the terms of the act creating it, the legislature passed a measure designed to coordinate and correlate all emergency poor relief work, activities, and administration with the federal emergency relief administration witch was authorized to administer and direct the distribution and expenditure of federal funds for relief in the state. Accordingly, all powers previously vested in the state relief commission were transferred to the county commissioners.

---

8. *Ibid.*, CXIV, pt. ii. 21-22.
9. *Ibid.*, CXIV, pt. ii. 17.
10. *Ibid.*, CXV, 22.
11. *Laws of Ohio*, CXV, 642, 649; CXV, pt. ii. 5, 33, 83, 177, 200, 247, 256.
12. *Ibid.*, CXV, 642.

Whenever in their discretion such action was necessary in order to continue the coordination and correlation of state, local, and federal funds they were authorized to appoint, with the approval of the director of finance of the state of Ohio, a representative or representatives of such emergency poor relief. If such officer were appointed, the representative succeeded to all powers and functions, which, under the act, were delegated to the county commissioners. This representative, however, was subject to such terms and conditions in respect to auditing, examinations, and reports as were directed by the county commissioners and such federal agency. In Adams County a relief director has been appointed under the provisions of this act. The county commissioners were directed to conduct relief activities outside limits of municipal corporations through the township trustees, insofar as practicable, and were to be guided by the recommendations of the township trustees with respect to relief heed in such political-subdivisions. Again, as in 1932, the commissioners were authorized, if the state tax commission found that no other means existed to provide funds, to borrow money, and issue bonds in the year 1935-1936. The maximum maturity date of such bonds was to be on or before March 1, 1944.[13] Other bonds, in addition to those secured by the county's share of the excise tax, might be issued not to exceed one- fifth of one percent of the general tax list of the county.[14] If the county was unable to issue bonds by reason of the limitations imposed by the constitution.[15] and section 5625-2 of the General Code, the taxing authority of each subdivision was authorized to submit the question of issuing bonds to the electorate either at a general or special session.[16]

---

13. *Ibid.*, CXVI, 571.
14. *Ibid.*, CXVI, 575.
15. *Ohio Const.* Art. XII, sec. 2.
16. *Laws of Ohio*, CXVI, 578.

The year 1936 saw the re-creation of the state relief commission. Consisting of four members appointed by the governor, this body was authorized to serve until January 31, 1937. Again, as in 1932, the commission was directed to study problems of relief, to receive advice from federal, state, and local governmental departments, to cooperate with agencies of the national and local governments and private agencies engaged in the administration or financial support of direct or indirect relief, to administer moneys appropriated to the commission for poor relief, to examine the conduct of local governmental agencies in administering relief, and to order the distribution and payment of moneys from the state treasury.

The county commissioners were authorized to administer all advances by the state to the relief commission and were directed to operate through duly authorized agencies of townships, municipalities, and school districts, Within the appropriations made by the commissioners and subject to the rules and regulations of the state relief commission, the commissioners were instructed to appoint assistants and such other employees as were necessary.

The county commissioners, like the state relief commission, were directed to cooperate with all agencies of the federal, state, and county governments, and with private agencies which were engaged in administering relief or financial support to the needy. It was made the duty of all county, township, and municipal governments administering relief or assistance to dependents to report to the county commissioners, at their request, the names and addresses of all persons to whom they were providing aid and the amount and character of aid given.[17]

The principle of issuing bonds and securing them by the county's share of the utility taxes was continued. Moreover, there was appropriated to the state relief commission from the general revenue fund the sum of $3,000,000 which was designated as the "state relief rotary fund." The various counties of the state which had not issued bonds and were not authorized to do so without the consent of the people, were empowered to obtain an advance from the state relief rotary fund in an amount equal to that of bonds which were permitted to be issued under the provisions of this act.

---

17. *Ibid.*, CXVI, pt. ii. 133-48, 240.

If the county failed to repay the total of all advances and interest at two percent before June 1936, the state relief commission was directed to refuse to make further allocations or distributions to the county.[18]

In the early months of 1937 the legislature authorized the state relief commission to serve until April 1937. Under this act the county commissioners are authorized to give temporary support and medical relief to nonresidents and to all needy persons possessing a legal residence in the county. Funds may be expended for both direct and work relief. However, all persons on relief able and competent to perform labor who refuse to accept private employment under prevailing conditions and prevailing wages, may be dropped from the relief rolls. This ruling does not apply, however, to areas where strikes are prevalent. On the other hand, any person receiving relief in the county is permitted to engage in any business without losing his relief status, during the period of such employment, he is required to forfeit the *pro rata* amount of relief received by him, and is eligible to his former relief status upon the conclusion of such employment.

The county commissioners are required to file with the state relief commission a budget and a detailed statement and plan showing how the funds to be received are to be expended, the purpose for which they are to be used, the nature and kind of work to be carried on, and the number of persons to be aided by such relief. Besides this, the county commissioners must file a complete analysis of their proposed expenditures, together with an estimate of all available resources, including the unencumbered proceeds of any bonds heretofore issued and the amount of bonds which the county commissioners have a right to issue without a vote of the people on the approval of the state tax commission of Ohio as authorized in 1935.

Of the funds allocated to the county by the state relief commission for direct relief, the commissioners may, when they believe that the cost of administration may be reduced, reallocate the funds on a percentage basis of relief requirements of the various subdivisions.[19]

The emergency relief measures passed during the period 1932-1937 gave the counties for the first time a centralized relief administration.

---

18. *Ibid.*, CXVI, pt. ii. 133-48.
19. George C. Trautwein, ed. *Page's Ohio Cumulative Code Service* (Cincinnati, 1337), no. 20, 65-67.

294. CASE CARDS
1936—. 1 file box. Prior records missing.
Case histories of applicants for relief as reported by investigator showing date, financial status, physical condition, number in family, and recommendations, Chronologically arranged. No index. Handwritten on printed forms. 12 x 12 x 24. County Home, Superintendent's office.

295. RECORD
November 1936—. 1 vol. Prior records missing.
Record of persons receiving relief showing date, name of client, amount received, and commodities given. Chronologically arranged. No index. Handwritten. 100 pages. 14 x 10 x 1.25. County Home, Superintendent's office.

296. WPA ELIGIBILITY RECORDS
1935—. 4 file boxes.
Record of relief clients certified to work on WPA showing date certified, name of client, and classification of work. Alphabetically arranged by names of clients. No index. Handwritten on printed forms. 6 x 10 x 5. Engineer's office.

297. [CCC] APPLICATIONS
1933—. 3 folders in 1 file box.
Applications for admittance to Civilian Conservation Corps showing date, name, age, and address of applicant. One folder for active records, one folder for discharge records, and one folder for records of rejections. Alphabetically arranged by names of clients. No index. Handwritten on printed forms. File box, 12 x 8 x 20. Engineer's office.

298. [CCC] ENR0LLMENT RECORD

1933—. 1 file box.

Record of enrollment in Civilian Conservation Corps showing name, age, and address of enrollee, and date enrolled. Alphabetically arranged by names of enrollees. No index. Typed. 6 x 5 x 10. Engineer's office.

299. NOTICE OF DISCHARGE

1934 1 file box.

Notices of expiration of enlistment or discharge from CCC camps showing date, name, and cause. Chronologically arranged. No index. Typed on printed forms. 12 x 6 x 20. Engineer's office.

The soldiers' relief commission was established by an act of the legislature passed May 19, 1886, entitled "An act to provide for the relief of indigent Union soldiers, sailors and marines, and the indigent wives, widows and minor children of indigent or deceased Union soldiers, sailors and marines." Under provisions of this act the commissioners of each county were authorized to levy a specified tax for the purpose of creating a fund for the relief of such beneficiaries; and the judge of the court of common pleas was authorized to appoint three county residents, at least two of whom were honorably discharged Union soldiers, to serve for a term of three years as members of the commission, which was organized by. the selection of a chairman and a secretary and was known as the soldiers relief commission.[1]

An amendment passed on March 4 , 1887, provided that councilmen of city wards, as well as the board of trustees of the townships, certify to the soldiers relief commission the names of those requiring and entitle d to aid under the act.[2]

By an act of the legislature, passed April 28, 1890 the soldiers' relief commission was required to appoint annually a committee of three in each township and a committee of three in each ward in any city in the county, whose duty it was to receive all applications for aid and to certify them to the soldiers' relief commission.[3]

Sections 2930 and 2933-4 of the General Code were amended, March 6, 1917, to provide for the appointment to each county commission of one member who is the wife, widow, son, or daughter of an honorably discharged soldier, sailor, or marine of the Civil War or of the Spanish-American War, the other two members to be honorably discharged soldiers, sailors, or marines of the United States; and for the appointment to each township and ward committee of a wife or widow of a soldier, sailor, or marine of the United States.[4] Two years later, in 1919, the provisions of the act were extended to include indigent veterans of the World War or to indigent parents, wives, widows, or minor children of such veterans.[5]

---

1. *Laws Ohio*, LXXXIII, 232.
2. *Ibid.*, LXXXIV, 100.
3. *Ibid.*, LXXXVII, 352.
4. *Ibid.*, CVII, 27.
5. *Laws of Ohio*, CVIII, pt. I. 633.

Sections 2930 and 2934 of the General Code were amended on April 6, 1929 to provide for the appointment by the court of common pleas in each county of a soldiers relief commission, to consist of three members, one to be the wife, widow, son or daughter of an honorably discharged soldier, sailor, or marine of the Civil War, of the Spanish-American War, or of the World War, the other two members to be honorably discharged soldiers, sailors, or marines of the United States, one of whom should, if possible, be a member of the Spanish-American War Veterans, the other a member of the American Legion.[6]

---

6. *Ibid.*, CXIII, 466.

300. SOLDIERS' RELIEF COMMISSION
1910-23. 1 vol. Prior records missing. Discontinued.
Record of minutes of meetings of the soldiers relief commission showing dates and proceedings. Chronologically arranged by dates of meetings. No index. Handwritten. 160 pages. 16 x 12 x 1. Auditor's vault.

301. SOLDIERS RELIEF RECORD
1910-23, 1 vol. Prior records missing;1924— in Commissioners Journal, entry 1.
Record of relief to indigent soldiers, sailors, and marines, or to their widows and minor children, showing name, service, disability, amount of award, and date. Chronologically arranged. Alphabetical index by names of soldiers, sailors, and marines. Handwritten. 200 pages. 16 x 12 x 1.5. Auditor's vault.

In 1884 the legislature made provision for a soldiers' burial commission in each county, to consist of three persons in each township appointed by the county commissioners, which was directed to defray the expense incurred in the interment of any honorably discharged Union soldier, sailor, or marine who died in poverty. The commission, serving at the pleasure of the appointing power, was required to report to the county commissioners the name, rank, and command of the decedent which report was transcribed by the county commissioners in a book kept for that purpose.[1] The original act, amended in 1891, extended the provisions of the act to include the interment of the wives or widows of Union soldiers.[2] In 1893 the act was again amended to provide for the interment of mothers of Union soldiers, sailors and marines, and any nurses.[3] In 1908 the personnel of the commission was reduced to two.

Under the present law which became effective in 1921 the county commissioners are authorized to appoint two suitable persons in each township and ward in the county, who are directed to contract with the undertaker selected by the family or friends of the deceased, and to direct the burial in a respectable manner of the body of any honorably discharged soldier, sailor, or marine having at any time served in the army or navy of the United States, or the mother, wife or widow of any soldier, sailor, or marine, or that of any war nurse who served at any time in the army of the United States who died in poverty.[4]

The burial commission is instructed to enforce all laws relative to the burial of indigent veterans, investigate the financial status of the decedent's family, and report its findings to the county commissioners, together with the name, rank, and command to which the deceased belonged, date of death, place of burial, occupation while living, and an itemized statement of the cost of burial.[5]

---

1. *Laws of Ohio*, LXXXI, 146-47.
2. *Ibid.*, LXXXVIII, 330-31.
3. *Ibid.*, XC, 177.
4. G.C. sec. 2950; *Laws of Ohio*, CVIII, pt. I. 34; CIX, 211.
5. *Laws of Ohio*, XCIX, 100.

Upon receiving this report of the burial commission, the county commissioners transcribe the information in a book kept for that purpose, and certify the expense to the county auditor who draws his warrant for payment to the person or persons specified by the county commissioners.[6]

The amount contributed by the county for the burial of an indigent veteran set by the legislature at $35 in 1884 was increased to $75 in 1908, and to $100 in 1921.[7] Since 1908 each member of the burial commission has been allowed one dollar for each service performed.[8]

No permanent records are kept by the soldiers' burial commission. Their report to the county commissioners is entered in the Soldiers' Burial Record, entry 6.

---

6. *Ibid.*, XCIX, 101.
7. *Ibid.*, LXXXI, 146-47; XCIX, 99; CIX, 212; G.C. sec. 2951.
8. *Laws of Ohio*, XCIX, 99; G.C. sec. 2951.

Provision for the relief of the indigent was made in 1805, but it was not until 1898 that the legislature provided separate relief for the indigent blind. The act authorized the township trustees to certify to the county commissioners an amount not to exceed $100 per person per annum for such relief, the certification to be made a record listing the name of the beneficiary and the amount required; and directed the county commissioners to, levy on the townships to the amount certified, this amount to be paid into the county treasury and thence to the township treasurer to be used for blind relief.[1]

Six years later, in 1904, certification authority was transferred from the township trustees to the probate judge, who was required to register the name and address of beneficiaries and to issue to each a certificate giving his name, address, and the amount to be drawn. Persons eligible for relief were blind males over twenty-one and blind females over eighteen years of age, without property or means of support. Not less than two county citizens, one a physician selected by the court, were required to testify that the applicant had been a resident of the state for five years and a resident of the county for one year immediately preceding the filing of an application for relief.[2]

The act of 1904 was declared unconstitutional for the reason that it required spending for a private purpose public funds raised by taxation.[3] Hence, in 1908, an act was passed authorizing the county commissioners to levy a stipulated tax to create a fund for relief of the needy blind, the maximum benefits not to exceed $150 per person per annum to be paid quarterly; and authorizing the probate judge to appoint a blind relief commission consisting of three members to serve for a three-year term, directed to meet annually in the office of the county commissioners to examine applications recorded in order of their receipt in a book furnished by the county commissioners.[4]

---

1. *Laws of Ohio*, XCIII, 270.
2. *Ibid.*, XCVII, 392-94.
3. *Auditor of Lucas County* v. *The State. Ohio State Reports.* LXXV, 114-37.
4. *Laws of Ohio*, XCIX, 56-58.

The blind relief commission was abolished by the legislature in 1913 and its powers and duties were transferred to the county commissioners who were authorized, on evidence furnished by a registered physician or surgeon that the applicant for blind relief might have such disability benefitted, or removed by medical or surgical treatment, and with the written consent of the patient, to expend all or part of a year's relief allowance for this purpose.[5]

Six years later, in 1919, this allowance for blind relief was raised to $200 per person per annum, and the county commissioners were authorized to appoint such clerks as they might deem necessary to investigate applications and to serve at the pleasure of the county commissioners.[6]

In 1927 the maximum benefit for blind relief was increased to $400 per person per annum, but in the event of a husband or wife both being blind and both applying for relief, the total maximum benefit for the two was fixed at $600 per annum.[7]

In April 1936 the state accepted the provisions of the federal social security act approved August 14, 1935, providing federal grants for state aid to the blind, and the legislature designated the Ohio commission for the blind the administration agency in the state, and the county commissioners were made the administration agency in the county. The county commissioners were directed to appropriate from the general fund of the county a sum sufficient when supplemented by federal and state grants to provide for the blind a subsistence "compatible with decency and health," and if they failed to make such appropriations the attorney general was directed to bring mandamus proceedings against them.

The act of 1936 provides that those entitled to blind relief are persons not less than eighteen nor more than sixty-five years old, who have lost their sight while residents of the state, and who have resided in the state for a period of five years in the nine years immediately preceding application, the last year of which period shall have been continuous.

---

5. *Ibid.*, CIII, 60.
6. *Ibid.*, CVIII, pt. I. 421-22.
7. *Ibid.*, CXII, 109.

Applications for blind relief are filed with the county commissioners who are required by statute to list such claims in their order of application in books kept for that purpose. At least ten days prior to action on a claim the applicant files a duly certified statement, including a certificate from a registered physician "skilled in diseases of the eye" stating to what extent the applicants vision is impaired, and written evidence from two reputable citizens that they know the applicant to be blind and that "he has the qualifications to entitle him to the relief asked." The county commissioners may allow the examining physician a fee not to exceed five dollars, and may employ an additional physician to examine the applicant. If after such inquiry the county commissioners are satisfied that the applicant is entitled to relief, they are directed by statute to issue an order for such sum as the board finds necessary, not to exceed the maximum fixed in 1927, such sum to be paid monthly from the fund created for that purpose. The ruling of 1913 concerning medical and surgical treatment for applicants remains in effect. Persons whose applications are denied by the county commissioners may appeal to the state commission for the blind which on its own motion may revise any decision of the county commissioners. Both the Ohio commission for the blind and the county commissioners have power to issue subpoenas, compel presentation of papers and examine witnesses.

At least once a year, oftener if directed by the Ohio commission for the blind, the county commissioners must examine the qualifications, disabilities and needs of all persons on the list of the blind, and may increase or decrease the amount of relief according to the budgetary requirements within the limits fixed by law. If the county commissioners remove a name from the list of the blind they are required to notify the county auditor and the Ohio commission for the blind as to their action.[8] Blind relief records are open to inspection of the public.

---

8. *Ibid.*, CXVI, pt. ii. 195-20.

302. RECORD OF BLIND PENSIONS
1911—. 1 vol. Prior records missing.
Blind relief records showing application, date, investigation report, physician's report on examination, amount granted, record of payment, and application for increase in grant. Alphabetically arranged by names of clients. No index. Handwritten. 200 pages. 18 x 12.x 1.25. Auditor's vault.

For related records, see entries 13, 249.

Old age pensions, although well known in Europe at the end of the nineteenth and beginning of the twentieth century and in a few American States during the same period, were not provided for in Ohio until recently.[1] During the depression years the sight of thousands of aged persons who had lost their homes and savings, and as a result of such losses faced starvation, touched the sensibilities of Ohioans. Accordingly, in 1933, an "Old Age Pension" law, proposed by initiative petition, was voted upon at the general election of that year, providing for the granting of aid to the aged in Ohio under certain conditions. The law was adopted by a majority of the electors voting thereon.[2] The act, as amended in 1936, provides, among other, things, that any person sixty-five years, of age or upward (unless confined in any penal or corrective institution or the state hospital) who is a citizen of the United States, who has resided in Ohio not less than five years during the nine prior to making application for aid, and who has resided for one year in the county wherein application for aid is made is eligible to receive a pension, providing his income from all and every source does not exceed $360 per year.[3] Moreover the applicant must be unable to support himself, and have no husband, wife, child, or other person who is legally responsible for his support, and found by the division of aid for the aged able to support him. In addition to this, the net value of all real and personal property of the unmarried applicant, less all encumbrances and liens, must not exceed $3,000; if the applicant is married the net value of the property of husband and wife shall not exceed $4,000. It may be required that such property, as a condition precedent to payment of aid, be transferred to the division of aid for the aged in trust. This provision does not, however, prohibit the applicant or his wife from occupying such property during their lifetime.[4] An amendment to the act in 1937 eliminated the transfer of property as a possible condition precedent to granting aid, leaving the transfer optional, The amended act further states that any property, either real or personal, which has heretofore been conveyed to the division in trust could be reconveyed to the grantor by the division.[5]

---

1. Arthur Lyon Cross, *A Shorter History of England and Greater Britain* (New York, 1925), 746-47; J. Salwyn Schapiro. *Modern and Contemporary European History 1815-1925* (New York, 1923), 295.
2. *Laws of Ohio*, CXV, pt. ii. 431-39.
3. *Ibid.*, CXVI, pt. ii. 86-88, 216-21.
4. *Ibid.*, CXV, pt. ii. 431-39.
5. G.C. sec. 1359-6.

For the purpose of administering the old age pension law there was created in 1933 in the state department of public welfare a division of aid for the aged. The chief of the division of the aid for the aged, appointed by the director of public welfare with the approval of the governor, is authorized to appoint all necessary assistants, clerks, stenographers, and other employees and fix their salaries, subject to approval of the director of public welfare.[6]

In each county the commissioners constitute a board for administering the act. However, if the commissioners by a majority vote decline to serve in such capacity, the chief of the division of aid for the aged is authorized, with the consent of the director of public welfare, to appoint a board consisting of three or five members, who, like the county commissioners, serve without compensation. The local boards are required to keep such records and make such reports aa the division may prescribe, and are also authorized to employ, subject to the approval of the division, such investigators, clerks, and other employees as are necessary for performances of their duties.[7]

In 1937 the chief of the division was directed to appoint an advisory board in each county consisting of five citizens of such county. The members of the board, appointed for two years, are required to take an oath of office before entering upon their duties.[8]

Applications for relief were made annually to the local board but an act of the legislature in 1937, reorganizing the division of aid for the aged, omitted the provision for annual re-application. [9] Each applicant is thoroughly investigated. In its investigations the local board is not bound by common law or statutory rules of evidence, but is authorized to make inquiries in such a manner as seems "best calculated to conform to substantial justice." For the purpose of its investigations, each county board has the power to compel the attendance and testimony of witnesses. Decisions of the local boards may be appealed to the division.[10]

---

6. *Laws of Ohio*, CXV, pt. ii. 431-39.
7. *Ibid.*, CXV, pt. ii. 431-39.
8. G.C. sec. 1359-12.
9. G.C. sec. 1359-14.
10. *Laws of Ohio*, CXV, pt. ii. 431-39.

After the applicants have been investigated by the local board, "certificates of aid" are granted to persons entitled to relief in conformity with the provisions of the law. Each certificate, bearing the applicant's name and the pension allowed, as well as the records pertaining to the investigation, is forwarded to the division, witch may approve, modify, or reject the certificate and findings of the board.[11]

Under the provisions of this act the state became the general guardian of public and private welfare. The pension system relieves the increasing burdens placed upon county homes, which, even under the most favorable conditions, are poor substitutes for homes. Although $2,625,000 was appropriated by the legislature for old age pensions in the early part of 1935,[12] the cost to the public, in the long run, should not be much greater than that of the antiquated system of support in charitable institutions.

All records are located in the office of the board of aid for the aged, West Main Street, West Union, Ohio.

---

11. *Laws of Ohio*, CXV, pt. ii. 435.
12 *Ibid.*, CXVI, 510.

303. OLD AGE PENSION RECORD
1935—. 4 file boxes.

Card record of all persons receiving old age pensions showing name, date of application, date approved and amount of pension granted. Alphabetically arranged by names of clients. No index. Typed on printed forms. 10 x 18 x 6.

304. CASE RECORDS
1935—. 1 file box.

Complete record of each application for aid showing name of applicant, residence in state, residence in county, physical condition, and amount of property owned. Alphabetically arranged by names of clients, No index. Handwritten and typed on printed forms. 12 x 12 x 24.

305. RECORD OF PROGRESS
1935—, 1 vol.

Complete record of each case from date of application showing name of client, date application filed, date of investigation, date application approved, and amount of aid granted. Alphabetically arranged by names of clients. No index. Handwritten. 250 pages. 12 x 20 x 1.75.

306. PROPERTY RECORD
1936—. 1 vol.

Record of property owned by old age pension clients showing description of property, value, and encumbrance. Alphabetically arranged by names of clients. No index. Handwritten.100 pp, 12 x 15 x .5.

307. STATISTICAL REPORTS
1935—. 1 file box

Copies of monthly reports to state office showing date, number of active cases, number added during past month, number closed, number denied, and time reports, Chronologically arranged. No index. Typed on printed forms. 12 x .12 x 24.

Aid to dependent children, although provided for by the, Ohio legislature in 1913 in the form of mothers' pensions, assumed a new significance, when, in April 1936, the Ohio legislature accepted the provisions of the federal social security act. With the acceptance of the act, the sections of the General Code[1] relative to mothers' pensions were repealed.

The administration of the act, in the state is delegated to the department of public welfare through the division of charities. In the administration of the act, the department was authorized to prescribe forms, certificates, reports, records, and accounts to be kept by the local departments.

The administration of the act in the counties is delegated to the juvenile judge or to the judge of the court of domestic relations, excepting in counties in which by charter or by law the powers were vested in or imposed upon "a county department, board, commission, or officer other than the juvenile judge." In Adams County the common pleas judge[2] performs this function. When he serves in the capacity of county administrator, the judge is directed to utilize the services of the employees of the court exercising juvenile jurisdiction. In the performance of his duties the judge is authorized to compel the attendance of witnesses and the production of books, and may institute contempt proceedings against persons refusing to testify. Except for this, powers conferred upon a judge are administrative powers only.

Those entitled to aid under the act include, among others, a child residing in the state less than sixteen years of age who has been deprived of parental support or care by reason of death, continued absence of a parent, or mental or physical incapacity of a parent. However, a child more than sixteen but less than eighteen years of age may receive aid at the discretion of the county administrator.

Application for aid is made to the court by the parent or a relative, with whom the child must be living. Before aid is granted, a careful examination of the name is made by the employees of the court. If the child is found to be eligible, the court may grant such amount as is deemed proper.

----

1. G.C. sec. 1683-2 - 1683-10.
2. See p. 78.

The amount of aid payable to any child is determined on the basis of actual needs "and shall be sufficient to provide support and care requisite for health and decency." In the event aid is granted, the home of such a child must be visited four times during each year. Each month the county auditor issues warrants upon the county treasurer for the payment of the warrants certified by the court. The decisions of the juvenile judge are subject to abrogation or modification by the department of public welfare. Any person attempting to receive aid on behalf of any child not entitled to such aid is deemed guilty of a misdemeanor and upon conviction may be punished by fine or imprisonment, or both.

Aid to dependent children is financed by federal, state, and local funds. The county commissioners are required to include in the annual tax budget an amount not less than that computed to yield a levy of fifteen one-hundredths of one mill on each dollar of the general tax list of the county. If the commissioners fail to comply with the provisions of the act relative to appropriations, the state department of public welfare is directed to request the attorney general to institute mandamus proceedings against them.[3]

---

3. G.C. secs. 1359-31 - 1359-45 *Laws of Ohio*, CXVI, pt. ii. 188-95

308. MOTHERS' PENSION RECORDS
1914—. 1 vol.
Record of pensions granted to mothers with dependent children showing date, name, case history, number of children, and amount granted. Kind of logically arranged. Alphabetical index by names of clients, Handwritten on printed forms. 206 pages. 16 x 12 x 1.5. Probate court vault.
For other records, see entries 240, 309.

309. MOTHERS' PENSIONS
1914—, 4 file boxes.
Original papers issued in mothers' pension cases. Chronologically arranged. For index, see entry 115. Handwritten on printed forms, 10 x 14 x 5. Probate court vault.
For other records, see entries 240, 308.

The office of county surveyor, another English institution transplanted to America during the colonial period, became an important office in frontier Ohio where land titles and boundary lines were often in dispute. The office is purely a creature of statute, there being no constitutional provision for its establishment.

The first act of the general assembly pertaining to the surveyor was passed during the first legislative session of 1803. Under this act the court of common pleas was authorized to appoint a person well qualified to act as county surveyor. He received his commission from the governor, was required to give bond conditioned for the faithful performance of the duties of his office, and was directed to survey all lands which were sold or were to be sold for taxes, and was authorized to appoint chairmen or markers whose function it was to establish corners. The surveys made by the surveyor or his deputies were the only ones to be accepted as legal evidence in any of law or equity. For remuneration, the surveyor was permitted to retain all fees collected by him in the operation of his office.

Although it made no fundamental change in the duties of the surveyor, the act of 1816 fixed his term of office at five years; authorized him to appoint deputies, and made him responsible for their official acts; and made him liable to removal by the court for negligence or incompetency, and, liable to suit by persons believing themselves damaged by his negligence or that of his deputies.[2] A year later, in 1817, provision was made for the appointment of a successor in the event the office became vacant because of death, resignation, or removal.[3]

The act of 1831 consolidated the previous acts, redefined the duties of the surveyor, increased the amount of his bond, and authorized him, when directed by the county commissioners, to procure from the surveyor general's office a "certified plat, together with the field notes of corners, and bearing trees to each section, quarter section, lot, or original survey in his county, and cause the same to be preserved in a book by him provided for that purpose; which shall be deposited in the county auditor's office, for the use of the landholders in the county."

---

1. *Laws of Ohio*, I, 90-93.
2. *Ibid.*, XIV, 424-31.
3. *Ibid.*, XV, 64.

It provided further, that the surveyor should keep a fair and, accurate record of all official surveys made by himself or by his deputies, in a suitable book to be kept by him for that purpose, and that he should number his surveys progressively. More significant, however, was the fact that the office was made elective for a three-year term by the act of 1831. The term remained at three years until 1906 when, it was reduced to a two-year period; and by the act of 1927, effective with the term of the surveyor elected in 1928, the term was increased to four years.[4]

During the years of the development of the office other duties have been delegated to the surveyor. In 1842 he was given the duty of ascertaining and reporting trespassing on public lands.[5] Ten years later, he was given the same powers as the justices of the peace to take and certify deeds, mortgages, powers of attorney, and other instruments affecting real estate, to administer oaths, and to take and certify affidavits.[6] In 1867 he was given authority, when directed by the county commissioners, to transcribe any and all dilapidated maps, records of plats, and field notes of surveys in other counties.[7] Similarly, in 1881, he was authorized to procure from any office in the state a certified plat together with the field notes of comers, quarter sections, lots, or original surveys and place them in a book provided for that purpose. Certified copies from his book were to be taken as *prima facie* evidence.[8]

With the increase in modern means of transportation, there developed a growing need for more efficient methods of road construction and maintenance. Accordingly, in 1906, the surveyor was directed to act, whenever the services of an engineer were required, in the capacity of an engineer with respect to roads, turnpikes, bridges, or ditches, except in cities of the first grade.[9] He was directed by statute to perform all duties in his county which would be done by a civil engineer or surveyor, to prepare all plans, specifications, and estimates of cost, and to submit forms for contracts for the construction and repair of all bridges, culverts, roads, draws, ditches, and other public improvements (except buildings) over which the county commissioners had authority.

---

4. *Ibid.*, XXIX, 399; XCVIII, 245-47; CXII, 179.
5. *Ibid.*, XL, 57.
6. *Ibid.*, LII, 70.
7. *Ibid.*, LXIV, 216-17; LXXVIII, 285.
8. *Ibid.*, XXIX, 399; LXXVIII, 285.
9. *Laws of Ohio*, XCVIII, 245-47.

At the same time, he was made responsible for the inspection of all public improvements, and was directed to keep a complete list of all estimates and bids received for such work, as well as of contracts awarded for improvements.[10]

Similarly, another measure enacted in 1919 increased the duties of the surveyor in regard to road construction and road maintenance. Under this act the surveyor was authorized to designate one of his deputies as maintenance engineer. This engineer, under the direction of the surveyor, was to have charge of all "road maintenance and repair work" in his county. Furthermore, when authorized by the county commissioners, the surveyor was to appoint a maintenance supervisor or supervisors to have charge of the maintenance of improved highways within a district or districts established by tho commissioners or the surveyor, and containing not less than ten miles of improved county roads.[11] In 1923 the surveyor was delegated to assist the county planning commission wherever such commission was established.[12]

Thus the general responsibility of planning and directing county road construction is vested, by statute, in the county surveyor. Because of this increased responsibility placed on this office there has been an attempt to raise the general qualifications of those seeking election to it. Accordingly, in 1935, an act was passed changing the title of the office to that of county engineer, and eligibility to the office was restricted to a registered professional engineer and registered surveyor licensed to practice in state of Ohio.[13] This act was amended in 1935 to permit the incumbent to continue in office upon re-election, regardless of lack of these qualifications.[14]

All records are located in the engineer's office unless otherwise specified.

---

10. *Ibid.*, XCVIII, 245-47.
11. *Ibid.*, CVIII, pt. ii. 497.
12. *Ibid.*, CX, 312.
13. *Ibid.*, CXVI, 283.
14. *Ibid.*, CXVI, pt. ii. 152.

310. SURVEYOR'S JOURNAL

1818—. 5 vols. Missing: 1854-1866.

Record of surveys made by county engineer showing date, for whom, amount of land, and description of boundary line; plat drawings showing watercourses, highways, and railways; also orders from county auditor for surveys of tracts to be sold for delinquent taxes. Prepared by county engineer. Chronologically arranged. No index. Handwritten and hand drawn, 1818-1853, condition poor. Scales vary. Average 281 pages. 12 x 8 x 1.5. 3 volumes. 1818-1853, Basement vault; 2 volumes. 1867—. Engineer's office.

311. SURVEYOR'S RECORDS

1818—. 7 vols.

Record of each survey by county engineer showing date, for whom, acreage, location, and plat drawing. Prepared by county engineer. Chronologically arranged. Alphabetical index by names of landowners. Handwritten and hand drawn. Scales vary. Average 475 pages. 20 x 12 x 3.5.

312. BLUEPRINTS AND MAPS

n.d. 12 file drawers (labeled by subjects).

Blueprints of highways, bridges, and county projects; also maps of proposed and existing roads. Prepared by county surveyor. No systematic arrangement. No index. Hand drawn, black on white. Scales vary. 3.5 x 5 x 3.

313. ESTIMATE RECORD

1911—, 2 vols. Prior records missing.

Engineer's estimates of costs on road and bridge construction, and repair projects showing date and estimated costs. Chronologically arranged. Alphabetical index by names of roads and bridges. Handwritten. Average 300 pages. 16 x 11 x 1.5.

314. CASH BOOKS

1923—. 2 vols,

Engineer's record of cash received showing date, from whom, what service, and amount. Chronologically arranged. No index. Handwritten. Average 160 pages. 20 x 12 x 1.25.

315. ACCRUED FEES

1917—. 2 vols.

Record of fees due engineer's office showing date, to whom charged, kind of service, *per diem*, amount of fees, total, and date paid. Chronologically arranged. No index. Handwritten. Average 320 pages. 18 x 12 x 2.

316. PAY ROLLS

1924—. 2 file boxes.

Engineer's certified pay rolls of employees of the engineer's office showing date, pay roll number, name of employee, and amount of salary. Chronologically arranged also numerically arranged by pay roll numbers. No index. Handwritten on printed forms. 20 x 12 x 10.

The Adams County agricultural society, an aggregate corporation whose object is the promotion of agriculture in the county, was established in December 1851, under provisions of sections. 9880 - 9921-1c of the General Code, authorizing such county societies and defining their powers and duties. The first fair was held in October 1852.[1]

County agricultural societies in Ohio were provided for by statute as early as 1846. On February 28 of that year the legislature passed an act authorizing the forming of such societies and making provisions for their aid by the counties.[2] On February 15, 1853, the legislature declared such societies to be bodies corporate and politic, capable of suing and being sued, and capable of holding in *fee simple* such real estate as they might purchase for sites whereon to hold fairs, the same to be paid for by the county commissioners.[3]

By act of the legislature passed February 20, 1861, county agricultural societies were required to report annually to the state board of agriculture, and to send a delegate to meet with the state board at Columbus once each year.[4] In 1883 the legislature provided for the organization of district or county agricultural societies. The act making this provision stimulated that when thirty or more persons, residents of any county or district embracing two counties, organized themselves into an agricultural society, under the rules and regulations of the state board of agriculture, the county might aid such society with a grant not to exceed $400 per year.[5] By act of April 21, 1896, provision was made for representation in a county society of thirty or more residents of any county or district embracing two or more counties.[6] In 1900 the legislature extended the amount of county aid to $800 per year,[7] Later, on May 6, 1902, the legislature passed an act authorizing thirty or more residents of a county or of a district embracing one or more counties, to organize themselves into an agricultural society.[8]

---

1. Ohio Department of Agriculture , *Annual Report*. 1936, 27.
2. *Laws of Ohio*, XLIV, 70.
3. *Ibid.*, LI, 333.
4. *Ibid.*, LVIII, 22.
5. *Ibid.*, LXXX, 142.
6. *Ibid.*, XCII, 205.
7. *Ibid.*, XCIV, 395.
8. *Ibid.*, XCV, 403.

On April 17, 1919, the legislature provided for the organization of county and independent agricultural societies, the payment of class premiums; defined the duties of persons competing for premiums; prescribed the publication of treasurers' accounts and the list of awards by societies; designated conditions of membership in a county agricultural society; authorized the society to elect a board of directors consisting of eight members, and prescribed their term of office and the manner of their election The act further stipulated how such societies might obtain state aid, and authorized the county commissioners to insure all buildings belonging to agricultural societies.[9]

The legislature in 1921 passed an act stipulating that the total amount of county aid to county agricultural societies should equal one hundred percent of the amount paid by the society in regular class premiums but not exceed $800.[10] By act of March 27, 1925, the county commissioners were authorized to purchase or to lease, for a term of not less than twenty years, real estate whereon to hold fairs under the management of county agricultural, societies, and to erect thereon suitable buildings.[11] On March 10, 1927, the legislature authorized the county commissioners to appropriate annually on the request of the agricultural society a sum not less than $1,500 nor more than $2,000 from the general fund for the purpose of "encouraging agricultural fairs."[12]

The most recent legislation affecting agricultural societies was that of March 19, 1935. This act provides that where no duly organized county agricultural society existed, and when no fair was held by a duly organized county agricultural society which had held an annual exposition for three years previous to January 1, 1933, the county commissioners should, on the request of an independent society, appropriate annually from the general fund a sum not more than $2,000 nor less than $500 for the encouragement of independent agricultural fairs.[13]

No records for the agricultural society were located in Adams County.

---

9. *Ibid.*, CVIII, pt. I. 381-85.
10. *Ibid.*, CIX, 240.
11. *Ibid.*, CXI, 238.
12. *Ibid.*, CXI I, 84.
13. *Ibid.*, CXVI, 47.

In 1914 the federal government passed an act providing for cooperative agricultural extension service between the state agricultural colleges and the United States department of agriculture. The purpose of the extension service was to give instructions and practical demonstrations in agriculture and home economics to persons not attending college, and to give such information through field demonstrations, publications, and other means. The funds for such work were to be supplied in part by the federal government and part by the state.[1]

A year following the federal legislation, the Ohio legislature accepted the provisions of the act by providing that when twenty or more residents of a county organized themselves into a "farmers institute society for the purpose of teaching better methods of farming, stock raising, fruit culture and business connected with agriculture," accepted a constitution and bylaws conforming to the rules and regulations prescribed by the trustees of the Ohio State University, and elected proper officers, the institute could be a corporate body. The Ohio State University was required to furnish speakers for their annual meeting. At the close of the session the trustees were authorized to publish the lectures in pamphlet or book form.

Besides maintaining an institute, the society was authorized to maintain a county experiment farm. Furthermore the county commissioners were authorized to select a county agent subject to the approval of the dean of the college of agriculture of the Ohio State University. The first agent in Adams County was appointed in 1925. It is the duty of the agent to inspect and study the agricultural conditions in his county, distribute agricultural literature, cooperate with the United States Department of Agriculture and the college of agriculture of the Ohio State University. In the event the commissioners failed to make such an appointment, the electorate could require them to do so on a referendum vote.[2]

In 1929 the original legislation was amended so as to authorize the trustees of the Ohio State University to employ home demonstration agents and boys and girls club agents.

---

1. *United States Statutes at Large*, XXXVIII, pt. I. 372-74.
2. *Laws of Ohio*, CVI, 356-59.

However, Adams County has not taken advantage of this legislation and has neither a home demonstration agent nor a club agent. The county extension agent was given the additional duty of carrying the teachings of the college of agriculture of the Ohio State University in agriculture and home economics to the residents of his county through personal visits, bulletins, and practical demonstrations. Furthermore it was his duty to render educational service not only in relation to agricultural production, but also in relation to economic problems including marketing, distribution, and the utilization of farm products.[3]

The initial legislation contained a clause which required the county commissioners to appropriate annually one thousand dollars if they wished to obtain the services of an agricultural agent. This amount was to be matched by the state. Under the present system the commissioners are empowered to levy a tax and to appropriate money from the proceeds thereof or from the general fund of the county an amount not in excess of three thousand dollars for each agent to be paid into the state treasury to the credit of the agricultural extension fund. Amounts in excess must have the unanimous consent of the commissioners.[4]

All records are located in office of county agricultural extension agent.

3. *Ibid.*, CXIII, 82-83.
4. *Ibid.*, CXIII, 82-83.

317. 4-H CLUB ADVISORS' RECORDS

1923—. 2 file boxes. Initiated 1923.

Record of 4-H club activities and accomplishments. Alphabetically arranged by names of projects and chronologically thereunder. No index. Typed on printed forms, 12 x 12 x 24.

318. 4-H CLUB ENROLLMENT RECORDS

1923—. 1 file box. Initiated 1923.

Registration and work records of 4-H members showing name of project, date, name of member, age, and progress. Alphabetically arranged by names of projects and chronologically thereunder. No index. Typed on printed forms. 12 x 12 x 24.

319. AAA RECORDS

1933-1936. 2 file boxes. Initiated 1933.

Records of individual farmers who operated their farms under AAA regulations; approximately 1,800 tobacco records, 89 wheat, and 300 corn-hog records. Arranged by types of projects and alphabetical thereunder by names of participants. No index. Typed on printed forms. 12 x 12 x 24.

320. AGRICULTURAL CONSERVATION RECORDS

1936—. 1 file box. Initiated 1936.

Record of agricultural conservation under federal program. Arranged by types of records. No index. Typed on printed forms. 12 x 12 x 24.

321. INDIVIDUAL [Conservation] RECORDS

1936—. 1 file box. Initiated 1936.

Records of farmers engaged in some special project work under the conservation program showing complete data concerning each farm; also a work sheet. Each case is in a separate folder. Alphabetically arranged by names of farmers. No index. Typed on printed forms. 12 x 12 x 24.

322. MONTHLY AND ANNUAL REPORTS

1923—. 1 file box. Initiated 1923.

Copy of agent's reports to state department of agriculture covering activities, progress, and finances of the program. Chronologically arranged by dates of reports. No index. Typed on printed forms. 12 x 12 x 24.

323. EXTENSION WORK REPORTS

1923—. 1 file box. Initiated 1923.

Progress reports of extension projects by county agent to agricultural extension service department of Ohio State University. Chronologically arranged. No index. Typed on printed forms. 12 x 12 x 24.

324. CORRESPONDENCE

1923—. 1 file box. Initiated 1923.

Record copies of outgoing correspondence and correspondence received. Chronologically arranged in folders labeled In and Out. No index. Handwritten and typed. 12 x 12 x 24.

The county dog warden, appointed by the county commissioners, has as his duty the enforcement of the provisions of the General Code relative to licensing dogs, the impounding and destruction of unlicensed dogs, and the payment of compensation for damages to livestock inflicted by dogs. This officer, like other county officials, is required to give bond conditioned for the faithful performance of the duties of his office. This bond, in the sum of not less than $500 nor more than $2,000, is filed with the county auditor. His compensation and tenure, like that of his deputies, is determined by the county commissioners.

In Adams County the duties of dog warden were under the jurisdiction of the sheriff from 1917 to 1927 as provided by statute.[1] In 1927 an act authorized the commissioners to appoint a county dog warden responsible to the commissioners,[2] under which act the Adams County dog warden was appointed in September 1927.

The warden is required to record all dogs owned, kept, or harbored in his county; to patrol the county; to seize and impound dogs more than three months of age found not wearing a valid registration tag. The latter provisions do not apply to dogs kept in a regularly licensed kennel. He is required to make weekly written reports to the commissioners of all dogs seized, impounded, redeemed, and destroyed. He is required to report all claims for damages to livestock inflicted by dogs.

The dog warden and his deputies have, in the performance of their legal duties, the same police powers as are conferred by statute upon sheriffs and police. They may summon the assistance of bystanders in performing their duties, serve writs and other legal processes issued by any court in the county with reference to enforcing the provisions of the laws relating to dogs.[3]

---

1. *Laws of Ohio*, CVII, 535.
2. *Ibid.*, CXI I, 348.
3. G.C. sec. 5652-7.

325. RECORD [Dog Warden's]
1925—. 1vol.

Dog warden's record of complaints investigated, dogs seized and impounded, end disposition made of dogs. Records for 1925-1927 were transferred from the sheriff's office. Chronologically arranged. No index. Handwritten. 280 pages. 18 x 12 x 2. Auditor's vault.

326. NOTICES [of Dogs Impounded]
1927—. 3 file boxes.

Copies of notices advertising dogs impounded showing date to be destroyed, if not claimed. Chronologically arranged. No index. 10 x 5 x 14. Auditor's vault.

Documentary Sources

Acts of the General Assembly. 1803-1938 (117 vols. published annually under state authority).

Baldwin, William Edward, ed. *Throckmorton's Ohio Code* (certified edn. Cleveland, 1936).

Carter, Clarence Edwin, ed. and comp. *The Territorial Papers of the United States* (4 vols. Washington, 1934, in progress). Vols. II and III of this monumental work treat of the Northwest Territory.

Chase, Salmon P., comp. *The Statutes of Ohio and of the Northwestern Territory*, 1788-1853 (3 vols., Cincinnati, 1833-1835).

Commissioners' Journal [Adams County], 1893—. 8 vols. This journal, as well as other records listed under the various offices included in the inventory, constitutes the most important source material on the history of Adams County.

Estrich, Willis A., ed. *Ohio Jurisprudence* (43 vols. Rochester, 1926-1938). Henry P. Farnham was editor in chief, 1928-1929.

Hammond Charles, and others, eds. *Reports of Cases Argued and Determined in the Supreme Court of Ohio in Bank . . .* (20 vols. Cincinnati, 1824-1852).

Howe, Henry, comp. *Historical Collections of Ohio* (2 vols. Norwalk, 1896). Contains much valuable material.

McCook, G. W. and others, eds. *Reports of Cases Argued and Determined in the Supreme Court of Ohio* (132 vols. Cincinnati, 1853—).

Ohio Auditor of State. *Annual Report*, 1836-1935 (72 vols. published under state authority).

Ohio Department of Agriculture, *Annual Report*, 1846-1936 (81 vols. published under state authority).

Ohio Secretary of State, *Annual Report*. 1857-1937 (90 vols. published under state authority).

_____. Commission Register, 1858-1938 (3 vols.). Manuscript volumes in the office of the secretary of state.

Ohio Tax Commission, *Annual Report*, 1913-1937 (25 vols. published annually under state authority).

Pease, Theodore Calvin, comp. *The Laws of the Northwest Territory 1788-1800. (Illinois State Bar Association Law Series. Springfield*, 1925, I).
The History of England (New York, 1921).

The Reorganization of County Government in Ohio: Report of the Governor's Commission on County Government (n.p., December 1934). An excellent analysis of the merits and defects of present-day county government as administered.

Report of the Joint Legislative Committee on Economy and Taxation of the Eighty-Sixth General Assembly (Columbus, 1926). In chapter xiii the Committee condemns the organization of county government in Ohio.

Shepard, Vinton R., ed., *The Ohio NISI PRIUS REPORTS* (32 vols., n.s., Columbus and Cincinnati, 1894-1934). Cases decided by the common pleas, probate, and municipal courts of the state of Ohio.

Trautwein, George C., ed., *Page's Ohio Cumulative Code Service* (22 vols., Cincinnati, 1927-1938).

_____, *Supplement to Page's Annotated General Code 1926 to 1935* (Cincinnati, 1935).

Biography, Journals, and Travel Accounts

[Burnet, Jacob], *Notes on the Early Settlement of the North-Western Territory*. (Cincinnati, 1847). An interesting contribution by a Cincinnati pioneer.

Darlington, William M., ed., *Christopher Gist's Journals, with Historical, Geographical and Ethnological Notes and Biographies of his Contemporaries* (Pittsburgh, 1893). A valuable source of early Ohio history as recorded by an agent of the Ohio company.

Massie, David Meade, *Life of Nathaniel Massie* (Cincinnati, 1896). The life story of the founder of Chillicothe as told by his grandson.

McDonald, John, *Biographical Sketches of General Nathaniel Massie, General Duncan MacArthur, Captain William Wells and General Simon Kenton: Who Were Early Settlers in the Western Country* (Cincinnati, 1838. Brief biographical sketches written by a resident of Ross County. The author was an actor in many of the events discussed which, of course, dims his objectivity.

Strickland, W.P., ed., *Autobiography of Rev. James B. Finley; or, Pioneer Life in the West* (Cincinnati, 1859) Contains significant observations of a circuit rider.

Thwaites, Reuben Gold, ed., *Early Western Travels 1748-1846*...(32 vols., Cleveland, 1904-1907). Accounts of the Western Country as told by contemporary Travelers. Valuable.

Secondary Sources

Adams, George Burton, *Constitutional History of England* (New York, 1921). A standard work.

Amer, Francis J., *The Development of the Judicial System in Ohio from 1787 to 1932* (Johns Hopkins University. Baltimore, 1932, *Institute of Law Bulletin* no. 6). This well-documented study treats of the evolution of the judicial system in Ohio.

Atwater, Caleb, *A History of the State of Ohio, Natural and Civil* (Cincinnati, c.1838). An old work containing some valuable information.

Ayer, N.W. & Son's, *Directory of Newspapers and Periodicals* (Philadelphia, 1937). A guide to publications printed in the United States and its possessions, the Philippines, dominions, etc.

Bannon, Henry T. *Scioto Sketches: An Account of Discovery and Settlement of Scioto County Ohio* (Chicago, 1920). A popular account written in an entertaining style undocumented and uncritical.

Bond, Beverley W. Jr., *The Civilization of the Old Northwest: A Study of Political Social, and Economic Development. 1788-1812* (New York, 1934). An excellent study in which the author develops the thesis that the Northwest was a laboratory in which the American Colonial system was developed.

Caldwell, J. A. comp., *Illustrated Historical Atlas of Adams County, Ohio* (Newark, 1880).

Chaining, Edward. *A History of the United States* (6 vols. New York, 1905-1925). A monumental work, but with the advance of historical scholarship the author's work becomes more inadequate as an authoritative treatment.

Cross, Arthur Lyon, *A Shorter History of England and Greater Britain* (New York, 1925). A standard textbook, but too sharp in outline.

Evans, Nelson W. and Stivers, Emmons B. *A History of Adams County, Ohio* (West Union,1900). Has the usual shortcomings of county histories.

Fess, Simeon D. ed. *Ohio Reference Library* (4 vols. Chicago and New York, 1937). A popular and uncritical work edited by a former United States senator.

Gwynne, A.E., *A Practical Treatise on the Law of Sheriff and Coroner* (Cincinnati, 1849).

Heiges, R.E. *The Office of Sheriff in the Rural Counties of Ohio* (Findlay, 1933). This volume has the usual limitations of a doctoral dissertation.

Hildreth, S.P., *Pioneer History: Being on Account of the First Examinations of the Ohio Valley, and the Early Settlements of the Northwest Territory* (Cincinnati, 1848). Although an old work, this volume is interesting and informative.

Jenkins, Warren, *The Ohio Gazetteer and Travellers Guide.* (Columbus, 1841). A continuation of Kilbourne's Gazetteer.

Karraker, Cyrus Harreld, *The Seventeenth-Century Sheriff: A Comparative Study of the Sheriff in England and the Chesapeake Colonies. 1607-1689* (Chapel Hill, 1930). Although interesting, this volume does not supersede the earlier studies made of that office.

Kennedy, Aileen Elizabeth, *The Ohio Poor Law and Its Administration* Sophonisba P. Breckinridge, ed. *Social Service Monographs*, no. 22, University of Chicago Press, Chicago, 1934). A biting criticism of the administration of poor relief in Ohio prior to 1932.

Kilbourn John, *The Ohio Gazetteer. . .* (Columbus, 1831). Edited by the distinguished Ohio journalist, this publication served as an immigrant guide to Ohio counties.

Mills, William C., *Archaeological Atlas of Ohio* (Columbus,1914). Contains map showing the location of Ohio mounds, villages, and other remains.

Moley, Raymond, *The Sheriff and the Coroner* (New York, 1926, *The Missouri Crime Survey*, pt. ii.) . This study treats of the present day aspects of the office of the sheriff and of the coroner

Ohio Study of Local School Units, *A Study of the Public Schools of Adams County.* (mimeographed, Columbus, 1937). An intensive study of the organization and operation of the schools in Adams County, Contains valuable statistical charts and tables.

McCarty, Dwight G., *The Territorial Governors of the Old Northwest. A Study in Territorial Administration* (Iowa City, 1910).

Pollock, Sir Frederick, and Maitland, Frederic William, *The History of English Law Before the Time of Edward I* (2 vols. Cambridge, 1895), A standard work.

Randall, Emilius O. and Ryan, Daniel J. *History of Ohio The Rise and Progress of an American State* (5 vols. New York, 1912). Inaccurate in detail.

_____ *The Serpent Mound, Adams County, Ohio* (Columbus 1805), A detailed treatment of an effigy mound in Adams County,

Robinson, Louis N., *Penology in the United States* (Philadelphia, 1922). Although an old work, this volume contains many significant conclusions,

Roseboom, Eugene Holloway, and Weisenburger, Francis Phelps, *A History of Ohio* (New York, 1954), The most satisfactory history of Ohio—scholarly and impartial,

Schapiro, J. Salwyn, *Modern and Contemporary European History 1813-1825* (New York, 1923). A standard textbook. Especially good on the intellectual and social history of the period.

Sutherland, Edwin H., *Principles of Criminology* (Chicago, 1934). An excellent study.

Van Waters, Miriam, *Youth in Conflict* (New York, 1925), An excellent study of the causes of delinquency written by the referee in juvenile court, Los Angeles.

Willoughby, W.F., *Principles of Judicial Administration* (Washington, 1929), A critical analysis of the enforcement of the laws as it exists in modern society. Excellent for bibliographical annotations.

Magazine Articles

Atkinson, R.C., "County Home Rule Developments in Ohio," *National Municipal Review*, XXIII (1934), 235.

_____. "Ohio County Charter Elections." *National Municipal Review*, XXIV (1935), 702-703.

_____. "Ohio Optional County Legislation," *National Municipal Review*, XXIV (1935), 228.

Becker, Carl, "Every Man His Own Historian," *The American History Review*, XXXVII (1932) 221-236

Binkley, Robert C., "History for a Democracy," *Minnesota History: A Quarterly Magazine* XVIII (1937), 1-27.

Boyd, W. W., "Secondary Educations in Ohio Previous to the Year 1840," *Ohio State Archaeological and Historical Quarterly*, XXV (1916), 118-134.

Downes, Randolph Chandler, "Evolution of Ohio County Boundaries," *Ohio State Archaeological and Historical Quarterly*, XXXVI (1927), 340-477.

Dykstra, C.A. "Cleveland's Effort for City County Consolidation," *National Municipal Review*, VIII (1919), 551-556.

Evans, Nelson W., "Colonel John O'Bannon, "*Ohio State Archaeological and Historical Quarterly*, XIV (1905), 319-327.

Gates, Charles M., "The Administration of State Archives," *The Pacific Northwest Quarterly,* XXIX (January 1938), no. 1.

Graham, A. A., "Legislation in the Northwest Territory,"*Ohio State Archaeological and Historical Quarterly*, I (1888), 303-318.

Grim, Paul R., "The Rev. John Rankin, Early Abolitionist," *Ohio State Archaeological and Historical Quarterly,*, XLVI (1937), 215-256.

Kaplan, H. Eliot, "A Personnel Program for County service," *National Municipal Review*, XXV (1936), 596-600.

Martzolff, Clement L. "Zane's Trace,"*Ohio State Archaeological and Historical Quarterly*, XIII (1904).

Miller, Edward A., "The History of Educational Legislation in Ohio from 1803 to 1850," *Ohio State Archaeological and Historical Quarterly*, XXVII (1918), 1-271.

Morris, William A., "The Office of Sheriff in the Anglo-Saxon Period," *English Historical Review,* XXXI (1916), 20-40.

Shilling, D.C., "Pioneer Schools and School Masters,"*Ohio State Archaeological and Historical Quarterly*, XXV (1916), 35-51.

Stone, Donald C., "The Police Attack Crime," *National Municipal Review*, XXIV (1935), 39-41.

Stout, Wilbur, "Early Forges in Ohio,"*Ohio State Archaeological and Historical Quarterly*, XLVI (1937), 27-41.

Newspapers

Ohio State Journal, 1932-1933.

Portsmouth *Blade*. 1910.

Commissioners**

Appointed under territorial government

James Scott	June 1798	James Edison	March 1800
Henry Massie	June 1798	Joseph Lucas	March 1801
Joseph Darlinton	June 1798	John Beasley	March 1801
George Gordon	March 1799	Needham Perry	March 1803

Elected under state government

Moses Baird	June 1804	Thomas Kinkaid	Oct 1827
(Three year term)		John Prather	Oct 1828
Robert Simpson	June 1804	Henry Rape	Oct 1829
(Two year term)		James Cole	Oct 1830
Nathaniel Beasley	June 1804	William Smith	Dec 1831
(One year term)		Seth Van Metre	Dec 1832
John Denning	1806 - 1814	William Kirker	Oct 1833
(Appointed November)		Jacob Treber	Oct 1833
James Baird	1809	Richard Noleman	Dec 1835
(Appointed December)		Elijah Leedom	Dec 1836
James Parker 1810		Asa Williamson	Nov 1838
James Baird 1812		William McVey	Dec 1839
Joseph Nielsen 1814		R.H. Anderson	Dec 1840
(Vice Denning, resigned)		Wm. Smalley	Dec 1842
Joseph Moore	1814	Daniel Burley	Dec 1844
James Baird	1814	(Died in office)	
James Parker	1816	Wm. T. Smith	Dec 1845
Joseph Moore	1817	James McNeil	Dec 1846
James Finley	1818	William Robe	Dec 1846
Joseph Curry	1818	(Vice Burley, deceased)	
John Matthews	Oct 1819	Jesse Wamsley	Dec 1847
John Fisher	Oct 1819	James McNeil	Dec 1849
Aaron Moore	Oct 1820	David C. Vance	Feb 1850
John Means	Nov 1821	(Vice Wamsley, resigned)	
Andrew McIntyre	Dec 1821	Christian Battleman	Dec 1850
John Sparks	Dec 1822	John Oliver	Dec 1851
John Lodwick	Dec 1823	John McGovney	Dec 1852
John McClanahan	Dec 1824	Christian Battleman	Dec 1853
Samuel R. Wood	Oct 1825	Wm. E. Grimes	Dec 1854
William Kirker	Oct 1825	R.S. Daily	Dec 1857

Commissioners (continued)

Andrew McHaffey	Dec 1858-1861	W.D. Early	Sep 1894 -1897
Joseph Spurgeon	Feb 1859-1862	F.M. Grimes	Jan-Sep 1895
J.C. Milligan	Dec 1861-1864	(Vice T.J. Shelton)	
Samuel S. Mason	Dec 1861-1864	M.H. Newman	Dec 1896 -
J.R. Stevenson	Dec 1862-1865	(Removed)	
John Pennywitt	Dec 1863-1869	R.H. Oursler	Jan-Sep 1896
Silas Marlatt	Dec 1864-1867	(Vice Robert Collins)	
John McClanahan	Dec 1865-1868	J.F. Cornelius	Sep.1895-1898
Stephen Reynolds	Dec 1867-1870	Darius Dryden	Jan-Sep 1897
Wm. B. Gregg	Dec 1868-1871	(Vice M.H. Newman)	
Thomas R. Leedom	Dec 1869-1872	R.H. Oursler	Jun-Nov 1898
Jesse Wamsley	Dec 1870-1873	(Appointed)	
John Williamson	Dec 1871–1874	F.B. Roush	Sep 1897-1900
John B. Allison	Dec 1872-1875	Sanford McCullough	Nov 1898-1902
Noah Tracy	Dec 1873-1876	J.F. Cornelius	Sep1898-1901
Wm. Treber	Dec 1874-1877	W.D. Early	Dec 1900-1903
Samuel P. Clark	Dec 1875-1878	W.H. Orebaugh	1902-1905
Jacob F. Weaver	Dec 1876-1879	D.W. Clark	1903-1906
Richard Moore	Dec 1877-1880	S.A. McCullough	1903-1904
Dugald Thompson	Dec 1878-1881	(Vice W.D. Early, Deceased)	
Alexander Stewart	Dec 1879-1882	William Baldwin	1904-1909
W.S. Battleman	Dec 1880-1883	W.H.Orebaugh	1905-1908
John V. Claxton	Jan-Dec 1881	John Graham	1906-1909
(Vice D. Thompson, resigned)		Milton"C. Ramsey	1908-1913
J.R. Zile	Dec 1881-1884	Lewis G. Blaine	1909-1911
F. Grinus	Apr-Dec 1882	Frank A. McCormich	1909-1913
(Vice Stewart, resigned)		G.B. Lewis	1911-1913
Wm. McGovney	Dec 1882-1885	J.H. McCoy	1913-1915
John Martin	Dec 1883-1886	J.G. Williamson	1913-1915
J.R. Zile	Dec 1884-1887	A.L. Jones	1913-1915
Thomas J. Shelton	Dec 1885-1888	J.L. Ryan	1915-1919
J.H. Crissman	Jan 1886-1889	W.H. McCreight	1915-1919
Mahlon Urton	Jan 1887-1890	Harry L. White	1915-1919
S.B. Truitt	Jan 1888-1891	Charles M. Wall	1919-1925
Robert Collins	Jan 1889-1892	Clayton Moore	1919-1925
P.M. Hughes	Jan 1890-1893	W.R. Mowery	1919-1921
M.H. Newman	Jan 1893-1896	M.F. Hooper	1923-1927

Commissioners (continued)

C.H. Botts	1925-1929
Paul Barnes	1925-1929
J.M. Swisshelm	1927-1931
Minor C. Wolfe	1929-1933
C.E. Kirkpatrick	1929-1933
Robert Henderson	1931-1935
V.E. Lewis	1933-1937
T.E. Shell	1935–
T.C. Alexander	1937–
W.E. Holt	1937–

*Compiled from: *Ohio Statistics*, 1869-1906 (Published annually by Secretary of State): Ohio Secretary of State: *Annual Report,* 1907 - 1938, Ohio Secretary of State, Commission Register, 1858 - 1938; Nelson W. Evans, *A History of Adams County* (West Union, Ohio), 1903.

**The board of County Commissioners, with three members each serving a three-year term, was established in 1804 (2 O.L. 150). 1806 the term of office was changed to two years (98 O.L. 271); In 1920 it was increased to four years, and so remains (108 O.L. pt. ii, 1300).

Recorders*

John Belli	1797-1803	Leonard Young	1886-1889
Joseph Darlinton	1803–1810	Wm. Cooper, Jr.	1889-1892
Samuel Bradford	1810-1813	Leonard Young	1892-1898
Joseph Darlinton	1813-1834	C.W. Murphy	1895
James Smith 1836-1838		(Jan to Sep)	
Wilson Prather	1838-1841	Jesse E. McCreight	1896-1907
John M. Smith	1841-1846	Will P. Tucker	1907-1909
(Resigned Aug 1846)		Oscar V. Holt	1909-1913
Robert Buck	1846-1849	John H. Smart	1913-1915
Henry Cursler	1849-1856	Charles D. Stroman	1915-1919
John T. Treber	1856-1859	C.E. Wamsley	1919-1923
W.W. Baird	1859-1862	John Gaskins	1923-1927
James T. Thoroman	1862-1865	Horace G. Pettit	1927-1935
John C. Dragoo	1865-1868	(Died in office)	
W.R. Thoroman	1868-1874	Mrs. AnnaLieu Pettit	1935-1937
J.M. Elllison	1874-1877	(Vice H.G. Pettit)	
James R. Stevenson	1877-1883	Authur Rothwell	1937–
C.T. Downing	1883-1886		

*Under the law of 1803, the associate judge of the court of common pleas appointed the recorder for a seven-year term. (1 O.L. 136). The office became elective for a three-year term in 1829, a two-year term in 1905, and a four year term in 1936 (27 O.L. 65; 116 O.L. pt. ii, 184; *Ohio Constitution 1851* Art. XVII, sec. 2).

Clerks of the Court of Common Pleas**

Gen. Joseph Darlinton***	1803-1806		Alexander C. Robe	1857-1859
(Appointed in Aug)			(Died Nov 1858)	
John M. Smith	Aug, Sep 1846		Wm. E. Hopkins	1859-1862
Joseph R. Cockerill	Sep 1846-1856		(Vice A. C. Robe)	
James N. Hook	1851-1854		L.E. Cox	1862-1865
George M. Puntenny	1854-1857		Charles N. Hall	1865-1868
Joseph Shinn	1868-1874		J.C. Foster	1910-1915
John P. Leedom	1874-1880		Blaine Nesbit	1915-1919
George W. Pettit	1880-1886		W.B. Thompson	1919-1923
William R. Mahaffey	1886-1892		Loran W. Grooms	1923-1927
Oscar C. Reynolds	1892-1901		Robert O. Black	1927-1933
B.F. Kimble	1901-1907		C.L. Murphy	1933-1935
Osba G. Gorman	1907-1910		De Loss Knox	1935–

** Called prothonotary under the laws of the Northwest Territory and appointed by the governor. Under the Ohio constitution of 1802 the court appointed its own clerk for a seven-year term (Art. III, sec. 9). The constitution of 1851 made the office elective for a three-year term (Art. IV, sec. 16). Under the constitutional amendment of 1905 the term was changed to two years and to four in 1936 (97 O.L. 641; 116 O.L. pt. ii, 184).

***Besides serving 43 years as clerk of court of common pleas, General Darlinton was the only man ever to serve as clerk of the supreme court of Adams County, having been appointed in 1803 and successively reappointed until his death August 2, 1851. The court expired the same year due to the constitution of 1851 (Evans, op. cit., 143).

Judges of the Court of Common Pleas*

President judges under the constitution of 1802 in the several judicial circuits which included Adams County

William Silliman	1803-1804	George Smith	1829-1833
Levin Belt	1804-1805	George Winston Price	1834-1841
Robert F. Slaughter	1805-1807	Owen J. Fishback	1841-1848
Levin Belt	1807-1810	George Collings	1848-1851
John Thompson	1810-1824	Shepherd F. Norris	1851-1852
Joshua Collett	1824-1828		

Associate judges under the constitution of 1802 in the judicial circuits which included Adams County

Joseph Darlinton	Apr 1803-Feb 1804	Robert Morrison	Feb 1822-Mar 1836
Needham Perry	Feb 1804-Sep 1813	John Kincaid	Feb 1828-Jul 1834
Hosea Moore	Apr 1803-Sep 1813	Jamuel C. McClanahan	1831-1838
David Edie	Apr 1803-Sep 1813	William Robbins	Jul 1834-Mar 1835
Moses Baird	Feb 1810-Apr 1821	Josepy Eylar	Feb 1835-May 1849
Andrew Livingston	Feb 1810-Aug 1831	David C. Vance	Mar 1836-Jul 1843
Willian Leedom	Sep 1813-Mar 1814	Robert Morrison	Apr 1838-1851
Job Dinning	Feb 1814-Mar 1828	William Robbins	Jul 1846-May 1849
Thomas Kirker	1821	Thomas Lockhart	Feb 1849-Apr 1852
	(Feb-Oct)		

*The president and associate judges under the first constitution were appointed for seven-year terms by joint ballot of both houses of the general assembly (*Ohio Constitution, 1802*, Art. III, sec. 8). The constitution of 1851 made the office elective for five-year periods and required the incumbent to be a resident of the district in which elected (*Ohio Constitution 1851,* Art. IV, sec. 12). The amendment of 1912 changed the term to six years, required the election of at least one judge for each county, who must be a resident of the county in which elected (Art. IV, sec. 12, as amended Sep 3, 1912).

Judges under the Constitution of 1851 in the judicial districts which included Adams County

Shepherd F.Norris	1852-1862	Noah Dever	1896-1897
Thomas Q. Ashburn	1862-1876	W.D. James	1896-1899
David Tarbell	1871-1876	John C. Milner	1897-1907
Thomas W. Lewis	1876	Henry Collings	1897-1905
(Feb to Oct)		(Died in office)	
Allen T. Cowen	1878-1888	W.H. Middleton	1899-1915
D.W.C. Loudon	1882-1892	A.Z. Blair	1905-1913
Frank Davis	1888-1898	(Vice Henry Collings,	
Henry Collings	1892-1897	deceased)	
		Edward E. Corn	1907-1919

Resident judges under the constitutional amendment of 1912

Will P. Stephenson**	Feb 1915-1932	J.R.B. Kessler	Nov 1932–

Judges of Probate Court***

John M. Smith 1852-1855	W.R. Mahaffey 1897-1897
James McColm 1855-1858	J.W. Mason 1897-1898
John M. Smith 1858-1864	J.O. McManis 1898
Henry Oursler 1864-1865	(Mar to Nov)
Joshua Gore 1865-1866	J.W. Mason 1898-1903
George Collings 1866-1870	J.H. Butler 1903-1906
B. McNeal 1879-1882	C.C. Reynolds 1906-1909
I.N. Tolle 1882-1894	Frank W. Kendall 1909-1917
	(See footnote*)

*Under the constitution of 1851 Adams was first placed in District V, first subdivision. In April, 1896 it was transferred to district VII, second subdivision, consisting of Adams, Scioto, Pike, Jackson, and Lawrence counties. (Evans, op. cit., 169).

**The same election that made Stephenson the first resident judge of Adams County merged the probate with the common pleas court, by authority of Art. IV, sec. 7 of the constitution, as amended September 1912. However, as the incumbent Frank W. Kendall had two years left of his term, Judge Stephenson did not assume the duties of probate judge until 1917.

***The probate court, established under the laws of the Northwest Territory in 1788, consisted of a probate judge and two judges of the court of common pleas (Pease, op. cit., 9). Under the constitution of 1802 it lost its identity completely in the court of common pleas. It emerged with its present form and functions, with a single judge serving a four-year term, under the constitution of 1851 (Art. IV, sec. 8). In Adams County the office was merged with that of the court of common pleas in 1914, by vote of the electorate under authority of Art. IV, sec. 7 of the constitutional amendment of 1912.

Prosecuting Attorneys*

John W. Campbell	1808-1817	David Thomas	1867-1869
Samuel Treat	1817-1820	Frank D. Bayless	1869-1873
Geo. R. Fitzgerald	1820-1821	John K. Billings	1873-1877
Richard Collins	1821-1822	Henry Collings	1877-1879
Daniel P. Wilkins	1822-1826	Wm. Anderson	1879-1884
George Collings	1826-1833	Philip Handrehan	1884-1890
Samuel Brush	1833-1835	Cyrus F. Wikoff	1890-1896
(The first to be elected)		C.F. McCoy	1896-1906
James Keenan	1835-1837	Will P. Stephenson	1906-1909
Nelson Barrere	1837-1838	C.C.W. Naylor	1909-1911
Joseph McCormick	1838-1839	F.A. Shiverly	1911-1915
Shepherd F. Norris	1839-1843	Edward A. Scott	1915-1919
Joseph McCormick	1843-1845	A. Harmon Holderness	1919-1923
Thomas McClausen	1845-1851	J.R.B. Kessler	1923-1927
John K. Billings	1851-1853	W.P. Tucker	1927-1929
John W. McFerran	1853-1857	E.S. Young	1929-1931
Thomas J. Mullen	1857-1861	J.R.B. Kessler	1931-1933
John K. Billings	1861-1863	E.S. Young	1933-1935
Reason T. Naylor	1863-1865	James W. Lang, Jr.	1935–
Thomas Downey	1865-1867		

*At first appointed by the supreme court and later 1805 by the court of common pleas, a law passed Jan. 23, 1833, made the office of prosecuting attorney elected for a term of two years (31 O.L. 13). In 1881 the term was increased to three years, in 1906 reduced to two, and in 1936 increased to four (78 O.L. 260; 98 O.L. 271; 116 O.L. pt. ii, 184).

Coroners**

William Killen	1852-1856	William Wade	1878-1880
John D. Hines	1856-1858	John W. Nelson	1880-1886
William Leach	1858-1859	Dr. George W. Osborne	1886-1888
John W. Nelson	1849-1863	Moses L. Wade	1888-1891
E. Kilpatrick	1863-1867	R.W. Purdy, M.D.	1891-1893
John W. Nelson	1867-1875	O.W. Robe	1893-1895
William Blake	1875-1876	C.W. Edington	1895-1897
William Rybolt	1876-1878	John M. Brooke	1897-1900

**Established in at 1788, the county coroner was appointed for two-year terms by the territorial governor (Pease, op. cit. 24-25). The Ohio constitution of 1802 (Art. VI, sec. 1) made the office elective without changing the term of office, which remained at two years until 1936, when it was increased to four years (116 O.L. pt. ii, 184). Andrew Ellison was the first coroner of Adams County while a coroner has been elected every two years from 1803 to 1852 (Evans, op. cit., 146), we can give the roster only from 1852 to date.

R.W. Purdy	1900-1904	H.W. Middleton	1915-1917
O.E. McHenry	1904-1906	W.T. Warner	1917-1927
S.T. Sproul	1906-1907	Charles Mack	1927-1929
(Vice McHenry, resigned)		C.R. Holmes	1928-1931
W. Lee Leedom	1907-1909	M.L. Purdin	1931-1935
R.Y. Littleton	1909-1911	E.T. Gibboney	1935–
John Shumaker	1911-1915		

Sheriffs*

David Edie	1797-1798	John Taylor	1863-1867
John Burritt	1798-1800	James T. Thoroman	1867-1871
Nathan Ellis	1800-1803	Lyman P. Slivers	1871-1873
John Lodwick	1803-1806	John Taylor	1873-1875
John Ellison	1806-1810	John K. Pollard	1875-1879
John Lodwick	1810-1812	Henry F. McGovney	1879-1883
Samuel Bradford	1812-1813	J. Matt Long	1883-1887
Mills Stephenson	1813-1815	W. Pierce Newman	1887-1889
Thomas Mason	1815-1819	Green N. McManus	1889-1893
John Lodwick	1819-1821	Marion Dunlap	1893-1897
Thomas Kinkaid	1821-1823	James W. McKee	1897-1899
John McDaid	1823-1827	James G. Metz	1899-1904
Robert McDaid	1827-1829	John W. Paul	1904-1908
John McDaid	1829-1833	Courtney M. Gibbony	1908-1910
James Cole	1833-1837	J.D. Williams	1910-1915
Samuel Foster	1837-1841	Charles A. Spears	1915-1919
Fields Marlatt	1841-1845	Charles H. Pettit	1919-1923
William Smith	1845-1847	J.L. Trefz	1923-1925
Jacob S. Rose	1847-1851	W.W.White	1925-1929
J.V. William	1851-1855	C.M. Mack	1929-1931
William Cochran	1855-1857	Harry Ogle	1931-1935
David S. Eyler	1857-1861	George S. Baldridge	1935–
Hazlett Sproull	1861-1863		

*Under the territorial government the sheriff was appointed by the governor from the time the office was created in 1792 (Pease, op. cit., 8). Under the first constitution the office was made elective for two-year terms (Ohio Constitution 1802, Art. VI, sec. 1) and was not changed until 1936, when the term was increased to four years (116 O.L. pt. ii, 184).

Treasurers*

Israel Donaldson	1797-1800	W.B. Brown	1888-1890
David Bradford**	1800-1832	P.H. Wickerham	1890-1894
James Hood	1832-1844	John R. Fristoe	1894-1898
Wilson Prather	1844-1850	H.B. Gaffin, Jr.	1898-1902
Andrew Smalley	1850-1854	S.S. Jones	1902-1906
George Moore	1854-1856	H.B. Gaffin	1906-1909
Robert Buck	1856-1858	Albert Q. Ebrite	1909-1913
Thomas Ellison	1858-1862	J.T. Ryan	1913-1915
George Moore	1862-1864	Omer S. Moore	1915-1919
W.R. Duffy	1864-1866	B.F. Games	1919-1923
John Duffy	1866-1868	J.O. Stultz	1923-1927
Elijah Leedom	1868-1872	W.J. Sproull	1927-1929
Henry Scott	1872-1876	E.T. Siddens	1929-1931
J.H. Connor	1876-1880	C.H. Nort	1931-1935
W.B. Brown	1880-1884	Berlin Thompson	1935–
C.W. Sutterfield	1884-1888		

*Omitted from the constitution of 1802, the office of Treasurer was created by legislative act in 1803 (1 O.L. 98). Appointive, by the associate judges in 1803 and, annually, by the county commissioners from 1804 to 1827, when the office became elective for two year terms (1 O.L. 98; 2 O.L. 154; 25 O.L. 25-32). The constitution of 1851 provided that no person should hold the office for more than four years of any six (Art. X, sec. 3). In 1859 the general assembly made the term two years (56 O.L. 105). In 1936 it was increased to four years, as at present (116 O.L., pt. ii,184).

**After 28 consecutive annual appointments David Bradford, in 1828, under the law of 1827 making the office elective, was elected and served two terms (Evans, op. cit. 147).

Auditors***

Joseph R. Baldridge	1820-1824	H.J. Thomas	1888-1894
Joseph Riggs	1824-1831	Dr. J.M. Wittenmeyer	1894-1900
Lenard Cole	1831-1844	R.A. Stephenson	1900-1903
A. Woodrow	1844-1846	F.H. Doyle	1903-1906
Francis Shinn	1846-1850	S.S. Jones	1906-1909
Robert Buck	1850-1854	Cyrus S. Daulton	1909-1911
Wm. E. Hokins	1854-1858	W.E. Spencer	1911-1913
Henry Oursler	1858-1860	Wesley McKenzie	1913-1915
James L. Coryell	1860-1864	Paris S. Clinger	1915-1919
J.N. Hook	1864-1868	Guy M. Smith	1919-1923
John L. Swearingen	1868-1874	C. Elbert Black	1923-1927
John F. Ellis	1874-1878	Guy Smith	1927-1931
R.H. Ellison	1878-1881	A.G. Lockhart, Jr.	1931-1935
J.W. Shinn	1881-1887	M.F. Hooper	1935–
J.W. Jones	1887-1888		

***Office established by legislative act Feb 18, 1820 (18 O.L. 70). At first appointment, it was made elective annually by an act of February 2, 1821, the person elected taking office March 1 each year (19 O.L. 116). In 1831 the term was set at two years, in 1877 at three years, in 1906 at two years, and in 1919 at four years (29 O.L. 280; 74 O.L. 381; 98 O.L. 271; 108 O.L. pt. ii, 1294).

Infirmary Directors*

William Hill	1886-1897	John W. Kincaid	1899-1903
James P. Wilson	1886-1888	Henry W. Middleton	1905-1907
William J. Graham	1887-1893	R.V. Howland	1906-1908
George W. Moomaw	1889-1892	Jacob Custer	1907-1909
John W. Kincaid	1892-1898	Henry W. Middleton	1909-1913
George W. Moomaw	1893-1896	Norman N. Park	1909-1911
William Young	1896-1899	Walker E. Warner	1909-1913
George J. Hill	1897-1906	A.L. Jones	1911-1913
J.T. Gaston	1898-1907		

*This office was created by a legislative act in 1816, authorizing the appointment by the commissioners of seven directors, to have charge of the county infirmary and choose its superintendent (14 O.L. 248-249). By an act of 1831, the membership of the board was reduced to three, and in 1865 the members were made elective for terms of three years (29 O.L. 319; 62 O.L. 24-25). The board was abolished by law in 1913, it's powers and duties being transferred to the board of County Commissioners and the infirmary superintendent(29 O.L. 399; 98 O.L. 245-247; 112 O.L. 179).

Surveyors**

James Stevenson	1801-1805	Jeremiah Bryan	1837-1840
Nathaniel Beasley	1805-1807	Joseph B. Cockerell	1840-1843
Richard Cross	1807-1810	Jeremiah Bryan	1843-1846
Andrew Woodrow	1810-1816	James N. Hook	1846-1851
James Pilson	1816-1818	Jesse Ellis	1851-1854
Joseph Wright	1818-1819	Jeremiah Bryan	1854-1857
Richard Cross	1819-1820	Jesse Ellis	1857-1863
Andrew Woodrow	1820-1822	R. Hamilton	1863-1869
James Criswell	1822-1823	Jesse Ellis	1869-1874
John Russell	1823-1824	Jeremiah Ellis	1874-1877
Andrew Ellison	1824-1826	A.V. Hutson	1877-1880
Richard McClanahan	1826-1829	Creighton Reynolds	1883-1886
Richard Cross	1829-1833	Captain Patterson	1886-1887
William Robe	1833-1836	A.V. Hutson	1887-1893
Richard Cross	1836-1837	A.S. Doak	1893-1899

Surveyors (continued)

J.H. Butler 1899-1903
    (Resigned Mar 1903)
F.M. Smart 1903-1906
D.B. Thomas 1906
    (Died in office)
Isaac W. Thomas Nov 1906-1909
Edward C. Zimmerman 1909-1913

B.F. Billings 1913-1915
M.J. Jones1915-1919
Edw. C. Zimmerman1919-1923
George G. Collier 1923-1929
C.W. Riffle 1929-1933
Frankie Newman 1933-1934
    (Died 1934)

**From 1803 to 1831 the surveyor was appointed by the court of common pleas and commissioned by the governor (1 O.L. 90-93). From 1831 to 1906 he was elected for a three-year term, from 1906 to 1928 for a two-year term, and since 1928 for a four-year term (29 O.L. 399; 98 O.L. 245-247; 112 O.L. 179).

Engineers*

Rufus Cox   1934-1937   Charles W. Riffle   1937–
    (Vice Newman, deceased)

*An act of 1935 change the title of surveyor to engineer (116 O.L. 283).

All addresses are West Union unless otherwise noted

Agency on Aging, 1 Acy Avenue, Jackson, OH 45640
    https://aging.ohio.gov/find-services/area-agency-on-aging-district-7
Agricultural Extension Department, 215 North Cross Street, #104
    https://extension.osu.edu/node/81
Agricultural Society, Fairgrounds, 836 Boyd Ave
Board of Election, 215 North Cross Street, Room #103
    https://www.boe.ohio.gov/adams/
Board of Health/Health Department, 923 Sunrise Avenue
    https://www.adamscountyhealth.org/
Children's Services, 300 North Wilson Drive
    http://www.adamscountychildren.org/
Clerk of Courts, 110 West Main Street, Room 207
    https://www.adamscountycourts.com/ClerkOfCourts/home/
Commissioners, 110 West Main Street
    https://adamscountyoh.gov/commissioners/
County Commissioners, 110 West Main Street
    https://adamscountyoh.gov/commissioners/
County Engineer, 75 Willow Drive
    https://adamscountyoh.gov/engineer/
Court of Common Pleas, 110 West Main Street
    https://www.adamscountycourts.com/CommonPleasCourt/jump/
Dog Warden, 11260 State Route 41
    https://adamscountyoh.gov/dog-and-kennel-department/
Family and Children First, *see* Board of Health/Health Department
Jury Commissioners, *see* Common Pleas
Juvenile Court, 110 West Main Street
    https://www.adamscountycourts.com/JuvenileCourt/home/
Probate Court, 110 West Main Street
    https://www.adamscountycourts.com/ProbateCourt/home/

Prosecuting Attorney, 110 West Main Street, Room #112
        https://adamscountyoh.gov/prosecutor/
Recorder, 110 West Main Street, Room #133
        https://adamscountyoh.gov/recorder/
Sheriff, 110 West Main Street
        https://adamscountyoh.gov/sheriff/
Treasurer, 110 West Main Street, Room # 138
        https://adamscountyoh.gov/treasurer/
Veterans' Affairs, 215 North Cross Street, Room #112
        https://adamscountyoh.gov/adams-county-veterans-service-office/
Wilson Children's Home, 300 North Wilson Drive
        http://www.adamscountychildren.org/

Check also the **https://adamscolibrary.org/resources/genealogy/** or Adams
County Library, P.O. Box 231, West Union, Ohio, as well as the Adams County
Genealogical Society at **acgsoh@yahoo.com** for further information.

Figures refer to entry numbers